Philosophy at the New Millennium

ROYAL INSTITUTE OF PHILOSOPHY SUPPLEMENT: 48

EDITED BY

Anthony O'Hear

CAMBRIDGE
UNIVERSITY PRESS

CAMBRIDGE UNIVERSITY PRESS
Cambridge, New York, Melbourne, Madrid, Cape Town, Singapore,
São Paulo, Delhi, Dubai, Tokyo, Mexico City

Cambridge University Press
The Edinburgh Building, Cambridge CB2 8RU, UK

Published in the United States of America by Cambridge University Press, New York

www.cambridge.org
Information on this title: www.cambridge.org/9780521005081

First published 2001

A catalogue record for this publication is available from the British Library

ISBN 978-0-521-00508-1 Paperback

Contents

Contents

Preface

Philosophy at the New Millennium consists of the lectures given in the Royal Institute of Philosophy's annual lecture series between October 2000 and March 2001. The lectures are here presented in the order in which they were given. The lecturers—who include some highly distinguished philosophers in their respective fields—were asked to consider where some significant part of philosophy stood at the end of the second millennium and where they hoped it might go at the start of the third. I am confident that readers of the volume will feel that all have fulfilled their brief with admirable vigour and style. On behalf of the Royal Institute of Philosophy, I would like to thank all participants most warmly for their contributions to the series, spoken and written.

Anthony O'Hear

Notes on Contributors

Ted Honderich
Grote Professor Emeritus of the Philosophy of Mind and Logic, University College, London; Vice-Chairman of the Council of the Royal Institute of Philosophy.

Daniel Dennett
University Professor and Austin B. Fletcher Professor of Philosophy; Director Centre for Cognitive Studies, Tufts University.

D. H. Mellor
Pro-Vice-Chancellor and Emeritus Professor of Philosophy, University of Cambridge; Member of the Council of the Royal Institute of Philosophy.

Anthony Quinton
Baron Quinton of Holywell; formerly President of Trinity College, Oxford; President of the Royal Institute of Philosophy.

Michael Redhead
Formerly Professor of the History and Philosophy of Science, University of Cambridge; Co-Director, Centre for the Philosophy of Natural and Social Science, London School of Economics.

Rom Harré
Emeritus Fellow of Linacre College, Oxford and Professor of Psychology, Georgetown University, Washington, DC; Member of the Council of the Royal Institute of Philosophy.

Mary Warnock
Baroness Warnock of Weeke; formerly Mistress of Girton College, Cambridge.

Ruth Garrett Millikan
Professor of Philosophy, University of Connecticut.

David E. Cooper
Professor of Philosophy, University of Durham; Member of the Council of the Royal Institute of Philosophy.

John Haldane
Professor of Moral Philosophy, University of St Andrews; Member of the Council of the Royal Institute of Philosophy.

Notes on Contributors

Anthony O'Hear
Professor of Philosophy, University of Bradford; Director of the Royal Institute of Philosophy.

John Skorupski
Professor of Moral Philosophy, University of St Andrews.

Margaret A. Boden
Professor of Philosophy and Psychology, School of Cognitive and Computing Sciences, University of Sussex; Member of the Council of the Royal Institute of Philosophy.

Jerry Fodor
Professor of Philosophy, Rutgers University.

Consciousness as Existence, and the End of Intentionality

TED HONDERICH

It was only in the last century of the past millennium that the Philosophy of Mind began to flourish as a part of philosophy with some autonomy, enough for students to face examination papers in it by itself. Despite an inclination in some places to give it the name of Philosophical Psychology, it is not any science of the mind. This is not to say that the Philosophy of Mind is unempirical, but that it is like the rest of philosophy in being more taken up with good thinking about experienced facts than with establishing, elaborating or using them. Logic, if not formal logic, is the core of all philosophy, and so of the Philosophy of Mind. The discipline's first question is what it is for a thing to be conscious, whatever its capabilities. The discipline's second question is how a thing's being conscious is related to the physical world, including chairs, brains and bodily movements—the mind-brain or mind-body problem.

The question of what it is for a thing to be conscious presupposes what is true, that we have some grip of what it is to be conscious from our own personal histories, presumably by remembering the last bits of them. In one sense, indeed the main sense, we have a complete grip, since consciousness itself is what we have without the aid of inference. Despite some light philosophy and a good deal of psychological and therapeutic stuff to the contrary, consciousness in itself it has no hidden depths—whatever may be under it, of whatever sort.

If you answer the first question by saying that what it is to be conscious somehow consists in nothing but physical facts now known elsewhere, neural or electrochemical facts as they are now known and understood in neuroscience, you do already answer one part of the second question, the part about consciousness and brains. Consciousness is related to the brain in that it is strictly identical with electrochemical activity in it. These answers of *Eliminative or Nothing-But Materialism* have remained the property of enthusiasts, usually in places of strong sunlight.

You could argue, despite the mediaevals and Hobbes and Descartes, that the Philosophy of Mind began in 1949 with Gilbert

Ted Honderich

Ryle's *The Concept of Mind*[1]. Certainly that book signalled the flourishing of the Philosophy of Mind. As the century ended, it was the most vigorous part of philosophy, what some called First Philosophy.[2] But the burden of my reflections will be that having learned a lot, we need in this new millennium to give up on what we have. We need to begin again, in a certain very different way.

Ryle certainly rejected *Substance-Dualism,* associated with Descartes and a lot of religion. That may be taken as the view that what it is to be conscious is something that can happen without dependency on any physical thing, and something not itself in space and hence not physical. Physical things may be understood as (1) space-occupiers that are perceived and (2) space-occupiers that are in causal or other lawlike connections with the space-occupiers that are perceived. Sofas are in the first category, atoms in the second. Ryle also rejected *Property-Dualism,* usually the view that what it is to be conscious is for a physical thing to have non-physical properties dependent on it, these themselves being out of space and thus the physical realm. These two rejections issue in *Naturalism* with respect to consciousness. This is the attitude that what consciousness comes to is somehow physical, but not necessarily nothing but physical facts as now known and understood elsewhere, say neuroscience. This distinction between Naturalism and Eliminative or Nothing-But Materialism is not easy, but let us not be delayed by it.[3]

Ryle rejected more than Substance-Dualism and Property-Dualism. Although the matter is bound up with doctrines of his that we need not enter into, he himself did not take consciousness in our species to be no more than the neural or electrochemical properties of neuroscience. He was not an Eliminative Materialist. He denied too that his doctrine was what it otherwise would have been taken as, a certain kind of Behaviourism. The trouble about

[1] London: Hutchinson.

[2] John Searle, *Mind, Language and Society: Philosophy in the Real World* (London: Weidenfeld & Nicolson, 1999), p. ix.

[3] By my understanding, Functionalism—serious and exclusive Functionalism—is within Naturalism, as is Cognitive Science with Philosophical Ambition, and also the doctrine that conscious events are physical events in heads but different from physical events recognized now in neuroscience. For a version of this latter view, see my 'Consciousness, Neural Functionalism, Real Subjectivity,' *American Philosophical Quarterly,* **32/4** (October, 1995). Thomas Hobbes, U. T. Place and Patricia Churchland count as Eliminative Materialists, as do those Behaviourists who said that conscious events are no more than behaviour, the latter being movements.

Consciousness as Existence, and the End of Intentionality

Ryle is that his several relevant doctrines, notably the large one about category mistakes, do not explain how consciousness is for him both physical and also more than neural and bodily properties.

Certainly Ryle contributed to *Functionalism*, one of the two ruling families of doctrines about consciousness in the last decades of the past millennium. Functionalism comes from the Behaviourism to which Ryle seems committed despite his denial. Functionalism's best source or motivation is not Turing Machines or computers but such a plain truth as that desires, for example, need partly to be conceived as things somehow owed to perception and as somehow issuing in or tending to issue in action. Functionalism gets out of sight of such truths by conceiving events of consciousness as *no more than* internal events that are effects of other such internal events and of inputs, and causes of other such internal events and of outputs. That is what it comes to freed of the lumber. What I mean is not only that such types of conscious events as desires are conceived as no more than certain internal effect-causes or functions, but that conscious events generally are conceived as some general class of such effect-causes and conceived in no other way. The general proposition is the philosophically fundamental one.

Against this family of doctrines, philosophically considered, there is the objection that begins with a question: *What* general class of effect-causes is it that consists in conscious events generally? It needs to be kept in mind, in trying to answer it, that serious and exclusive Functionalism is different from certain hybrid and commonsensical doctrines. It does not allow that there is *more* to conscious events than a large class of effect-causes. It does not allow, for example, that conscious events involve some funny subjectivity, maybe an 'inside,' or 'qualia' as usually understood.

To come towards the crux of the matter of serious Functionalism, and to put the question one way, in terms of just our species, it needs to be remembered that our lives are replete with effect-causes internal to us. In any hour of my life, my weight changes. Of these myriad effect-causes, as we non-Functionalists know and can say, only *some* are conscious—the ones that have some character *other than* being just any old internal effect-causes. The point is not that they have non-causal properties, which they may have, but that they have certain special causal properties rather than *any* old causal properties having to do with other such internal events and with input and output. They fall under a different conception.

Such a conception is officially impossible for Functionalism. In fact, in elaborating itself and concerning itself with just beliefs, desires and so on, it is incoherent. Evidently it depends on some-

3

thing whose existence it denies, a conception of conscious events as other than effect-causes of whatever sort. It uses this to exclude my unnoticed weight changes from its study.

Can this objection be put aside as somehow over-punctilious? An attempt to do so may be made by a scientist of mind. Suppose he says what is true, that we do all depend in our thinking about consciousness on having some grip of what it is to be conscious, got from our personal histories. Suppose he says that what the Functionalist does is to use this grip to locate a subject-matter of which he then discovers, coherently, that it consists in no more than his or her effect-causes. This reply is no good. It cannot conceivably end with the conclusion that Functionalism plainly needs, that our grip was *only* of effect-causes. If the conclusion were true, our grip *would* include effect-causes that patently are not included, such as my hourly weight-change.[4]

There is the same objection of incoherence, although I will not go into the matter, with the other and related ruling family of doctrines about consciousness in recent decades. That is *Artificial Intelligence or Cognitive Science With Philosophical Ambition*. Here conscious events are taken as only something like logical states, or states of a computation. The simple fact is that we are at every moment in myriad states that fall under such a description and are certainly not all conscious states.

If you are a card-carrying Functionalist or member of the Artificial Intelligentsia, you will take more convincing of the need to turn in your card. Many others in and around philosophy, however, are persuaded that we need to start the new millennium with something a lot different. Thomas Nagel is one—see his 'Conceiving the Impossible and the Mind–Body Problem,' his Royal Institute Annual Lecture for 1998.[5] Certainly we have had enough of accounts of consciousness that are in fact denials of its existence—denials of that on which we have a grip. Thomas Kuhn spoke of a period of what he called *normal science* coming to an end with a paradigm shift.[6] Have we not come to an end of some normal

---

[4] For some more along these lines, and also the objection that Functionalism despite its pretensions is in fact no advance on Eliminative Materialism, see my 'Functionalism, Identity Theories, The Union Theory,' in R. Warner & T. Szubka, (eds), *The Mind-Body Problem: A Guide to the Current Debate* (Oxford: Blackwell, 1994), pp. 215–35.

[5] Thomas Nagel, 'Conceiving the Impossible and the Mind-Body Problem,' *Philosophy* July, 1998.

[6] T. S. Kuhn, *The Structure of Scientific Revolutions* (Chicago: University of Chicago Press, 1962).

Consciousness as Existence, and the End of Intentionality

Philosophy of Mind? Do we not need a new paradigm with consciousness? With that want of humility so natural to the philosophical temperament, I would like to carry forward the proposing of one. It was begun in two previous papers.[7]

What is it for you in the room you are in to be *perceptually* conscious at this moment? What is it for you to be aware of your surroundings? *It is for a world somehow to exist.*

What it is for you to be perceptually conscious is not, on this view, for *a world somehow to exist—of which you are conscious or aware or the like.* There is no such circular addition. The sum of the view is that for you to be aware of your surroundings is just for a world somehow to exist. It is the beginning of an analysis of perceptual consciousness, one that takes the claim that someone is perceptually conscious to be a certain existence-claim.

The nub is what that existence claim is or comes to. It is that a collection of things, reasonably referred to as chairs and the like, are in space and time and have other properties, but are not exactly physical.

Recall the earlier quick definition of the physical—space-occupiers that are perceived or space-occupiers that are in lawlike connections with space-occupiers that are perceived. To say that something is physical in the first sense may be to say that it has a several-sided dependency on *perceivers in general* or some of them, most familiarly on their perceptual apparatus. Their contribution to secondary properties of things, the founding fact of British Empiricism, is one large side of this story of dependency. In contrast, to say that your being aware of this room now is for a world somehow to exist—for a particular world of perceptual consciousness to exist—is to say that things are in space and time and have other properties, but have a several-sided dependency on *you alone*.

The chairs now in your world of perceptual consciousness are certainly not in your head or mind, or out of space, but right there in space outside of you. This is perfectly consistent with their having a dependency not only on the atoms and so on in the other half of the physical world, what we can call the scientific world, which

[7] 'Consciousness as Existence,' in Anthony O'Hear, (ed.), *Current Issues in the Philosophy of Mind*, Royal Institute of Philosophy lectures for 1996–7 (Cambridge: Cambridge University Press), pp. 137–55; 'Consciousness as Existence Again,' *in Proceedings of the Twentieth World Congress of Philosophy*, Vol. 9, *Philosophy of Mind*, (ed.) B. Elevitch (Bowling Green: Philosophy Documentation Center, 1999), and also forthcoming in *Theoria*. The second paper corrects the first in certain important respects.

dependency certainly is important to the view in question, but also a unique dependency on you alone among perceivers.

Their existence in this way, this state of affairs, is no more mysterious than things existing physically, that other state of affairs. It is in several ways *less* mysterious. The first sort of existence, personally-dependent, is in fact somehow fundamental to the second. We get to or make up or posit the physical world from the material of our perceptual worlds. In short, what we have are two related ways of conceiving of *what there* is, where by those latter words we can gesture at whatever it is to which we bring our perceiving, conceptualizing, science and so on, something like a Kantian noumenal world.

Taking Naturalism as before, as the attitude that we should somehow or in a way restrict our thinking to the physical world, this doctrine of *Perceptual Consciousness As Existence* is not exactly Naturalism. But it is not far off, and it is as good as identical in spirit. This existentialism about perceptual consciousness could not be regarded as Substance-Dualism, and is remote from Property-Dualism as traditionally and now conceived. It does not turn perceptual consciousness into ghostly stuff or events whose character goes unexplained. It has a considerable if accidental affinity with meaning-doctrines of Anti-Individualism, Externalism and Wide Content—it might be thought to make sense of them.[8] It can properly be spoken of as *Near-Naturalism*. To repeat, your being conscious of this room is for chairs etc. to be in a way in space and time and to be brown, etc., where this is dependent, in so far as it is dependent on persons, on you as against anyone else.

So much for a quick sketch of the doctrine of perceptual consciousness as existence. Does it make clear that it is an analytic advance rather than a circularity? That it is far from saying, in a common way, that what it is to see something is for the thing to exist in one's mental world? I hope so, and hope too that it may be a basis for an account of consciousness generally—its other two parts. These are reflective consciousness, which roughly speaking is thinking without perceiving, and affective consciousness, which has to do with desire, emotion and so on. Let me as quickly note what I take to be some recommendations of existentialism about perceptual consciousness.

(1) To say that for me to be aware of my surroundings is for a world somehow to exist is certainly to be true to what is called the

---

[8] More sense than made by me in 'The Union Theory and Anti-Individualism,' John Heil and Alfred Mele, (eds), *Mental Causation* (Oxford: Clarendon Press, 1993).

phenomenology or seeming nature of the awareness. That is a really good start. Suppose, as seems pretty undeniable, and as was remarked at the start, that the seeming nature of perceptual conscious is *it's* only nature, since consciousness itself contains only what we have without inference. Then the recommendation of truth to so-called phenomenology is the greater.

(2) Despite a temptation to etherealize consciousness, we do, to speak a little loosely, take it to be a reality. Something does go out of existence when I lose consciousness. Consciousness *is* such a reality in the view under consideration. Compare, for example, conscious events as merely logical states, the stock in trade of Artificial Intelligence or Cognitive Science With Philosophical Ambition.

(3) Any view of perceptual consciousness must account for what we call its subjective character, its real subjectivity. The view under consideration does this uniquely, without being elusive. It explains how there is a difference between your awareness and mine, these being different worlds of perceptual consciousness, and, more important, differences between both awarenesses and the physical world in its particular objectivity. These three worlds have different things in them, numerically and qualitatively. The first two involve different real points of view.

(4) With any view of perceptual consciousness, its upshot for the mind-body or mind-brain problem is crucial. We demand, almost above all, that a view of consciousness should explain, or at any rate not make more obscure, how it is that consciousness can be both effect and cause of physical things. The view in hand, I take it, passes the test. The nub is that being perceptually conscious, as was not the case for Descartes and his followers, *is* something that is not only in time but also in space. This it can be, clearly, without also being exactly physical. The fact has to do in part with its other dependency, on what was called the scientific world.

As it seems to me, the two Naturalist families of accounts of consciousness mentioned, Functionalism and the Artificial Intelligence, fail to satisfy the first three of these four requirements—about phenomenology so-called, a reality, and real subjectivity. This is so, perhaps, because they are responses above all to the fourth, the mind-body problem, this fact having something to do with their kinship to the sciences of consciousness. Perceptual consciousness as existence, by contrast, satisfies all four requirements. However there may be another one. It is the main concern of this paper.

It has been a philosophical commonplace that most of non-perceptual consciousness, and perceptual consciousness as well, has a property or nature that is its *intentionality*. In the Philosophy of Mind since Roderick Chisholm's *Perceiving* of 1957,[9] an awful lot has been heard about it. Many have contemplated that this intentionality may be the mark of the mental, and taken consciousness as at least a main part of the mental, the remainder being our various capabilities and dispositions. Intentionality is typically introduced by way of certain remarks.

(i)   In consciousness there is something before the mind.

(ii)   The mind has a capacity to direct itself at things.

(iii) Conscious events are directed at or have reference to things.

(iv) They are *about* things.

(v)   They are *of* things.

(vi) We do not just believe, or just desire, or just see, but believe, desire or see something.

(vii) We can believe what is not the case, want what does not exist, and so on

Do you suppose, on hearing or rehearing these remarks, that you have already been told what intentionality is? That would perhaps be in line with Dennett's initial definition of intentionality in *The Cambridge Dictionary of Philosophy* as simply 'aboutness.'[10] But of course there is something philosophically more important that has the name of intentionality. This is some more clarified property or character of conscious events, this property or character being their intentionality properly speaking. Such a property or character is given to us in a philosophical doctrine, one of a family of philosophical doctrines.

Thus we can take the initial remarks as parts of what has been called *folk-psychology*—that of which it is tempting to say that it is what we actually know about the mind. The subsequent doctrines of intentionality are not part of folk-psychology. They are in a way on a level with the Dualisms, Eliminative Materialism, Functionalism, philosophical Artificial Intelligence, certain doctrines of the subjective character and of the content of conscious events[11], and so forth. This is so although the doctrines of intentionality may not compete with but may enter into the Dualisms

---

[9] R. M. Chisholm, *Perceiving: A Philosophical Study* (Ithaca: Cornell University Press, 1957).

[10] 'Intentionality,' in Robert Audi, (ed.), *The Cambridge Dictionary of Philosophy* (Cambridge: Cambridge University Press, 1995)

[11] I take the opportunity to affirm that existentialism about perceptual consciousness is no continuation at all of my positive lines of thought in 'Seeing Things,' *Synthese* **98**, 1, January 1994, and 'Consciousness, Neural Functionalism, Real Subjectivity.'

and so on. Nearly all of these, save Eliminative Materialism, have somehow added to their materials at least a recognition of a somehow clarified property or character of intentionality.

The general question in front of us, then, is whether the various philosophical doctrines of intentionality satisfy a requirement on accounts of consciousness that is given in the various remarks, and also whether the account of perceptual consciousness as existence satisfies the requirement.

Of course, it is not very clear how much of a requirement it is. On reflection, we do not have much of a test of philosophical doctrines of intentionality or the doctrines of Dualism etc. into which they enter in the particular truth (vi) that to see is always to see something—that being understood as a remark in an ordinary unphilosophical tone of voice. Functionalists have not yet become so insecure as to claim the recommendation that they too can allow that when we see, we always see things. Perhaps the day is coming but we are not yet there.

What about the remark that (i) in consciousness there is something before the mind, or the remark that (ii) the mind has a capacity to direct itself upon things? Does the latter introduce a bit of *folk doctrine*, if there can be such a thing—something beyond the truth that seeing is always seeing something? To the extent that the term 'the mind' can be assigned a plain man's meaning, do we get more of a requirement on accounts of consciousness?

Let us not reflect further on the use of the opening remarks about intentionality. Let us assume that the remarks may be *some* guide as to perceptual consciousness, but leave the matter a little unsettled. Let us not struggle, either, to arrive at the single best understanding of the philosophical doctrines of intentionality. One reason for not doing so is that we would lose things of interest and possibly of value. Rather, let us look at seven philosophical doctrines of intentionality or the like. No doubt there are more, yet more obscure, but these seven will serve my dark purpose.

(1) Consciousness involves a relation of directedness or reference between something or other, this being unspecified, and an object or content internal to the conscious event in question. The event in question takes place in the head of the perceiver, as must its contained object or content.

This doctrine of intentionality does not have in it something often associated with the matter—this being a mediaeval embarrassment about the object or content existing only in some funny way, being halfway between nothing and something. In fact, it is closer than many doctrines to what Brentano actually says in his famous and often misread paragraph on the subject: 'Every mental phenomenon is characterized by what the Scholastics of the Middle Ages called the intentional (or mental) inexistence of an object, and what we might call, though not wholly unambiguously, reference to a content, direction towards an object (which is not to be understood here as meaning a thing), or immanent objectivity. Every mental phenomenon includes something as object within itself, although they do not all do so in the same way. In presentation something is presented, in judgement something is affirmed or denied, in love loved, in hate hated, in desire desired and so on.'[12]

Doctrine (I) rather than Brentano's paragraph is my concern. Evidently it has in it nothing whatever about objects or contents *outside* the head of the perceiver—objects or contents of which it is remarked, by other doctrinalists to whom we will come, that they may not exist. Also, this first doctrine is in accord with the truism that a relation requires the existence of its terms, and in particular that a dyadic relation requires the existence of two terms. If the second term in the doctrine, the mentioned object or content in consciousness and the head of the perceiver, did not exist, the token relation would not exist, and hence the particular event of perceptual consciousness would not exist. But there is no reason whatever to raise a question of such an inner object or content not existing.

What is to be said of (I)? It seems out of touch with the initial remarks as ordinarily understood that (i) in consciousness there is something before the mind, that (ii) the mind has a capacity to direct itself at things, and that (vi) in seeing we see something. According to them, do I not have before me, direct myself at, and see, *ordinary rooms outside my head*? Folk-psychology is not the Sense-Datum or Representative Theory of Perception, not Phenomenalism. Even when a supposed external object in fact does not exist, say the fountain of youth in Hampstead, what I seem to get in hallucinating it is not what I as a member of the folk would then describe as a fountain *in my head*. Very definitely this first doctrine of intentionality as applied to perceptual consciousness is wonderfully incomplete. Seeing involves *some* relation to something outside the head in question. That is built into the concept.

---

[12] *Psychology From an Empirical Standpoint*, Oskar Kraus, Linda L. McAlister (eds) (London, Routledge & Kegan Paul, 1973), p. 88. For interpretation of the paragraph, in particular in connection with existence-in rather than non-existence, see David Bell, *Husserl* (London: Routledge, 1990), Ch. 1.

Consciousness as Existence, and the End of Intentionality

We need to object, too, that the relation in this first doctrine, inside the head, is left about as metaphorical and obscure as in the ordinary remarks with which we began. Certainly the relation, although *reference* to the object or content is mentioned, could not possibly be one of *representation*, like that between a word or picture and what it stands for. What the account evidently wants to bring in as the first term of the relation is something like *the mind*, which itself, whatever it is, can be no representation or symbol. Also, what *is* this thing called the mind? We are doing philosophy now, not chatting, and so we need to know.

A further objection will have counterparts with respect other doctrines of intentionality to which we are coming. We have it that an event of perceptual consciousness in a head includes within itself an object or content. The account says nothing of the nature of this item, about whether it is conceptual or not and so on, but leave that. The relevant fact is that the object or content is understood as being *within or a part of the consciousness of the perceiver*. It is as much so as if it were a sense-datum—which, for all we are told, it may be. It would also be within or a part of the consciousness of the perceiver if it were the original sort of thing in the intentionality tradition, the *intentio* of the mediaevals, this being an idea, concept or notion.[13]

But when I am aware of this room now, what is within my consciousness is *the room* and no other relevant thing. Seeing isn't always seeing double. Seeing isn't seeing by way of using some conscious means to that end, an image or idea or whatever else. There's no picture or word or the like in the story of my perceptual consciousness now. There is no minimizing this objection. The very centrepiece of this first account of intentionality is missing from its subject-matter, from the reality of perceptual consciousness. The reality is *Hamlet* without the prince.

Does some scientist of consciousness now say that this last objection is beside some large point? And say that that point is that the object or content need not be within or part of the conscious event? Well, that is not at all like the account we have been considering, the one closest to Brentano's paragraph, but of course we *can* contemplate something distant from Brentano's paragraph but yet related to it.

[13] For introductory sketches of intentionality, see Stephen Priest, *Theories of the Mind* (London: Penguin Books, 1991); Owen Flanagan, *The Science of the Mind* (Cambridge MA: MIT Press, 1984), Robert Stalnaker, *Inquiry* (Cambridge MA: MIT Press, 1984), Ch. 1, and Tim Crane, 'Intentionality,' *Routledge Encyclopedia of Philosophy* (London: Routledge, 1998), Edward Craig (ed.).

(II) An event of perceptual consciousness involves a relation of directedness between something or other, more congenial to the late 20th Century than *the mind*, maybe a neural system, and an object or content not internal to the event of perceptual consciousness, but within the head of the perceiver. This object or content has an explanatory role with respect to the conscious event itself.

The objections to the first doctrine having to do with incompleteness and an obscure relation also apply to this second one. This story of non-conscious intentionality does escape the largest objection, since its centre-piece is not known to be missing. The escape, however, is by means of what is hardly less than philosophical disaster. This is not because the account is in a certain way false. No doubt at all—there are *many* things that may be dubbed contents or objects that are within or on the surface of a perceiver and are within the directedness of something else, and are somehow explanatory of events of perceptual consciousness. The most familiar one is a real retinal image. Neuroscience provides a lot more candidates. The philosophical disaster of this account is, rather, that it is in fact *no account whatever* of the kind promised, an account of perceptual experience itself, this consciousness. It merely changes the subject while pretending to stick to it.

Is there a reason for changing the subject, for contemplating this second account? Could it be that someone's reason, so-called, is just some fuller account of perceptual consciousness, something that calls for the relocation of intentionality outside of consciousness as we have a grip on it? Maybe hybrid or modified Functionalism, having in it the story of inner causal relata but also something about 'qualia,' these being a matter of consciousness but not intentionality? But that is not a *defence* of non-conscious intentionality, a *reason* in favour of it. It is in effect pretty much the opposed doctrine—and thus near to begging the question. We want a *ground* for moving from intentionality within consciousness to non-conscious intentionality, not an assertion of the latter. By contrast, as it seems to me, the objection that this doctrine of non-conscious intentionality gives no account whatever of something, as implicitly promised, is not the question-begging assertion of another account.

One of the initial remarks about intentionality was that (vii) we can believe in or want what does not exist—and of course hope for it and so on. This plain fact is thought to be catered for in *some* doctrine of intentionality. It is not catered for in the first doctrine, as noticed, or presumably the second. There is nothing in either doctrine about any relation one of whose terms does not or may not exist. The plain fact that we can believe in or want or hope for what does not exist may be turned into something else, as it was by Chisholm.[14] It may be replaced by a fact about language now philosophically familiar, the fact of *intensionality* with an 's'. This linguistic fact is;

> (III) It does not follow, from the use of a referring expression, that the thing referred to actually does exists.

It does not follow from the truth that someone wanted to find the fountain of youth in Hampstead that it exists. But the unusual entailment-failure, as is now well-known, occurs with other things than consciousness and the like. It tells us nothing of the distinctiveness of consciousness. I mention this so-called account of intentionality only to put it aside quickly. Even if the linguistic fact turned up only and always with consciousness, of course, it *by itself* would tell us little worth knowing of consciousness itself.[15] It would not be an account of how it was that consciousness gave rise to the linguistic fact. Our subject is not language.

Is there some doctrine of intentionality, as distinct from anything else, that does cater for the fact that we can believe in or want what does not exist—some doctrine that does involve us in the problem, as it called, of a relation to something that does not exist? Indeed there is. Consider the following candidate, anticipated in passing earlier.

> (IV) An event of perceptual consciousness is such that a mind is in a relation of directedness with respect to an object or content internal to the event, as before, but there is a second relation between the object or content and something outside the event and the head in question. This second relation may hold between the content or object and something that does not exist.

The doctrine is complete in the way that the first two are not. We get outside the head. It faces the objections noticed earlier having to do with the obscurity of the first relation between the mind and internal object or content, and the obscurity of the mind itself, and, as might have been said before, an objection having to do with the probable circularity of recourse to the mind in an account of consciousness. It is also entirely open to the major objection that we

---

[14] *Perceiving.*

[15] See my *A Theory of Determinism: The Mind, Neuroscience, and Life-Hopes* (Oxford: Clarendon, 1988) or *Mind and Brain* (Oxford: Clarendon, 1999), both p. 71 ff.

have no awareness at all of the supposed object or content. It is just missing. *Hamlet* without the prince again.

There is also the fact that the second relation, to say the least, is obscure. If it is said to be *representation*, what is that in general? No philosophical question is further from an answer. As for the philosophical question of what this sort of conscious representation, as against representation with real sentences and pictures, is supposed to be, this is a philosophical question often regarded as unanswerable.[16]

That is not the end of the trouble. There is worse. It is no good tripping lightly past the so-called 'problem' of a non-existent term of a relation. This is in fact a simple contradiction. The relation of representation or whatever is indeed presented as a relation. What we are thus offered is nothing other than the nonsense of the possibility of a dyadic relation with one term, the nonsense of a relation between something and nothing.

Do some of us come to tolerate the so-called problem by concentrating on the many happy cases where the thing outside the conscious event and the head *does* exist—say the fountain in South End Green rather than the fountain of youth? Can it be supposed that despite the contradiction in the second case, we can have a clear and good account of this relation in the first case? Exactly the opposite can be argued. The so-called relation of representation, it seems, is the same in both cases. Well then, what is clear about the first case is *not* part of that relation.

Let me be brief about something else, a once hopeful doctrine that is best regarded as a part of our serious and exclusive Functionalism and hence something we have put aside. It could, however, be made part of doctrine (IV) just considered or of something else. It is distinctive in being a certain attempt to make an escape from the obscurity of the second relation at which we have been glancing, regarded as one of representation, aboutness or whatever. What it does is to suppose that:

> (V) The relation between the internal object or content and the particular thing outside the head is just that the latter causes the former.

This seems hopeless. The simplest reason for saying so is that the internal object or content must be the effect of myriad things other than the particular thing it is said to represent or whatever—it is the effect of a real image on a retina for a start. Complicating the the simple causal story has not succeeded, and further attempts, more

[16] Tim Crane, 'Representation,' *Routledge Encyclopedia of Philosophy.*

epicycles, seem unlikely to do better. *Of course* the truth about per-ceptual consciousness is causal, but it is a different kind of truth. You do not get to it by fiddling with the central causal story in the science of perception.[17]

Before turning to the fullest and best-known account of inten-tionality, let us consider a very recent one, by Tim Crane.[18] It has to do with something so far not mentioned, a consensus that inten-tionality is *not* a feature of certain conscious or mental states—such bodily sensations as having a pain and such moods or feelings as undirected anxiety or depression. This doctrine is also different in another way. The previous ones, those that do not change the sub-ject, have at least the smell of the Sense-Datum Theory of Perception about them. Here, we get rid of it.

In this exposition, tentative and not doctrinally-burdened, the consensus about bodily sensations and moods not being intentional is questioned. The essential first move in this connection, certainly arresting, is simply to detach intentionality from a mental state's being (iv) *about* anything, or (v) *of* anything, or *representing* any-thing. The facts that a pain and being gloomy about nothing in par-ticular are not *of* or *about* anything and do not *represent* anything—these were of course just the reasons that those states were *not* regarded as intentional. Now they can be. The main plank of the doctrine is said to be captured by or expressed in or inspired by what we have treated as a guiding remark, that (vi) we do not just believe or desire or see, but believe or desire or see *something*.[19] This main plank is:

(VI) What it is for something to be an intentional state is for it to be given to the mind.

Particular accounts are given of the pain and gloom. With respect to the pain, it is first contemplated that an internal mental object is presented to the mind. However, an alternative account is preferred, one that takes being in pain to be being aware of something non-mental—one's body, or a state of it, or bodily events in it.[20] With respect to the undirected gloom, what is mainly said is that really it

[17] Cf. Jerry A. Fodor, *Psychosemantics: The Problem of Meaning in the Philosophy of Mind* (Cambridge, MA.: Bradford Book, 1987).

[18] 'Intentionality as the Mark of the Mental,' in *Current Issues in the Philosophy of Mind*, Royal Institute of Philosophy Lectures for 1996–97, pp. 229–51.

[19] Op. cit., pp. 246, 238, 243.

[20] M. G. F. Martin, 'Setting Things Before the Mind,' in *Current Issues in the Philosophy of Mind*.

is in a way or ways directed. As Sartre held, emotions in general are a mode of apprehending the real world. This is a kind of Direct or Naive Realism about pains and gloom.

So we have these two instances of something being 'given to the mind,' which fact is the fact of intentionality. The view is said to be close to previous doctrines of intentionality for two reasons. One, alas, is that it involves what appears to be a relation between thinkers and the objects of their thoughts—despite, as is allowed, the fact that this cannot be true in general. Secondly, the view is true to the idea so far unmentioned that when something is apprehended as the object of an intentional state, it is apprehended in a certain way. This is an idea closely associated with intensionality with an 's.'

This view must prompt a number of reflections. One, of some importance, has to do with the initial remarks, also a matter of consensus, that an intentional state certainly is *about* something or *of* something. There is also the philosophical commonplace that an intentional state *represents* something. Are these items not pretty much the heart of the matter? The ease with which this heart is jettisoned should go some way to curing anyone of the thought that with intentionality we have philosophical doctrines that at least have agreed foundations. To say the least, things are not that clear. And, putting aside foundations, there is not even a decent consistency. But another reflection is still more important.

We have long had philosophical accounts of the various kinds of consciousness—including accounts of seeing and other perceiving, and of sensations like pain, and of being subject to the emotions. Accounts of the latter two things are offered in the doctrine we are considering. A view of seeing and other perceiving is also favoured in the doctrine—Direct or Naive Realism, in line with what is preferred in connection with the pain and gloom. The doctrine's main aim, however, is to characterize a wholly pervasive character of consciousness. The aim is rightly higher than a certain disjunction: consciousness is either such-and-such, as when it consists in seeing and the like, or such and such, with pain and the like, or. ... The aim, rather, is to come up with a *common* character of conscious events, their intentionality.

We have the sum total of that character, I take it, when we are told that in consciousness something is *given to mind*. Regarded as a philosophical account, this is very safe, because it says so very little. In fact it would fit well into the initial remarks which we began. Presumably more than a metaphor is intended, but what? My apprehension is that we learn nothing from this account. If it goes beyond the remark that (vi) in believing, desiring and seeing we believe, desire and see *something*, where does it go? Is it helped on its way at all by additional unexplained talk of 'directedness?'

The thinness can be madé clear in a particular way. Consider the 'of-ness,' 'about-ness' and representativeness of other mental states than pain and gloom etc., those that do indeed seem to have it, belief above all. Is this what it is for them to be instances of something's being *given to the mind* or is it not? If it is, then we have no general philosophical account of intentionality, one that also applies to the pain and gloom. This is the disjunctive failure. But if the 'of-ness' etc. is *not* what it is for something to be given to the mind, then what *is* this givenness? Could it be that what we have here is no more than a generalized Direct or Naive Realism—something pretty unlikely to throw light on consciousness itself or a fundamental character of *it*. In its talk of direct awareness, it has never analysed awareness, but only asserted it to be direct.

The doctrine under consideration also has in it something else to give us pause. Not only *conscious* states can have things *given* to them. Unconscious ones can. What is it for something to be given to something else if the latter thing is not conscious—if it is, as presumably it is, a neural structure? Do remember, by the way, if you are willing to tolerate non-conscious *representation*, that this givenness of something is specifically *not* its being represented by or to anything.

Let me also remark quickly, as in another case earlier, that if we are giving an analysis of a fundamental fact of consciousness or mentality, and something called 'the mind' turns up in it essentially, we are not a long way forward. Finally, and as important as anything else, there is that matter of a wonky relation between thinkers and the objects of their thoughts. Can you say, in effect, as our philosopher does in this case, that something is *usually* a relation but sometimes is not? That in general intentionality is a relation, but not always?[21] No you can't. At best you face immediate questions. *What* is that thing? One thing it isn't is a relation.

(VII) Let us finish this survey by looking a little more closely at John Searle's doctrine in his book *Intentionality*.[22] There is too much of it to be summarized in a sentence or two, but it is in part that *in your now being aware of this room, there exists something called a content, but no directedness towards it.* Nor, then, is there anything that is directed towards it. What can be said, at most, is that a person has the experience. The content, then, is no object

---

[21] 'Intentionality as the Mark of the Mental,' p. 244.
[22] Cambridge: Cambridge University Press, 1983.

of awareness. It is not a sense-datum, sensum, impression, copy, kind of picture or the like—this doctrine, like the previous one, is a version of Direct Realism as against the Sense-Datum Theory or Phenomenalism. The content is not a 'linguistically realized' item either.[23] Despite not being any of these things, however, it *is* something else. *This content is directed to something.* It *is a propositional content* or *representative content.* It may represent an object or state of affairs, as in the case of your awareness of a yellow station wagon or this room. Or, it may represent without there being any object or state of affairs that it represents.

Several other things are said of contents in general. One is that instead of taking a conscious experience to be a relation between a person and the content, it would be more accurate to say the experience was *identical* with the content somehow realized. With respect to the representative character of the content, gestured at by what is admitted to be only the metaphor of directedness, it is allowed that it is not possible to give an *analysis* of it in simpler terms. Intrinsic intentionality is a ground-floor property of the mind.

Despite this, however, light can be shed on it by way of the derived intentionality or representativeness of sentences of language, real pictures, and so on. These latter things, in what is called their logical character as against any of their ontological realizations, are a matter of (i) a truth condition or other 'condition of satisfaction,' (ii) a psychological mode, such that the sentence or whatever is a belief, desire or the like, which mode determines (iii) direction of fit. In the case of a sentence that is a belief, the belief needs to fit the world, rather than the world be changed to fit the belief, as in the case of a command. So with your awareness of this room, and perceptual consciousness in general. To speak of any content being a representation is just shorthand for such 'logical' facts about it.

To return to perceptual experience in particular, it is added that it has what are spoken of as phenomenal properties. Above all, while it is true that your being aware of this room is more or less a representation, it is more natural to regard it as a *presentation* of a state of affairs—directly of it, immediate, and involuntary. Also, with perceptual experience, it enters into the content somehow that the content is caused by the object it represents. This is 'shown' in the experience. Finally, a perceptual content may involve an aspect under which an object is presented, as in the case of the duck/rabbit drawing.

---

[23] *Intentionality*, p. 6.

Consciousness as Existence, and the End of Intentionality

This account of intentionality seems to me both admirable and a disaster—being philosophy, it can be both. If it escapes metaphor, scientism and spirituality, it faces some of the same seemingly insuperable difficulties as its predecessors. Also, for a large reason not yet given, it seems in the end to raise a question about itself, a general question about its own interpretation.

The exclusion of anything about a relation of a content to anything so vague as the mind or the like is of course understandable. But the exclusion is also impossible. It runs up against the seeming necessity that a representation *is* something that is *to* or *for* someone or something. A mark or propositional content or whatever such that there is no possibility of there being a reading or understanding of it by something is no representation. This remains true if representation is reduced to satisfaction-conditions and so on. It thus seems that eschewing of the vagueness of a *mind* or whatever in relation to the content will not do. An account of that thing to which something is a representation is needed, and no account at all is given. Nor, secondly, is any account given of any relation from the thing to the representation. That is quite as bad, not an incidental failing.

To come on to the other relation, content to object, there is the other old difficulty of there being no sense in talk of a dyadic relation with only one term. There still is a relation asserted, of course, when representation is conceived in the way just mentioned, by way of the several notions—satisfaction-conditions and so on. It is no good saying, as it is said, that intentionality cannot be 'an ordinary relation' since the object or state of affairs at one end of it need not exist.[24] It obviously cannot be a relation *at all*, ordinary, extraordinary, plain, fancy or of any other kind whatever.

To come on to other difficulties of this account, they involve us in what seems to be a general question of how to interpret it. It may seem in a way clear enough. The content of a perceptual experience is not an object of awareness, not seen, not a sense-datum or the like, and not a linguistically realized item. However, that does not exclude a related possibility—very likely exactly what you have had in mind in contemplating the whole story. It is just that the content is *within* or *a part of* the experience, in consciousness, something reportable without inference.

One reason for this interpretation is that the content, as you will remember, is on the way to being identical with the experience, and that the experience is of course something had by the perceiver, something that is *experienced* by the perceiver. It is at least indicative,

[24] *Intentionality*, p. 4.

19

too, that it is said that such a content, which has a self-referential side having to do with causation mentioned in passing earlier, can be made explicit in a certain form. 'I have a visual experience (that there is a yellow station wagon there and that there is a yellow station wagon there is causing this visual experience.)'[25]

That same conclusion, that the content is within consciousness as a part, can be based as well on the content's having, as you will remember, such phenomenal properties as being a *presentation*. It seems we can tell or indeed are given this difference of perceptual experience from other consciousness. Remember as well that perceptual experience may involve an aspect under which an object is presented. It is certainly worth keeping in mind, too, that Searle's official position with respect to the ontology of conscious events is against *Reductionism*—against, as it seems, their having only neural properties.[26] Further, while he does indeed distinguish his position from the Representative Theory of Perception and Phenomenalism, he stresses that for him experiences are *real* in a way that he takes to be denied in some other versions of Direct Realism.

The burden of all this is that the account we are considering is that in seeing the room we have the content *in* our experience—and, as we know, it is certainly not the object, which is such a thing as the yellow station wagon out there in the world. This is all very well, but there are reasons for hesitation. There are reasons to consider a very different interpretation. It is that the content of which we have heard so much is *not* in consciousness.

We have learned in recent Philosophy of Mind that the language of consciousness is easily degraded. The meanings of terms can be reduced to what is far less than the realities the terms are supposed to be about. This is true of 'consciousness,' of course, and 'content' itself, but also such other terms as have turned up in the exposition of this doctrine of intentionality, including 'experienced,' 'representation,' 'aspect' and so on. It does indeed seem unlikely that Searle should be among the degraders, given his role as the hammer of the Artificial Intelligentsia. But for certain reasons it is not impossible.

One reason is that he insists that his doctrine gives the *logical* properties of intentionality, and not the *ontology* of the experiences that realize those properties. The distinction is perhaps sufficiently

---

[25] *Intentionality*, p. 48.

[26] John Searle, *The Rediscovery of the Mind* (London & Cambridge MA: MIT Press, 1992), p. xi ff, p. 1 ff, p. 113 ff

clear, and it does certainly leave us with the question of the ontology or actual nature of perceptual consciousness. We hear about that in another book.[27] We are told there that a Reductionist account of that nature is not intended, but it is uncertain how such an account is avoided. To come to a principal contention of mine in the past, it certainly is *not* avoided by what is mainly said of consciousness, that it consists in higher-level biological events of the brain caused by lower-level wholly neural events in the brain.[28] *That* description, certainly, allows the higher-level events to be wholly neural.

It is not reassuring either that in one place in *Intentionality* where he says his contents are not objects, that there are no internal objects of awareness, he also goes further. 'The visual experience is not the object of visual perception, and the features which specify the intentional content are not in general literal features of the experience.'[29] That does not sound at all like the first interpretation. Do we need to hear *all* the lines about experience, awareness and so on in a way very differently from before?

Let me notice in passing, on the way to a conclusion about the interpretation of the doctrine, that there is a special difficulty in saying that no analysis is possible of the intrinsic intentionality of consciousness. If this ground-floor property of the mind *does* defy any analysis, how can we know that light is shown on it by the intentionality of language, pictures and so on derived from it? This is not obvious, if only for the reason that there is no sense in which causes have to be *like* their effects.

Let me notice, too, that there is a remarkable difference between derived intentionality and intrinsic intentionality. With derived intentionality we have actually *got* representations—words in English, sentences, pictures, images and so on. When I use your name in saying good morning to you, that representation of you is about as real as you. If we cannot actually find any analogue with intrinsic intentionality, why should it be thought that it can have light cast on it by derived intentionality? How could something so unlike intrinsic intentionality cast any light at all?

I shall not attempt to settle the general question of interpretation that has emerged. Like much impressive philosophy, what we have may be an attempt to have it both ways. Let me suggest, rather, that

[27] *The Rediscovery of the Mind*

[28] For a general assessment of Searle as reductionist, dualist or whatever, see my 'Consciousness, Neural Functionalism, Real Subjectivity,' especially pp. 337–338.

[29] *Intentionality*, pp. 44, 45.

we have a dilemma. If content *is* taken to be within consciousness, there is a large problem, and if it is not so taken, there is as much of a problem.

With respect to the first supposition, that contents are within consciousness, parts of perceptual experience—this is false. It is not only false that in perceptual experience we have a content as a sense-datum or other object of awareness, but *as false* that we have the content otherwise conceived somehow within or as a part of the experience. What I have in my awareness of this room is nothing more than this room. What we get, in Searle's terms, is just the object. We just get the station-wagon itself. That is the so-called phenomenology of it, as noted already with several other doctrines of intentionality. So on this interpretation of the doctrine what we again get is *Hamlet* without the prince. No more needs to be said.

The second interpretation is that really Searle wishes to relocate all that stuff about content *out* of consciousness as we have a grip on it. On his account correctly understood, it is really somewhere else. The proper response to this is the same as before, with another doctrine of intentionality, the second we looked at it. It is that we are left with no account at all of perceptual consciousness itself, and no reason for changing the subject.

So much for this last doctrine of intentionality—now let me rehearse a bit.

It seemed possible that an adequate account of perceptual consciousness needs to satisfy a requirement having to do with intentionality conveyed by a number of remarks, the first being that in consciousness there is something before the mind. The remarks in question have issued in a number of philosophical doctrines of or related to intentionality, seven noticed by us, which doctrines can enter into dualisms and the like. We have looked at these doctrines of intentionality in order to see if they satisfy a requirement of intentionality conveyed by the remarks. Do they?

They do not. They do not satisfy *any* requirement of interest. This is because these doctrines are a mess. I have been a little relentless in laying out objections to them, some of which may have been noted by you before. My aim has partly been to reinforce a suspicion or at any rate a tentativeness that should have become a suspicion—maybe a suspicion or tentativeness less expressed because of the idea that there is no alternative to some doctrine of intentionality or other. In any case, the doctrines *are* a mess.[30]

The largest reason for saying so, now familiar, is that what most

[30] Searle takes the intentionality tradition before him to be 'something of a mess.' *Intentionality*, p. 1.

of them centrally affirm, an object or content internal to perceptual consciousness, is a fiction. The reality of perceptual consciousness is no prince. The second reason is the nonsense of a relation to
an object or state of affairs that does not or need not exist, a dyadic
relation with one term. The third is the vagueness of that to which
something is a representation, maybe a mind. The fourth is obscurity about the second relation, often said to be representation. A
fifth, as with Crane, is the obscurity of some relation or other,
givenness, in the Direct or Naive Realism. A sixth, in the case of
several doctrines, is incompleteness. A seventh, in two cases, is
missing the subject entirely. Finally, there is the uncertainty about
the general interpretation of the fullest account, Searle's, which
helps to open it to all of the objections already mentioned.

The first of my principal conclusions in this paper, then, is that
we need to give up on doctrines of intentionality—anything of the
sort we have considered. Doctrines of intentionality should be
regarded as having no future. We should give up on them. The second conclusion is that reflection on these philosophical doctrines
has results for something else. It has results for the proposition that
what it is for you to be perceptually conscious is for a world in a way
to exist.

Existentialism about perceptual consciousness does not exactly
follow from, but is certainly suggested by, there being no object or
content within perceptual consciousness. Might it be that it is only
this existentialism that that is both arguable and also consistent with
the fact of the missing object or content?

Existentialism about perceptual consciousness is suggested too by
the nonsense about a relation lacking a term. In this existentialism,
there is no such relation—and no relation which can tempt anyone
in the direction of the nonsense. You are right to suppose there are
other relations, between a world of perceptual consciousness and
the scientific world, and between a world of perceptual consciousness and a brain, and between such a world and the perceived part
of the physical world, but no question whatever arises of a relation
existing in the absence of one of its terms. If existentialism about
perceptual consciousness has to fit in illusion and hallucination,
which it does, and about which nothing has been said, it does not
have to do so by pretending that a non-relation is a relation.

There is the very same story with our other reflections on the
doctrines of intentionality—incompleteness, vagueness about the
possessor or whatever of a representation, obscurity about the relation of this thing to the representation, obscurity of the relation of
representation to an object, and missing the subject-matter entirely.

Ted Honderich

These shortcomings of philosophical doctrines of intentionality—
not to mention startling inconsistencies between them—point to
something very different, arguably our existentialism.

Let us return briefly to the bundle of remarks with which we
began, the folk psychology as against the developed philosophical
accounts of intentionality. How does perceptual consciousness as
existence stand to that bundle? Also, how much of a requirement on
accounts of perceptual consciousness *is* the bundle? Does perceptual consciousness as existence, for a start, accord with the remark that
in consciousness (i) there is something before the mind?

Well, you could say that the view actually gets rid of the distinction between 'the mind' and 'something before it'—thereby meaning just the central proposition that to be perceptually conscious is
for a world in a way to exist. You could also say, however, that the
view gives a certain sense to the remark that in consciousness something is before the mind—that in a perceptual experience there
exists a particular world rather than any other. You could say, too,
that our existentialism about consciousness does better than did
certain doctrines of intentionality in accommodating the remark.
My own first reaction, however, is one that does not accord too
much respect to the remark. It is that it is a recommendation of the
view that it gets rid of the mind as a ghostly entity, which the
remark seems to take it to be.

So too with the remark that (ii) the mind has a capacity to direct
itself at things. Of this it can also be said that in a perceptual experience there exists a particular world rather than any other. But I
leave to you further reflection on the bundle and the extent to which
we have catered for it, and how far we should be constrained by it.

Finally, three general reflections on intentionality from elsewhere.

The first is by the distinguished Brentano and Husserl scholar,
Reinhardt Grossman.[31] It is about dilemmas, and begins with what
can seem to be one—that in perceptual and other consciousness
either the mind is related to what is before it or it is not. The second horn of this dilemma *is* a horn because there is no plausible
non-relational account. The first horn is a horn because it leads to
difficulties of which you have heard something from me. That is, a
relational account must deal with the proposition that we can
believe in and desire things that do not exist. Thus what we have is
either that there can be a relation to things that do not exist, a weird

[31] Reinhardt Grossmann. 'Intentional Relation,' in *The Oxford
Companion to Philosophy* (Oxford: Oxford University Press, 1995), Ted
Honderich (ed.).

relation, or certain things that do not really exist do somehow exist—another dilemma.

In the tradition of Brentano and Husserl, I take it, the response to the first dilemma has indeed been that there is no non-relational account of perceptual consciousness. Thereafter a lot of fortitude has gone into trying to make sense of a relation underdescribed as weird, or to make sense of objects that somehow do not and also do exist. As you will anticipate, my response is different. We need not get into all that deep water, since, to go back to the first dilemma, so-called, there now *is* a non-relational account of perceptual consciousness—as a kind of existence.

The second reflection is by Quine.[32] It has to do with both the tradition of Brentano and also his idea, so far unmentioned, that intentionality is not only the mark of the mental but something that cannot be accounted for in physical terms. There can be no account of it that preserves a Naturalism. Quine's response in effect is that if there is inconsistency between a supposed fact of intentionality and Naturalism, then it is the supposed fact that must be given up. Does this response come to an entire disregarding of the requirement we have been considering on an account of consciousness? Does it come to supposing there is *no* sense or truth in the remark that in the consciousness on which we have a grip something is before the mind? Then it is no tolerable conclusion.

But that does not drive us far from Quine's position. If the choice *was* between something about the mind inconsistent not only with Naturalism but also with the Near-Naturalism of perceptual consciousness as existence, my own inclination would be to give up that thing. That is not the choice we face. It may be a recommendation of taking perceptual consciousness to be a kind of existence that we can satisfy what requirements we need to satisfy in connection with intentionality and still remain philosophically respectable.

The third reflection is Fodor's, often reported, that '... if aboutness is real, it must really be something else.'[33] What is supposed to stand in the way of taking aboutness to be real? Fodor's answer, and the answer of many, is that it has seemed not to fit into naturalism at all, and particularly has not been open to the hopeless causal analysis mentioned earlier.[34] That is, there is no serious chance of taking *B*'s being a representation of *A* as just the fact that *A* causes *B*.

[32] W. V. O. Quine, *Word and Object* (New York: Wiley, 1960), p. 221.

[33] *Psychosemantics: The Problem of Meaning in the Philosophy of Mind*, p. 97

[34] See intentionality doctrine V, p. 14.

Ted Honderich

A response to Fodor is that getting near to Naturalism is enough, and certainly that it would be absurd to suppose that intentionality is somehow non-causal. But of course consciousness as existence *is* Near-Naturalism and *is* a causal account of perceptual consciousness. Aboutness *is* real, and no doubt is more a fact of more of consciousness than perceptual consciousness. But, given our account of perceptual consciousness as the basis of consciousness generally, aboutness really *is* something else than has been supposed. He's right about that.

The Zombic Hunch: Extinction of an Intuition?

DANIEL DENNETT

Here is a good way of looking at the problem of consciousness:

Daniel Dennett

If Saul Steinberg's 1967 *New Yorker* cover is the metaphorical truth about consciousness, what is the literal truth? What is going on in the world (largely in this chap's brain, presumably) that makes it the case that this gorgeous metaphor is so apt?

1. The Naturalistic Turn

Our conception of this question at the end of the twentieth century is strikingly different from the ways we might have thought about the same issue at the beginning of the century, thanks very little to progress in philosophy and very much to progress in science. Steinberg's *pointillist* rendering of our conscious man gives us a fine hint about the major advances in outlook that promise—to many of us—to make all the difference. What we now know is that each of us is an assemblage of trillions of cells, of thousands of different sorts. Most of the cells that compose your body are descendants of the egg and sperm cell whose union started you (there are also millions of hitchhikers from thousands of different lineages stowed away in your body), and, to put it vividly and bluntly, *not a single one of the cells that compose you knows who you are, or cares.*

The individual cells that compose you are alive, but we now understand life well enough to appreciate that each cell is a mindless mechanism, a largely autonomous micro-robot, no more conscious than a yeast cell. The bread dough rising in a bowl in the kitchen is teeming with life, but nothing in the bowl is sentient or aware—or if it is, then this is a remarkable fact for which, at this time, we have not the slightest evidence. For we now know that the 'miracles' of life—metabolism, growth, self-repair, self-defence, and, of course, reproduction—are all accomplished by dazzlingly intricate, but non-miraculous, means. No sentient supervisor is needed to keep metabolism going, no *élan vital* is needed to trigger self-repair, and the incessant nano-factories of replication churn out their duplicates without any help from ghostly yearnings or special life forces. A hundred kilos of yeast does not wonder about Braque, or about anything, but you do, and you are made of parts[1] that are fundamentally the same sort of thing as those yeast cells, only with different tasks to perform. Your trillion-robot team is gathered together in a breathtakingly efficient regime that has no dictator but manages to keep itself organized to repel outsiders, banish the weak, enforce iron rules of discipline—and serve as the headquarters of one conscious self, one mind. These communities of cells are fascistic in the extreme, but *your* interests and values

[1] Eukaryotic cells.

have almost nothing to do with the limited goals of the cells that compose you—fortunately. Some people are gentle and generous, others are ruthless; some are pornographers and others devote their lives to the service of God, and it has been tempting over the ages to imagine that these striking differences must be due to the special features of some *extra* thing—a soul—installed somehow in the bodily headquarters. Until fairly recently, this idea of a rather magical extra ingredient was the only candidate for an explanation of consciousness that even *seemed* to make sense. For many people, this idea (dualism) is *still* the only vision of consciousness that makes any sense to them, but there is now widespread agreement among scientists and philosophers that dualism is—must be—simply false: we are each *made of* mindless robots and nothing else, no non-physical, non-robotic ingredients at all.

But how could this possibly be? More than a quarter of a millennium ago, Leibniz posed the challenge to our imaginations with a vivid intuition pump, a monumentally misleading grandfather to all the Chinese Rooms (Searle), Chinese Nations (Block) and latter-day zombies.

> Moreover, it must be confessed that *perception* and that which depends upon it are *inexplicable on mechanical grounds*, that is to say, by means of figures and motions. And supposing there were a machine, so constructed as to think, feel, and have perception, it might be conceived as increased in size, while keeping the same proportions, so that one might go into it as into a mill. That being so, we should, on examining its interior, find only parts which work one upon another, and never anything by which to explain a perception. Thus it is in a simple substance, and not in a compound or in a machine, that perception must be sought for. (Leibniz, *Monadology*, 1714:parag. 17 [Latta translation]).

There is a striking *non sequitur* in this famous passage, which finds many echoes in today's controversies. Is Leibniz's claim epistemological—we'll *never understand* the machinery of consciousness—or metaphysical—consciousness *couldn't be* a matter of 'machinery'? His preamble and conclusion make it plain that he took himself to be demonstrating a metaphysical truth, but the only grounds he offers would—at best—support the more modest epistemological reading.[2] Somebody *might* have used Leibniz's wonderful

---

[2] Leibniz makes this particularly clear in another passage quoted in Latta's translation: 'If in that which is organic there is nothing but mechanism, that is, bare matter, having differences of place, magnitude and figure; nothing can be deduced or explained from it, except mechanism, that

Daniel Dennett

Gulliverian image to *illustrate and render plausible*[3] the claim that although consciousness is—must be, in the end—a product of some gigantically complex mechanical system, it will surely be utterly beyond anybody's intellectual powers to explain how this is so. But Leibniz clearly intends us to treat his example as demonstrating the absurdity of the very idea that consciousness could be such an emergent effect of a hugely complex machine ('Thus it is in a simple substance, and not in a compound or in a machine, that perception must be sought for.') The same mismatch between means and ends haunts us today: Noam Chomsky, Thomas Nagel and Colin McGinn (among others) have all surmised, or speculated, or claimed, that consciousness is beyond all human understanding, a mystery not a puzzle, to use Chomsky's proposed distinction.[4] According to this line of thought, we lack the wherewithal—the brain power, the perspective, the intelligence—to grasp *how* the 'parts which work one upon another' could constitute consciousness. Like Leibniz, however, these thinkers have also hinted that they themselves understand the mystery of consciousness a little bit—just well enough to able to conclude that it *couldn't* be solved by any mechanistic account. And just like Leibniz, they have offered nothing, really, in the way of arguments for their pessimistic conclusions beyond a compelling image. When they contemplate the prospect they simply draw a blank. and thereupon decide that no further enlightenment lies down that path *or could possibly* lie down that path.

[3] It would not, of course, *prove* anything at all. It is just an intuition pump.
[4] Most recently, in the following works: Noam Chomsky, 'Naturalism and Dualism in the Study of Mind and Language', *Int. J. of Phil. Studies*, vol. 2, pp. 181–209 (his Agnes Cuming lecture of 1993), 1994. Thomas Nagel, 'Conceiving the Impossible and the Mind-Body Problem', *Philosophy*, **73**, 1998, pp. 337–52. Colin McGinn, *The Mysterious Flame: Conscious Minds in a Material World* (New York: Basic Books, 1999).

is, except such differences as I have mentioned. For from anything taken by itself nothing can be deduced and explained, except differences of the attributes which constitute it. Hence we may readily conclude that in no mill or clock as such is there to be found any principle which perceives what takes place in it; and it matters not whether the things contained in the 'machine' are solid or fluid or made up of both. Further we know that there ence of magnitude. Whence it follows that, if it is inconceivable how perception arises in any coarse 'machine', whether it be made up of fluids or solids, it is equally inconceivable how perception can arise from a fine 'machine'; for it our senses were finer, it would be the same as if we were perceiving a coarse 'machine', as we do at present.' [from *Commentatio de Anima Brutorum*, 1710, quoted in footnote in Latta, p. 228.]

The Zombic Hunch: Extinction of an Intuition?

Might it be, however, that Leibniz, lost in his giant mill, just couldn't see the woods for the trees? Might there not be a birds-eye view—*not* the first-person perspective of the subject in question, but a higher-level third-person perspective—from which, if one squinted just right, one could bring into focus the recognizable patterns of consciousness in action? Might it be that somehow the organization of all the parts which work one upon another yields consciousness as an emergent product? And if so, why couldn't we hope to understand it, once we had developed the right concepts? This is the avenue that has been enthusiastically and fruitfully explored during the last quarter century under the twin banners of cognitive science and functionalism—the extrapolation of *mechanistic naturalism* from the body to the mind. After all, we have now achieved excellent mechanistic explanations of metabolism, growth, self-repair, and reproduction, which not so long ago also looked too marvellous for words. Consciousness, on this optimistic view, is indeed a wonderful thing, but not *that* wonderful—not too wonderful to be explained using the same concepts and perspectives that have worked elsewhere in biology. Consciousness, from this perspective, is a relatively recent fruit of the evolutionary algorithms that have given the planet such phenomena as immune systems, flight, and sight. In the first half of the century, many scientists and philosophers might have agreed with Leibniz about the mind, simply because the mind seemed to consist of phenomena *utterly unlike* the phenomena in the rest of biology. The inner lives of mindless plants and simple organisms (and our bodies below the neck) might yield without residue to normal biological science, but nothing remotely mindlike could be accounted for in such mechanical terms. Or so it must have seemed until something came along in midcentury to break the spell of Leibniz's intuition pump; computers. Computers are mindlike in ways that no earlier artifacts were: they can control processes that perform tasks that call for discrimination, inference, memory, judgment, anticipation; they are generators of new knowledge, finders of patterns—in poetry, astronomy, and mathematics, for instance—that heretofore only human beings could even hope to find. We now have real world artifacts that dwarf Leibniz's giant mill both in speed and intricacy. And we have come to appreciate that what is well nigh invisible at the level of the meshing of billions of gears may nevertheless be readily comprehensible at higher levels of analysis—at any of many nested 'software' levels, where the patterns of patterns of patterns of organization (of organization of organization) can render salient *and explain* the marvellous competences of the mill. The sheer existence of computers has provided an existence proof of undeniable influence:

Daniel Dennett

there are mechanisms—brute unmysterious mechanisms operating according to routinely well-understood physical principles—that have many of the competences heretofore assigned only to minds.

One thing we know to a moral certainty about computers is that there is nothing up their sleeves: no ESP or morphic resonance between the disk drives, no action-at-a-distance accomplished via strange new forces. The *explanations* of whatever talents computers exhibit are models of transparency, which is one of the most attractive features of cognitive science: we can be quite sure that *if* a computational model of *any* mental phenomena is achieved, it will inherit this transparency of explanation from its simpler ancestors.

In addition to the computers themselves, wonderful exemplars and research tools that they are, we have the wealth of new concepts computer science has defined and made familiar. We have learned how to think fluently and reliably about the cumulative effects of intricate cascades of micro-mechanisms, trillions upon trillions of events of billions of types, interacting on dozens of levels. Can we harness these new powers of disciplined imagination to the task of climbing out of Leibniz's mill? The hope that we can is, for many of us, compelling—even inspiring. We are quite certain that a naturalistic, mechanistic explanation of consciousness is not just possible; it is fast becoming actual. It will just take a lot of hard work of the sort that has been going on in biology all century, and in cognitive science for the last half century.

2. The Reactionaries

But in the last decade of the century a loose federation of reactionaries has sprung up among philosophers in opposition to this evolutionary, mechanistic naturalism. As already noted, there are the *mysterian*s, Owen Flanagan's useful term for those who not only find this optimism ill-founded but also think that defeat is certain. Then there are those who are not sure the problem is insoluble, but do think they can titrate the subtasks into the 'easy problems' and the 'Hard Problem' (David Chalmers) or who find what they declare to be an Explanatory Gap (Joseph Levine) that has so far—and perhaps always will—defy those who would engulf the mind in one unifying explanation.[5] A curious anachronism found in many

[5] David Chalmers, 'Facing Up to the Problems of Consciousness', *J. Consc. Studies*, **2**, pp. 200–19, and *The Conscious Mind: In Search of a Fundamental Theory* (Oxford University Press, 1996). Joseph Levine, 'Materialism and Qualia: The Explanatory Gap', *Pacific Philosophical Quarterly*, **64**, pp. 354–61, 1983.

but not all of these reactionaries is that to the extent that they hold out any hope at all of solution to the problem (or problems) of consciousness, they speculate that it will come not from biology or cognitive science, but from—of all things—physics!

One of the first to take up this courtship with physics was David Chalmers, who suggested that a theory of consciousness should 'take experience itself as a fundamental feature of the world, alongside mass, charge, and space-time.' As he correctly noted, 'No attempt is made [by physicists] to explain these features in terms of anything simpler'[6] a theme echoed by Thomas Nagel:

> Consciousness should be recognized as a conceptually irreducible aspect of reality that is necessarily connected with other equally irreducible aspects—as electromagnetic fields are irreducible to but necessarily connected with the behaviour of charged particles and gravitational fields with the behaviour of masses, and vice versa.[7]

And Noam Chomsky:

> The natural conclusion ... is that human thought and action are properties of organized matter, like 'powers of attraction and repulsion', electrical charge, and so on.[8]

And Galen Strawson, who says, in a review of Colin McGinn's most recent book: 'we find consciousness mysterious only because we have a bad picture of matter' and adds:

> We have a lot of mathematical equations describing the behaviour of matter, but we don't really know anything more about its intrinsic nature, The only other clue that we have about its intrinsic nature, in fact. is that when you arrange it in the way that it is arranged in things like brains, you get consciousness.[9]

Not just philosophers and linguists have found this an attractive idea. Many physicists have themselves jumped on the bandwagon, following the lead of Roger Penrose, whose speculations about quantum fluctuations in the microtubules of neurons have attracted considerable attention and enthusiasm in spite of a host of

[6] Chalmers, 'Facing Up to the Problems of Consciousness', *J. Consc. Studies*, **2**, pp. 200–19.

[7] Nagel, op.cit., p. 338.

[8] Chomsky, op. cit., 189. Chomsky is talking about the conclusion drawn by La Mettrie and Priestley, but his subsequent discussion, footnoting Roger Penrose and John Archibald Wheeler, makes it clear that he thinks this is a natural conclusion today, not just in early post-Newtonian days.

[9] Galen Strawson, 'Little Gray Cells,' *New York Times Book Review*, 7/11/99, p. 13.

problems.[10] What all these views have in common is the idea that some revolutionary principle of physics could be a *rival* to the idea that consciousness is going to be explained in terms of 'parts which work one upon another,' as in Leibniz's mill.

Suppose they are right. Suppose the Hard Problem—whatever it is—can only be solved by confirming some marvellous new and irreducible property of the *physics* of the cells that make up a brain. One problem with this is that the physics of your brain cells is, so far as we know, the same as the physics of those yeast cells undergoing population explosion in the dish. The differences in functionality between neurons and yeast cells are explained in terms of differences of cell anatomy or cytoarchitecture, not physics. Could it be, perhaps, that those differences in anatomy permit neurons to respond to physical differences to which yeast cells are oblivious? Here we must tread carefully, for if we don't watch out, we will simply reintroduce Leibniz's baffling mill at a more microscopic level—watching the quantum fluctuations in the microtubules of a single cell and not being able to see how any amount of *those* 'parts which work one upon another' could explain consciousness. If you want to avoid the bafflement of Leibniz's mill, the idea had better be, instead, that consciousness is an irreducible property that inheres, somehow, 'in a simple substance,' as Leibniz put it, 'and not in a compound or in a machine.' So let us suppose that, thanks to their physics, neurons enjoy a tiny smidgen (a quantum, perhaps!) of consciousness. We will then have solved the problem of how large ensembles of such cells—such as you and I—are conscious: we are conscious because our brains are made of the right sort of stuff, stuff with the micro-*je-ne-sais-quoi* that is needed for consciousness. But even if we had solved *that* problem, we would still have the problem illustrated by my opening illustration: how can cells, even *conscious* cells, that themselves know nothing about

[10] Incurable optimist that I am, I find this recent invasion by physicists into the domains of cognitive neuroscience to be a cloud with a silver lining: for the first time in my professional life, an interloping discipline beats out philosophy for the prize for combining arrogance with ignorance about the field being invaded. Neuroscientists and psychologists who used to stare glassy-eyed and uncomprehending at philosophers arguing about the fine points of *supervenience* and *intensionality-with-an-s* now have to contend in a similar spirit with the arcana of *quantum entanglement* and *Bose-Einstein condensates*. It is tempting to suppose that as it has become harder and harder to make progress in physics, some physicists have sought greener pastures where they can speculate with even less fear of experimental recalcitrance or clear contradiction.

art or dogs or mountains compose themselves into a thing that has conscious thoughts about Braque or poodles or Kilimanjaro? How can the whole ensemble be so knowledgeable of the passing show, so in touch with distal art objects (to say nothing of absent artists and mountains) when all of its parts, however conscious or sentient they are, are myopic and solipsistic in the extreme? We might call this the *topic*-of-consciousness question.

I suspect that this turn to physics looks attractive to some people mainly because they have not yet confronted the need to answer *this* question, for once they do attempt it, they find that a 'theory' that postulates some fundamental and irreducible sentience-field or the like has no resources at all to deal with it. Only a theory that proceeds in terms of how the parts work together in larger ensembles has any hope of shedding light on the topic question, and once theory has ascended to such a high level, it is not at all clear what use the lower-level physical sophistications would be. Moreover, there already are many models of systems that uncontroversially answer *versions* of the topic question, and they are all computational. How can the little box on your desk, whose parts know nothing at all about chess, beat you at chess with such stunning reliability? How can the little box driving the pistons attached to the rudder do a better job of steering a straight course than any old salt with decades at sea behind him? Leibniz would have been ravished with admiration by these mechanisms, which would have shaken his confidence—I daresay—in the claim that no mechanistic explanation of 'perception' was possible.[11]

David Chalmers, identifier of the Hard Problem, would agree with me, I think. He would classify the topic question as one of the 'easy problems'—one of the problems that *does* find its solution in terms of computational models of control mechanisms. It follows from what he calls the principle of organizational invariance.[12] Consider once again our *pointillist* gentleman and ask if we can tell from the picture whether he's a genuinely conscious being or a zombie—a philosopher's zombie that is behaviourally indistinguishable from a normal human being but is utterly lacking in consciousness. Even the zombie version of this chap would have a head full of

---

[11] A classic example of the topic problem in nature, and its ultimately computational solution, is Douglas Hofstadter's famous 'Prelude ... Ant Fugue' in *Gödel Escher Bach* (1979), the dialogue comparing an ant colony ('Aunt Hillary') to a brain, whose parts are equally clueless contributors to systemic knowledge of the whole. In his reflections following the reprinting of this essay in Hofstadter and Dennett, (eds), *The Mind's I*, (1981), he asks 'Is the soul more than the hum of its parts?'

[12] Chalmers, 1996, op. cit., esp. chapter 7.

Daniel Dennett

dynamically interacting data-structures, with links of association bringing their sequels on-line, suggesting new calls to memory, composing on the fly new structures with new meanings and powers. Why? Because only a being with such a system of internal operations and activities could non-miraculously maintain the complex set of behaviours this man would no doubt exhibit, if we put him to various tests. If you want a theory of all that information-processing activity, it will have to be a computational theory, whether or not the man is conscious. According to Chalmers, where normal people have a stream of consciousness, zombies have a stream of unconsciousness, and he has argued persuasively that whatever explained the *purely informational competence* of one (which includes every transition, every construction, every association depicted in this thought balloon) would explain the same competence in the other. Since the literal truth about the mechanisms responsible for all the sworls and eddies in the stream, as well as the informational contents of the items passing by, is—*ex hypothesi*—utterly unaffected by whether or not the stream is conscious or unconscious, Steinberg's cartoon, a brilliant metaphorical rendering of consciousness, is exactly as good a metaphorical rendering of what is going on inside a zombie. (See, e.g., the discussion of zombie beliefs in Chalmers, 1996, pp. 203–5.)

3. An Embarrassment of Zombies

Must we talk about zombies? Apparently we must. There is a powerful and ubiquitous intuition that computational, mechanistic models of consciousness, of the sort we naturalists favour, *must leave something out*—something important. Just what must they leave out? The critics have found that it's hard to say, exactly: qualia, feelings, emotions, the what-it's-likeness (Nagel)[13] or the ontological subjectivity (Searle)[14] of consciousness. Each of these attempts to characterize the phantom residue has met with serious objections and been abandoned by many who nevertheless want to cling to the intuition, so there has been a gradual process of distillation, leaving just about all the reactionaries, for all their disagreements among themselves, united in the conviction *that there is a real difference between a conscious person and a perfect zombie*—let's call that intuition the *Zombic Hunch*—leading them to the thesis of

[13] Thomas Nagel, 1974, 'What is it Like to be a Bat?' *Phil. Review*, **83**, pp. 435–50.
[14] John Searle, *The Rediscovery of the Mind*, (MIT Press, 1992).

The Zombic Hunch: Extinction of an Intuition?

Zombism: that *the fundamental flaw in any mechanistic theory of consciousness is that it cannot account for this important difference.*[15] A hundred years from now, I expect this claim will be scarcely credible, but let the record show that in 1999. John Searle, David Chalmers, Colin McGinn, Joseph Levine and many other philosophers of mind don't just *feel the tug* of the Zombic Hunch (I can feel the tug as well as anybody), they *credit* it. They are, however reluctantly, Zombists, who maintain that the zombie challenge is a serious criticism. It is not that they don't recognize the awkwardness of their position. The threadbare stereotype of philosophers passionately arguing about how many angels can dance on the head of a pin is not much improved when the topic is updated to whether zombies—admitted by all to be imaginary beings—are (1) metaphysically impossible, (2) logically impossible, (3) physically impossible, or just (4) extremely unlikely to exist. The reactionaries have acknowledged that many who take zombies seriously have simply failed to imagine the prospect correctly. For instance, if you were surprised by my claim that the Steinberg cartoon would be an equally apt metaphorical depiction of the goings on in a zombie's head, you had not heretofore understood what a zombie is (and isn't). More pointedly, if you *still* think that Chalmers and I are just wrong about this, you are simply operating with a mistaken concept of zombies, one that is irrelevant to the philosophical discussion. (I mention this because I have found that many onlookers, scientists in particular, have a hard time believing that philosophers can be taking such a preposterous idea as zombies seriously, so they generously replace it with some idea that one *can* take seriously—but one that does not do the requisite philosophical work. Just remember, by definition, a zombie behaves *indistinguishably* from a conscious being—in all possible tests, including not only answers to questions [as in the Turing test] but psychophysical tests, neurophysiological tests—all tests that any 'third-person' science can devise.)

Thomas Nagel is one reactionary who has recoiled somewhat from zombies. In his recent address to this body, Nagel is particularly circumspect in his embrace. On the one hand, he declares that naturalism has so far failed us:

> We do not at present possess the conceptual equipment to understand how subjective and physical features could both be essential aspects of a single entity or process.

[15] In the words of one of their most vehement spokespersons, 'It all comes down to zombies.' Selmer Bringsjord, 'Dennett versus Searle: It All Comes Down to Zombies and Dennett is Wrong,' (APA December, 1994).

Daniel Dennett

Why not? Because 'we still have to deal with the apparent conceivability of ... a zombie.' Notice that Nagel speaks of the *apparent* conceivability of a zombie. I have long claimed that this conceivability is *only* apparent; some misguided philosophers *think* they can conceive of a zombie, but they are badly mistaken.[16] Nagel, for one, agrees:

> the powerful intuition that it is conceivable that an intact and normally functioning physical human organism could be a completely unconscious zombie is an illusion.[17]

David Chalmers is another who is particularly acute in his criticisms of the standard mis-imaginations that are often thought to support the zombie challenge (his 1996 chapter 7, 'Absent Qualia, Fading Qualia, Dancing Qualia,' bristles with arguments against various forlorn attempts), but in the end, he declares that although zombies are in every realistic sense impossible, we 'non-reductive functionalists' still leave something out—or rather, we leave a job undone. We cannot provide *'fundamental* laws' from which one can deduce that zombies are impossible (p. 276 and elsewhere). Chalmers' demand for fundamental laws lacks the independence he needs if he is to support his crediting of the Zombie Hunch, for it arises from that very intuition: *if* you believe that consciousness sunders the universe in twain, into those things that have it and those that don't, *and* you believe this is a fundamental metaphysical distinction, then the demand for fundamental laws that enforce and explain the sundering makes some sense, but we naturalists think that this elevation of consciousness is itself suspect; supported by tradition and nothing else. Note that nobody these days would clamour for fundamental laws of the theory of kangaroos, showing why pseudo-kangaroos are physically, logically, metaphysically impossible. Kangaroos are wonderful, but not *that* wonderful. We naturalists think that consciousness, like locomotion or predation, is something that comes in different varieties, with some shared functional properties, but many differences, due to different evolutionary histories and circumstances. We have no use for fundamental laws in making these distinctions.

We are all susceptible to the Zombic Hunch, but if we are to credit

---

[16] Daniel Dennett, 1991, *Consciousness Explained,* New York and Boston: Little Brown, esp chapters 10–12; 1994, 'Get Real,' reply to 14 essays, in *Philosophical Topics,* **22,** no. I & 2, 1994, pp. 505–68; 1995, 'The Unimagined Preposterousness of Zombies,' *J. Consc. Studies,* **2,** pp. 322–36.

[17] Nagel, 1998, op. cit., p. 342.

it, we need a good argument, since the case has been made that it is a persistent cognitive illusion and nothing more. I have found no good arguments, and plenty of bad ones. So why, then, do so many philosophers persist in their allegiance to an intuition that they themselves have come to see is of suspect provenance? Partly, I think, this is the effect of some serious misdirection that has bedevilled communication in cognitive science in recent years.

4. Broad Functionalism and Minimalism

Functionalism is the idea that handsome is as handsome does, that matter matters only because of what matter can do. Functionalism in this broadest sense is so ubiquitous in science that it is tantamount to a reigning presumption of all of science. And since science is always looking for simplifications, looking for the greatest generality it can muster, functionalism in practice has a bias in favour of minimalism, of saying that less matters than one might have thought. The law of gravity says that it doesn't matter what stuff a thing is made of—only its mass matters (and its density, except in a vacuum). The trajectory of cannonballs of equal mass and density is not affected by whether they are made of iron, copper or gold. It *might* have mattered, one imagines, but in fact it doesn't. And wings don't have to have feathers on them in order to power flight, and eyes don't have to be blue or brown in order to see. Every eye has many more properties than are needed for sight, and it is science's job to find the maximally general, maximally noncommittal—hence minimal—characterization of whatever power or capacity is under consideration. Not surprisingly, then, many of the disputes in normal science concern the issue of whether or not one school of thought has reached too far in its quest for generality.

Since the earliest days of cognitive science, there has been a particularly bold brand of functionalistic minimalism in contention, the idea that just as a heart is basically a pump, and could in principle be made of anything so long as it did the requisite pumping without damaging the blood, so a mind is fundamentally a control system, implemented in fact by the organic brain, but anything else that could *compute the same control functions* would serve as well. The actual matter of the brain—the chemistry of synapses, the role of calcium in the depolarization of nerve fibres, and so forth—is roughly as irrelevant as the chemical composition of those cannonballs. According to this tempting proposal, even the underlying micro-architecture of the brain's connections can be ignored for many purposes, at least for the time being, since it has been proven by computer scientists that any function that can be computed by one specific computational architecture can also be computed (perhaps much less efficiently) by another architecture. If all that matters is the computation, we can ignore the brain's wiring diagram, and its chemistry, and just worry about the 'software' that runs on it. In short—and now we arrive at the provocative version that has caused so much misunderstanding—in principle you could replace your wet, organic brain with a bunch of silicon chips and wires and go right on thinking (and being conscious, and so forth).

This bold vision, computationalism or 'strong AI' [Searle], is composed of two parts: the broad creed of functionalism—handsome is as handsome does—and a specific set of minimalist empirical wagers: neuroanatomy doesn't matter; chemistry doesn't matter. This second theme excused many would-be cognitive scientists from educating themselves in these fields, for the same reason that economists are excused from knowing anything about the metallurgy of coinage, or the chemistry of the ink and paper used in bills of sale. This has been a good idea in many ways, but for fairly obvious reasons, it has not been a *politically* astute ideology, since it has threatened to relegate those scientists who devote their lives to functional neuroanatomy and neurochemistry, for instance, to relatively minor roles as electricians and plumbers in the grand project of explaining consciousness. Resenting this proposed demotion, they have fought back vigorously. The recent history of neuroscience can be seen as a series of triumphs for the lovers of detail. Yes, the specific geometry of the connectivity matters; yes, the location of specific neuromodulators and their effects matter; yes, the architecture matters; yes, the fine temporal rhythms of the spiking patterns matter, and so on. Many of the fond hopes of opportunistic minimalists have been dashed—they had hoped they could leave out various things, and they have learned that no, if you leave out x, or y, or z, you can't explain how the mind works.

This has left the mistaken impression in some quarters that the underlying idea of functionalism has been taking its lumps. Far from it. On the contrary, the reasons for accepting these new claims are precisely the reasons of functionalism. Neurochemistry matters because—and *only* because—we have discovered that the many different neuromodulators and other chemical messengers that diffuse through the brain have *functional roles* that make important differences. What those molecules do turns out to be important to the *computational* roles played by the neurons, so we have to pay attention to them after all. To see what is at stake here, compare the neuromodulators to the food that is ingested by people. Psychologists and neuroscientists do not, as a rule, carefully inventory the food intake of their subjects, on the entirely plausible grounds that a serving of vanilla ice cream makes roughly the same contribution to how the brain goes about its tasks as a serving of strawberry ice cream. So long as there isn't any marijuana in the brownies, we can ignore the specifics of the food, and just treat it as a reliable energy source, the brain's power supply. This *could* turn out to be mistaken. It might turn out that psychologically important, if subtle, differences, hinged on whether one's subjects had recently had vanilla ice cream. Those who thought it did make a difference would have a significant empirical disagreement with those who thought it didn't, but this would not be disagreement between functionalists and anti-functionalists. It would be a disagreement between those who thought that functionalism had to be expanded downward to include the chemistry of food and those who thought that functionalism could finesse that complication. Consider the following:

> there may be various general neurochemical dispositions [based on the neuropeptide systems] that guide the patterning of thoughts that no amount of computational work can clarify. (Panskepp, 1998) Panskepp, J. 1998, *Affective Neuroscience: The Foundations of Human and Animal Emotions,* Oxford and NY, CUP.

This perfectly captures a widespread (and passionately endorsed) attitude, but note that there is nothing oxymoronic about a computational theory of neuromodulator diffusion and its effects, for instance, and pioneering work in 'virtual neuromodulators' and 'diffusion models of computational control' is well underway. Minds will turn out not to be simple computers, and their computational resources will be seen to reach down into the sub-cellular molecular resources available only to organic brains, but the theories that emerge will still be functionalist in the broad sense.

So within functionalism broadly conceived a variety of important controversies have been usefully playing themselves out, but an intermittently amusing side effect has been that many neuroscientists and psychologists who are rabidly anti-computer and anti-AI for various ideological reasons have mistakenly thought that philosophers' *qualia* and *zombies* and *inverted spectra* were useful weapons in their battles. So unquestioning have they been in their allegiance to the broad, bland functionalism of normal science, however, that they simply haven't imagined that philosophers were saying what those philosophers were actually saying. Some neuroscientists have befriended *qualia,* confident that this was a term for the sort of functionally characterizable complication that confounds oversimplified versions of computationalism. Others have thought that when philosophers were comparing zombies with conscious people, they were noting the importance of emotional state, or neuromodulator imbalance. I have spent more time than I would like explaining to various scientists that their controversies and the philosophers' controversies are not translations of each other as they had thought but false friends, mutually irrelevant to each other. The principle of charity continues to bedevil this issue, however, and many scientists generously persist in refusing to believe that philosophers can be making a fuss about such a narrow and fantastical division of opinion.

Meanwhile, some philosophers have misappropriated those same controversies within cognitive science to support their claim that the tide is turning against functionalism, in favour of qualia, in favour of the irreducibility of the 'first-person point of view' and so forth. This widespread conviction is an artifact of interdisciplinary miscommunication and nothing else.

5. The future of an illusion

I do not know how long this ubiquitous misunderstanding will persist, but I am still optimistic enough to suppose that some time in the new century people will look back on this era and marvel at the potency of the visceral resistance[18] to the obvious verdict about the Zombic Hunch: it is an illusion.

[18] It is visceral in the sense of being almost entirely a-rational, insensitive to argument or the lack thereof. Probably the first to comment explicitly on this strange lapse from reason among philosophers was Lycan, in a footnote at the end of his 1987 book, *Consciousness* (MIT Press) that deserves quoting in full:

> On a number of occasions when I have delivered bits of this book as talks or lectures, one or another member of the audience has kindly praised my argumentative adroitness, dialectical skill, etc., but added that cleverness—and my arguments themselves—are quite beside the point, a mere exercise and/or display. Nagel (1979 [Preface to *Mortal Questions* Cambridge University Press]) may perhaps be read more charitably, but not much more charitably:
>
> > I believe one should trust problems over solutions, intuition over arguments .... [Well, excuuuuuse me!—WGL] If arguments or

The Zombic Hunch: Extinction of an Intuition?

Will the Zombic Hunch itself go extinct? I expect not. It will not survive in its current, toxic form but will persist as a less virulent mutation, still psychologically powerful but stripped of authority. We've seen this happen before. It still *seems* as if the earth stands still and the sun and moon go around it, but we have learned that it is wise to disregard this potent appearance as mere appearance. It still *seems* as if there's a difference between a thing at absolute rest and a thing that is merely not accelerating within an inertial frame, but we have learned not to trust this feeling. I anticipate a day when philosophers and scientists and laypeople will chuckle over the fossil traces of our earlier bafflement about consciousness: 'It still *seems* as if these mechanistic theories of consciousness leave something out, but of course that's an illusion. They do. in fact, explain everything about consciousness that needs explanation.'

If you find my prediction incredible, you might reflect on whether your incredulity is based on anything more than your current susceptibility to the Zombic Hunch. If you are patient and open-minded, it will pass.

---

systematic theoretical considerations lead to results that seem intuitively not to make sense ... then something is wrong with the argument and more work needs to be done. Often the problem has to be reformulated, because an adequate answer to the original formulation fails to make the *sense* of the problem disappear (pp. x–xi).

If by this Nagel means only that intuitions contrary to ostensibly sound argument need at least to be explained away, no one would disagree (but the clause 'something is wrong with the argument' discourages that interpretation). The task of explaining away 'qualia'-based intuitive objections to materialism is what in large part I have undertaken in this book. If I have failed, I would like to be *shown why* (or, of course, presented with some new anti-materialist argument). To engage in further muttering and posturing would be idle. (pp. 147–8)

The Time of Our Lives

D. H. MELLOR

Early last century an article appeared which transformed the philosophy of time. The article was James Ellis McTaggart's 'The unreality of time', published in 1908.[1] As his title implies, McTaggart argued in this article that there is in reality no such thing as time. But that claim, although startling enough, is not what makes the article so remarkable. The same claim had after all been made long before McTaggart, for example by Kant in 1781[2], and in McTaggart's sense it is still made by those who think that time is merely one of the four dimensions of an unchanging 'block universe'. However, most of those who think this are more influenced by Minkowski's comment, also made in 1908,[3] that relativity has doomed space and time to 'fade away into mere shadows' of a unified spacetime than they are by McTaggart's more substantial arguments.

Actually, what is even more significant than McTaggart's arguments is his way of stating them. For here as elsewhere, the key to answering a hard question is seeing how to put it, which for McTaggart meant drawing his now-standard distinction between two ways of saying when things happen. One way is to say whether they are past, present or future and, if not present, then how past (yesterday, last week, ten years ago) or how future (tomorrow, next week, ten years hence). Events ordered in this way, by their temporal relations to the present, form what McTaggart called the 'A-series'. His other way of ordering events, into what he called the 'B-series', is by how much earlier or later they are, not than the present but than each other. And McTaggart's first great contribution to the philosophy of time was to show how many of the most important questions about time are really questions about his two series.

To see why this is so, we must start by comparing time with space, whose dimensions are obviously more like time than is any other way of ordering things, e.g. by their temperatures. The reason

[1] J. M. E. McTaggart, 'The Unreality of Time', *Mind* 18, 457–484.
[2] Immanuel Kant, *Critique of Pure Reason*, trans. N. Kemp Smith, (London: Macmillan, 1781), 76.
[3] H. Minkowski, 'Space and Time', trans. W. Perrett and G. B. Jeffrey, *The Principle of Relativity*, A. Einstein *et al.* (London: Methuen, 1908), 75.

is that time and space form a four-dimensional array of possibilities —namely spacetime points—each of which enables two things to coincide or be in contact, i.e. to be able to interact immediately, at that point. So to say that there are four dimensions of space-time is just to say that there are four ways in which things can *fail* to coincide, by having different locations in at least one of these dimensions. In other words, what distinguishes time and space from everything else is the fact that people and things can—literally— contact each other by, and only by, being in the same place at the same time. Whether they share the same temperature, colour, shape or any other property is irrelevant to whether or not they are in contact and thereby able to interact immediately. So the first, easiest and largest part of the answer to the question 'What is time?', which tells us how it differs from everything else except space—and is, incidentally, quite independent of the special theory of relativity— is that it is one of the four dimensions of spacetime.

That of course still leaves the question of how time differs from the other dimensions of spacetime, a question which nothing in the theories of relativity either answers or makes redundant. McTaggart's answer is that time is the dimension of *change*. And so of course it is: change is something's having incompatible properties at different times. To move, i.e. to change one's place, is to be first at one place and then at another; to change colour is to have first one colour and then another; and similarly for size, shape, temperature and all other changeable properties. A change is the variation over time of one or more properties of some thing.

But why should this fact distinguish time from space? After all many properties also vary across space. Take that venerable philosophical weapon, the poker, and imagine one stuck in a fire, thus making it hot at one end and cold at the other. Why should we not call this spatial variation of temperature a change? It is not enough to reply that what we *mean* by change is variation over time rather than across space. That just prompts the question of why we draw this distinction between temporal and spatial variation. And how, if we do draw it, are we then to distinguish time from space? We cannot do it by defining time as the dimension of change if we then define change as variation over time but not across space.

Or can we? McTaggart thinks we can, because he thinks there must be more to change than having incompatible properties at different times. Suppose your central heating comes on at 6 o'clock and warms your house by 7 o'clock. What, McTaggart would ask, makes this rise in temperature a change? Not just the facts that your house is cold at 6 and warm at 7, for those facts never change. If your house is cold at 6, it cannot later on *not* have been cold then; nor, if it was warm at 7, can it ever not have been *warm* then. If these are ever facts, they are always facts. But how can two such unchanging facts constitute a change?

According to McTaggart, they cannot. Changes are not facts about how cold or warm your house is at 6 or at 7 but about how cold or warm it is *now*. So at 6, i.e. when it is *now* 6, the relevant fact is that your house is *cold now;* and at 7, i.e. when it is *now* 7, the relevant fact is that your house is *warm now*. Those are the changeable facts. The fact that your house is cold now is *not* always a fact, since it is a fact at 6 but not at 7; just as the fact that your house is warm now is a fact at 7 but not at 6. Those are the facts whose comings and goings make the warming up of your house a case of change.

Thus, for McTaggart, what makes temporal variation change is that it entails changing facts about how things are now. And what makes these facts change is that the present *time* keeps changing. What makes your house first cold now and then warm now, given that it is cold at 6 and warm at 7, is that first it is now 6 and then it is now 7. When it is now 6, everything whose time is 7 is one hour into the future, meaning that it will be present in an hour's time; and when, an hour later, it is now 7, everything whose time is 6 is one hour into the past, meaning that it was present one hour ago. In short, what makes change possible is the so-called flow or passage of time, and hence of everything in it, from the future *via* the present to the past. So what makes time differ from space, by making it the one and only dimension of change, is the fact that time flows and the dimensions of space do not.

And here, for McTaggart, lies the rub, since he argues also that time *cannot* flow, and hence that in reality there can be no change, and thus, for him, no time. He admits of course that there is a fourth dimension of what we call spacetime, a dimension which we mistake for time. But as he thinks variation in this dimension no more entails change in his sense than spatial variation does, he declines to call it time. That is what he means by saying that time is unreal.

Put like this, McTaggart's claim may be more credible; and indeed, as I have said, it is in substance still widely accepted, albeit differently expressed and held less for his reasons than as a false inference from relativity. But even if McTaggart's own objection to the flow of time is still disputed, no one disputes his distinction between the A- and the B-series, which is what his objection rests on. And it is that distinction, and what it can tell us about how we should think, not only about time but also about ourselves, that has made McTaggart's work on time so prescient and so fruitful.

To see why, consider the personal analogue of the *present,* namely one's own *self.* We can relate people to each other in two ways, analogous to McTaggart's two ways of relating events in time. In what I shall call the *personal* way, analogous to McTaggart's A-series, we relate people to ourselves. The relations may be familial, like being a parent, a cousin, an in-law, etc.; or they may be spatial, as in being a neighbour; or social or political, as in being an employee or a leader of a political party; or indeed of any other kind. What matters here is not what the relation is but whether it is directly or indirectly to *us:* as in *my* parents, *my* neighbours, *my* cousin's employees, *my* nephew's flatmate's party leader, and so on.

This is what I mean by the personal way of identifying and describing people, namely by relating them directly or indirectly to ourselves. The other, *impersonal* way, analogous to McTaggart's B-series, is to relate people not to ourselves but to each other, as in Jill's parents, John's neighbours, David's cousin's employees, Fred's flatmate's party leader, and so on.

Now let us ask how these two ways of relating people differ, first in reality and then as ways of thinking about reality. In reality, the personal way is obviously parasitic on the impersonal way. For the latter is simply defined by who is related in what way to whom, regardless of which of the people concerned, if any, is me; and these impersonal relations between people then fix all the personal ones. Thus if John is Hugh's cousin and I am Hugh, John must be my cousin; and similarly in all other cases. So personal and impersonal reality can only differ if there is in reality more to John's being my cousin than there is to his being Hugh's cousin; which in turn will be the case only if *my* being Hugh is itself a substantial part or aspect of reality.

Now you may think it obvious that it is. But it cannot be, as the following analogue of McTaggart's argument against the flow of time shows. In asserting this I am not of course denying that when I say 'I am Hugh', that statement is true, or that when my cousin says 'I am John', that statement is also true. The question is what *makes* these statements true. It cannot be the fact that in reality I am Hugh and not John, since that would make John's statement false. Nor can it be that in reality I am John and not Hugh, since that would make Hugh's statement false. And nor can I be both Hugh and John, since at most one person can be me. The fact is therefore that taking personal truths like 'I am Hugh' to be made true by corresponding personal facts only generates contradictions, by requiring the fact that I am Hugh both to exist, in order to make Hugh's statement 'I am Hugh' true, and also not to exist, to enable John's statement 'I am John' also to be true.

What then does make these personal statements true? The answer is simple. For example, for any X, statements of the forms 'I am X', 'X is my cousin' and 'I live in X' are made true respectively by being said by X, by a cousin of X and by someone who lives in X. But those are all impersonal facts about who says what, lives where and is related in a certain way to whom, regardless of which if any of those people is me—which is why these facts imply no contradiction. And that is why, if we are to say without contradiction what in reality makes personal statements true, we must take reality itself to be impersonal, i.e. to contain no such facts as *my* being Hugh, or *my* being John's cousin or *my* living in Cambridge, over and above Hugh's being and doing those things.

The simplicity and obvious soundness of this argument against a personal reality makes it remarkable how few philosophers accept its equally sound and simple temporal analogue, namely McTaggart's argument against the flow of time. Here again we need not deny that when, at 6 o'clock, I say 'It is now 6', that statement is true, and when at 7 o'clock I say 'It is now 7', that statement is also true. But again the question is what *makes* these statements true. It cannot be the fact that in reality it is now 6, or that would make my 7 o'clock statement false. Nor can it be that in reality it is now 7, or that would make my 6 o'clock statement false. And nor can it now be both 6 and 7, since at most one time can be now. The fact is therefore that taking A-series truths like 'It is now 6' to be made true by corresponding A-series facts only generates contradictions, by requiring the fact that it is now 6 o'clock both to exist, in order to make my 6 o'clock statement 'It is now 6' true, and also not to exist, to enable my 7 o'clock statement 'It is now 7' also to be true.

What then does make A-series statements true? Again the answer is simple. For example, for any X, statements of the forms 'It is now X', 'X was last week' and 'X is due tomorrow' are made true respectively by being said at X, in the week after X, and the day before X is due. But those are all B-series facts, about when things happen and are said, regardless of which if any of those things and sayings are present—which is why these B-series facts imply no contradiction. And that is why, if we are to say without contradiction what in reality makes A-series statements true, we must take reality itself to contain no A-series facts, i.e. no such facts as X's being now, or a week before now, or due a day after now.

Sound and simple though this argument is, to call it contentious

D. H. Mellor

would be an under-statement. But I have no space here to defend it against its many perverse but ingenious critics.[4] Instead I shall try to make it more palatable by showing why, even in a purely B-series world, we are bound to think about that world in A-series terms, i.e. in terms of past, present and future. And here again it will help to bring in the personal analogue. For as Thomas Nagel wrote in 1986, 'If it is not a fact about the ... world that I am [Thomas Nagel], then something must be said about what else it is, for it seems not only true but ... one of the most fundamental things we can say about the world'.[5] Similarly, if less self-centredly, I say that if it is not a fact about the world that such-and-such events are happening now, then something must be said about what else it is, for this too seems not only true but a most important thing to say and believe.

To see what we should say about this, consider first how what we want, and what we believe, affects how we act. The connection, as quantified in modern decision theory, is roughly that, as Frank Ramsey put it in 1926, 'we act in the way we think most likely to realize the objects of our desires',[6] a thesis that is now a stock if contentious ingredient of so-called functionalist theories of belief and desire. However, for present purposes, all I need is the simpler and less contentious qualitative claim that, usually, we do what we think will get us what we want, a claim that I hope no one will deny.

That for example was what caused me to go to London on 22 October 1999 in order to give the lecture at the Royal Institute of Philosophy of which this (with minimal and obvious variations) is the text. I went there then because I wanted to give that lecture, which I believed I was due to give there on that day. But for that belief to cause this action of mine it had, as John Perry, using other examples, showed in 1979,[7] to be both a personal and an A-series belief. Believing that Hugh Mellor was due to speak in London on 22 October would not have been enough. That belief did not after all make anyone else go to London to speak, simply because no one else believed 'I am Hugh Mellor'. Nor would that belief have made *me* go to London then if I had forgotten who I was, and thereby ceased to believe that the speaker was not only Hugh Mellor but *me*.

[4] See L. Nathan Oaklander and Quentin Smith (eds), *The New Theory of Time* (New Haven: Yale University Press, 1994).

[5] Thomas Nagel, *The View from Nowhere* (Oxford: Oxford University Press, 1986), 57.

[6] F. P. Ramsey, 'Truth and Probability', *Philosophical Papers* (Cambridge: Cambridge University Press, 1926), 52–109. 69.

[7] John Perry, 'The Problem of the Essential Indexical', *Noûs* **13** (1979), 3–21.

And similarly with the date. Wanting to be at the lecture, and believing it to be on 22 October, would not have taken anyone there on 22 October unless and until they also acquired the A-series belief 'Today is 22 October'.

It is obvious therefore *that* we need personal and A-series beliefs to make us act when we do. What is less obvious is *why* we need these beliefs, a question whose answer lies in an underrated fact about truth: namely, that truth is the property of our beliefs which enables us to get what we want. Consider again my going to London to give this lecture on 22 October because I believed I was due to do so then. That belief would have made me go to London even had it been false, i.e. even if I had made a mistake and was not in fact due to speak on that date. And as in this case, so in general: the truth or falsity of our beliefs does not in general affect what they make us do. What it does affect is whether what they make us do will *succeed*, i.e. get us what we want to get by doing it. It is only because the belief that took me to London on 22 October was true then that my going there succeeded in 'realizing the object of my desire', namely to give this lecture. Had my belief been false, i.e. had I not been due to lecture then, the action (going to London) which my belief caused me to do would have failed to achieve the object for which I did it.

This link, between the truth of our beliefs and the success of our actions, is the grain of truth in so-called pragmatic theories of truth, such as that published by William James in 1909.[8] I think in fact that, as Jamie Whyte has argued,[9] this link enables us to define truth, although that again is not a case I need to make here. All I need here is the undeniable fact that actions do generally depend for their success on the truth of the beliefs that cause them. For that fact is enough to explain why we, like all agents, need personal and A-series beliefs even in a wholly impersonal and B-series world.

This explanation, of our need for personal and A-series beliefs, starts with the obvious fact that almost all actions depend for their success on who does them and when. Thus for my action in going to London to give my lecture to succeed, it had to be done by the person who was due to give the lecture, namely Hugh Mellor, and on the day set for the lecture, namely 22 October. So far, so obvious. But to see what this obvious fact implies about the beliefs that cause our actions we need another obvious fact, namely that I will only be caused to act by beliefs that *I* have, and then only *when* I have them. No one else's belief that I was due to speak would have taken *me* to

[8] William James, *The Meaning of Truth* (Cambridge, Mass.: Harvard University Press, 1909).

[9] J. T. Whyte, 'Success Semantics', *Analysis* **50** (1990), 149–57.

D. H. Mellor

London: the person who needed to believe that was me. And for even that belief of mine to make me go to London on 22 October, I had to have it not on the day before, or the day after, but on that very day.

All this follows from the fact that, for reasons I need not go into, causes never act immediately at a distance in either space or time. Our actions are therefore bound to occur roughly when and where the beliefs and desires which cause them occur, namely where we are when we have those beliefs and desires. I say 'roughly' because our beliefs and desires do not in fact cause our actions immediately, but only via such effects as contracting our muscles, moving our limbs, or generating the sound, light or even radio waves by which we act on people and things at a distance.[10]

Now combine all this with the fact that our actions usually succeed only if the beliefs that cause them are true. It follows then that, for an action's success to depend on who does it and when, it must be caused by a belief whose truth also depends, in the same way, on who has that belief and when. That is why, in order to make me go to London to lecture when I did, I had to believe at the time that the lecturer was *me* and the date of the lecture was *today*. For since my action in going to London would succeed only if done on the due day and by the advertised speaker, the belief that caused it had to be true only if it was held by that person on that day. But the only beliefs which respectively fit those two bills are the A-series belief that today is the due day, and the personal belief that the speaker is me.

This is why we, as agents, need personal and A-series beliefs. We need them to enable us to act *when* we need to act, and when *we* need to act, in order to make our actions succeed. And not only in such minor matters as the giving and hearing of lectures on time, but in matters of life and death. No species could survive whose members' reactions to food, predators and prospective mates were not right, timely and made by themselves. So the members of any species whose actions are, like ours, caused by their beliefs and desires,

[10] For present purposes we can neglect all such distances and delays. For first, they may be negligible, as they are for so-called 'basic actions' like moving our limbs (see Arthur Danto, 'Basic Actions', *American Philosophical Quarterly* 2 (1965), 141–148). And second, even when they are not negligible, they mostly only affect when an action ends. not when it starts. Thus my action, going to London, *started* almost as soon as I acquired the belief that it was time to leave Cambridge. That belief is what caused my action, i.e. caused it to start, then and there, even though the action ended sixty miles away and ninety minutes later. So even in this case it is true enough to say that our actions are caused by the beliefs and desires we have when we do them, meaning when we start to do them.

52

must have personal and A-series beliefs—and must generally acquire them when, and only when, they are true.

This therefore is the original and basic function of our senses: to make the appearance and disappearance of food, predators and prospective mates cause us respectively to believe and to disbelieve '*I* am *now* facing food/a predator/a prospective mate' when and only when those beliefs and disbeliefs are true. And as in these situations, so in all others where we need or want to act. Only personal and A-series beliefs that are reliably formed (i.e. formed only in whom and when they have a high chance of being true) will enable us generally to act when we need to act in order to act successfully. This is why I call the present-centred A-series conception of time, this practically indispensable way of thinking of events as being past, present or future, 'the time of our lives': for we literally could not live without it.

And yet, I say, this is not in reality how time is, since there is in reality no distinction between past, present and future, and hence no flow of time and no changing A-series facts. But then what in reality does distinguish time from space'? The answer, proposed by A. A. Robb in 1914 and elaborated by Reichenbach in 1928,[11] is *causation:* time is the *causal* dimension of spacetime. This answer exploits the fact that while causes have effects in all spatial directions, as when a fire gives off heat all round, they have them in only one temporal direction, since causes only ever precede their effects. That is why nothing we do ever affects anything that happens before we do it, and also why we never see anything before it happens, since to perceive something is always, among other things, to be affected by it.

There are admittedly objections to this causal theory of time, based on apparent or allegedly possible cases of simultaneous or backward causation. Of these all I can say here is that all such objections can be met.[12] And to this claim I would add that I know of no serious alternative to a causal theory of how time differs from space. In particular, none of the other ways of defining time and its direction that have been touted—for example, as the dimension and direction in which entropy increases, or the universe expands, or radiation travels away from small sources—explains why we never affect the past or perceive the future.

[11] A. A. Robb, *A Theory of Time and Space* (Cambridge: Cambridge University Press, 1914); Hans Reichenbach, *The Philosophy of Space and Time,* trans. Maria Reichenbach and John Freund, (New York: Dover, 1928).

[12] See my *Real Time II* (London: Routledge, 1998), chs 10–12.

D. H. Mellor

This however does not tell us why we should call the causal dimension of spacetime the dimension of *change,* i.e. why variation along spacetime's non-causal and therefore spatial dimensions should not also count as change. To see why it might not, we must first ask what distinguishes change from mere difference. Why is *my* house being cold and *your* house warm merely a difference, while mine being cold at 6 and warm at 7 is a change? The answer is of course that we only call a difference in properties a change if there is a single thing—the thing that changes—which has the different and incompatible properties.

Yet how can a single thing have incompatible properties? In the spatial case, of a poker simultaneously hot at one end and cold at the other, the answer is that it does not: the poker as a whole is neither all hot nor all cold; and the part of it that *is* hot is not the same as the part of it that is cold. That is why spatial variation in the properties of a single thing is not a change, but merely a difference, since what has the different properties in these cases is not the thing itself but merely different parts of it.

Why should we treat temporal variation differently? We certainly do treat it differently, precisely because we do not normally think of people and things as having temporal parts. The audience at my lecture may not have thought I was all there mentally, but they certainly thought I was all there temporally: they thought it was me, and not just a part of me, that they were seeing and hearing. And the same goes for the building in which I gave the lecture. That is why everyone—or at least everyone untainted by philosophy— would take any temporal variation in someone's properties, or those of a building, to be a change and not just a difference: because in each case they think there is a single entity whose varying properties are all properties of *it* and not just of different parts of it.

However, many B-series philosophers, such as David Armstrong,[13] say that we are wrong to think like this, and argue that in reality people and things *do* have temporal parts. But although I disagree with them, I shall not rebut their arguments here. For even if we do have temporal parts, our normally failing to think and talk as if we do still explains why it is only temporal variation that we *call* change. So the real question for me is not why we do that, but why we only apply the concept of change to variation along the *causal* dimension of space-time.

The answer to this question lies in the fact that we take the identity

[13] David Armstrong, 'Identity Through Time', *Time and Cause: Essays Presented to Richard Taylor,* Peter Van Inwagen (ed.) (Dordrecht: Reidel, 1980), 67–80.

of things to depend on their keeping some at least of their properties. For example, some of my properties, such as being human, may be essential to me, i.e. such that I could not lose them, because nothing that lacked them would be me. But even if no one property is in this sense essential to me, so that I might conceivably change by suffi- ciently gradual stages into a beetle or a rhinoceros, no one thinks that I could survive the simultaneous loss of *all* my properties. And this means that, while any one changeable property of mine *is* changing, I must, in order to preserve my identity through that change, keep enough of my other properties *un*changed.

But what keeps most of my properties unchanged over time is the same as what makes some of them change, namely causation. My present height, weight, views of time and other fairly constant properties of mine are what they are now because—literally be*cause* —since nothing has happened to change them, that is what they were a minute ago. The causation of stasis may be less obvious than the causation of change; but it is no less real, and no less necessary to secure the identity that is needed to make a difference a change.

This is why a merely spatial variation in a thing's properties, for example from the hot to the cold end of a poker, is never a change. Because causes are never simultaneous with their effects, no poker can have any property at one end just because it has the same prop- erty at the other end at the same time. That is what stops a poker's two ends being a single thing in two places at once—as opposed to two parts of a single thing—and thereby makes any difference of properties between them merely a difference, and not a change in the poker as a whole.

This explanation of why we limit change to the causal dimension of spacetime is fairly new, and not yet as widely held as it should be. Still, what matters here is that no one doubts the fact which it pur- ports to explain, namely that, rightly or wrongly, we apply the con- cept of change to, and only to, temporal variation. For given this fact, there are undeniable changes in us which explain why we feel that time flows despite the fact that in reality it does not. These changes are those we need to keep making in our A-series beliefs in order to keep them true, as we have seen that they must be if our actions are to get us what we want. That is why, for example, when I woke up on the morning of 22 October, my previous belief that my lecture was *tomorrow,* which had been true the day before but was now false, turned into the belief that my lecture was *today,* a belief that was false the day before but was now true. And as these two beliefs are clearly incompatible properties of a single thing (me), my having one of them on 21 October and the other one the next morning was a real change in me, a change with real causes, such as my hearing the date on the radio that morning, and real effects, such as my going to London on that day.

Again, as in this case, so in general. Our beliefs about what is past, present and future are changing all the time: your beliefs about what you are reading right now, for example, are changing every second. These, and all the other changes we are continually making in our A-series beliefs, are real changes, with real causes and real mental and physical effects. They are the changes that embody our experience of the flow of time. Even though time does not flow in reality, in our minds the time of our lives really does flow, a fact whose recognition will I hope make the B-series view of time itself more credible.

Note however two things that what I have just said does *not* imply. First, it makes no concession to the A-series view of time itself. In particular, it does not mean that the flow of time is a real but so-called 'mind-dependent' phenomenon, i.e. that time really does flow in our world, but only because our world contains minds which somehow make it flow. That is not so: there is no possible world, with or without minds, in which time flows. So in particular, whatever else may make psychology irreducible to physics, it is not the flow of time, which psychology no more needs to postulate than physics does.

Nor, on the other hand, have I implied that the A-series beliefs whose continual changes are what make us experience time as flowing are false. Mine is not a so-called 'error theory' of A-beliefs, such as my belief, held on 22 October, that that was today's date. That belief, held then, was as absolutely true as the belief that the earth is round. There need be no error at all in any of our A-beliefs, about whether an event is past, present or future, provided we have them all at the right times. Consequently, our experience of time flowing can be not only real but true, as when I came to believe, on the morning of 22 October, that my lecture was today. In that sense the flow of time is no more illusory than, for example, what we call mirror images are. For just as it is not my beliefs about what I see in a mirror that are false, only the theory that what makes them true is an array of visible but intangible objects behind the mirror, so it is not our A-beliefs about what is past, present and future that are false, only the A-theory of what makes them true.

Where, finally, do we get the ever-changing A-beliefs that constitute the time of our lives? Just as our theory of mirrors must explain how a world without mirror images can give us true beliefs about what we see in mirrors, so a B-theory of time must explain how a world without A-facts can give us true A-beliefs. How can my hear-ing a clock strike 6 tell me truly that it is now 6 o'clock if in reality there is no such fact as its now being 6 o'clock'?

The answer to that rhetorical question is that we are born with the default habit of letting our senses make us believe that what they show us is happening *now*. Where does this habit come from? The answer must I think lie in evolution. What makes it generally useful to see events as being present is that the light which shows us near-by events travels much faster than we need to react to those events. In particular, this is true of events, like the approach of predators, partners and food, on our timely reaction to which we and our species depend for our survival. If our eyes made us believe that such events were still future when we saw them, we would not act on them in time, and if they made us believe that they were very past, we would not act on them at all; and either way we would die out. In order to survive in our world we need the default habit of believing that what we see happening is happening now. That is why evolution has bred this habit into us, precisely because, when it mat-ters, the habit makes our senses almost always give us A-beliefs only when they are true.

This completes my tale of what I have called the time of our lives, a tale I have told for two main reasons. First because, although still contentious, I think it is true and, I hope, interesting. My other reason is this. Too many philosophers, especially of the footnotes-to-Plato, French waffle, philosophy-as-therapy and analytic nit-picking schools, conspire with scientists to perpetuate the canard that philosophy never makes progress or settles any questions. The canard arises in part from philosophy's frontier work, of clearing the conceptual around for new sciences—ranging in the last centu-ry from relativity through computer science to theoretical linguis-tics—and then moving on, so that in many cases the settling of a philosophical question makes it cease *ipso facto* to count as philo-sophical. But even within philosophy there is still far more progress than some of my colleagues will admit, the philosophy of time being a good example, whether or not what I have said about it here is true.

For just consider the developments in the last hundred years that have advanced and now inform all serious philosophical work on time. First, there is relativity, which has greatly refined our under-standing of how time does and does not differ from space, and in particular of how it relates to causation.[14] Then there are new

[14] A. Einstein *et al.*, *The Principle of Relativity* (London: Methuen, 1923).

semantic theories of so-called indexicals like 'now' and 'I',[15] which show why our A-series talk of events being past, present or future cannot be translated into non-indexical B-series talk, as B-theorists once thought it could.[16] These theories also show why this untranslatability does not force us *either* to accept the flow of time *or* to reject all our everyday A-series talk as false.

The debate about time has thus been moved on, as it has also been moved on by new work in the philosophy of mind, and especially by the development first of behaviourist and then of functionalist theories of mind, which relate the contents of our beliefs and desires to how they make us act.[17] These theories have shown both how and—combined with the new theory of truth referred to above[18]—why our A-series way of seeing the world is as indispensable as it is irreducible.

Our metaphysical debates about time have also been advanced by philosophical work on meaning and truth,[19] which has shown how the meaning of A-series and B-series statements is related to their so-called truth conditions and thereby, more recently and usefully, to their so-called truthmakers, i.e. to what in the world *makes* such statements, and the beliefs they express, true or false.[20]

And these are just some of the developments inside and outside philosophy that have contributed to the progress the philosophy of time has made since McTaggart's article appeared. There is also a mass of work relating the direction and origin of time to theories of cosmology, causation, decision making, thermodynamics, statistical mechanics and quantum theory. There is all the semantic and metaphysical work on theories of change and identity through time, on the links between theories of time and theories of possibility and necessity, and—as advertisers used to say—much, much more.[21]

[15] E.g. David Kaplan, 'On the Logic of Demonstratives', *Journal of Philosophical Logic* **8** (1979), 81–98.

[16] See e.g. Perry, op. cit.; *Real Time II*, ch. 6.

[17] Peter Smith and O. R. Jones, *The Philosophy of Mind: an Introduction* (Cambridge: Cambridge University Press, 1986). chs 10–13.

[18] Whyte, op. cit.

[19] E.g. Donald Davidson, 'Truth and Meaning', *Synthese* **17** (1967), 304–23; Kaplan op. cit.

[20] *Real Time II*, chs 2–3.

[21] For an introduction to some of this literature, see for example: 'Time' and related entries in Edward J. Craig (ed.), *Routledge Encyclopedia of Philosophy* (London: Routledge, 1998); Paul Horwich, *Asymmetries in Time: Problems in the Philosophy of Science* (Cambridge, Mass.: MIT Press, 1987); Raymond Flood and Michael Lockwood (eds), *The Nature of Time* (Oxford: Blackwell, 1986); Jeremy Butterfield (ed.), *The Arguments of Time* (Oxford: Oxford University Press, 2000).

Of course some large philosophical questions about time are still open—or at least still debated—but that no more shows a lack of progress than do the ups and downs of atomic theories in physics. Is matter atomic? Well, yes and no, depending on what you mean by an atom. Does time flow? Well, yes and no, depending on what you mean by the flow of time. In both cases the devil, and the progress, is in the details. And just as this century has seen a vast increase in our detailed knowledge of the microstructure of matter, so it has seen a vast increase in our detailed philosophical understanding of time. And much of that increase has been, as I have tried to show, prompted and enabled by McTaggart's distinction between his A- and B-series, or, as I would put it, between the time of our lives and the time of reality. Anyone who does half as much for the philosophy of time in the coming century as McTaggart did for it in the last one will have done pretty well.

The Rise, Fall and Rise of Epistemology

ANTHONY QUINTON

I began the study of philosophy in an organized fashion after I was demobilised in 1946. My first steps were firmly Lockean. Innate idea, substance, primary and secondary qualities and personal identity were the topics of the first term's essays, along with smaller infusions of Descartes, Berkeley and Hume. The fundamental examination paper in those days in Oxford was General Philosophy and that meant the problems in the theory of knowledge that had exercised the great philosophers of the seventeenth and eighteenth centuries and, beyond them, Russell, Moore, Price and Ayer. The syllabus was very clearly set out by the chapter headings of Russell's *Problems of Philosophy*.

But that all changed in the late 1950s and early 1960s. Where once phenomenalism, knowledge of other minds, knowledge of causal connections, knowledge of the past had reigned supreme they were replaced by such matters as reference, identity (in general, not just of persons), truth, meaning, conditionals (particularly counterfactual ones). A fairly reliable indicator of British philosophical fashion is supplied by the appropriate supplementary volumes of the proceedings of the Aristotelian Society in which the symposium subjects for each year's Joint Session are to be found.

Originally this new domain of primary concentration was called 'philosophical logic'. The expression seems to have fallen into comparative neglect. No important books have had it as all or part of their titles, although some useful ones have. Sir Peter Strawson's Oxford Readings volume with this title dates from 1967 when it was, perhaps, already on the turn. It has been replaced by 'philosophy of language'. That may reflect a squeamishness brought on by the indiscriminate use of the word 'logic' in the high days of postwar analytic philosophy when works about the logic of personality, of prayer, of history and so on abounded. Another factor may have been a desire to mark it off from the much more restricted field of the philosophy *of* logic.

The epistemological tradition that ended, it may be suggested, around 1959 or 1960, with the publication in those years of Strawson's *Individuals* and Quine's *Word and Object*, was really established by Locke. Descartes had contributed indispensably to its inauguration with his radical scepticism and consequent endeavour to reinstate the human capacity for knowledge. But for all the massiveness of his influence, he was an epistemologist only *per accidens*. The entirely suitable subtitle of his *Meditations* is 'in which the existence of God and the real distinction of mind and body are demonstrated'. These are matters of ontology, not theory of knowledge, and his more local, more legitimate intellectual progeny—Spinoza and Leibniz—are builders of comprehensive metaphysical systems.

Locke, too, had a system, but it was an epistemological one, more particularly of a foundationalist variety. The basis was simple ideas of sensation and reflection. From them complex ideas, most notably that of substance were constructed and from some of them the existence of qualities and substances in the actual, objective world were inferred (at least according to a conventional interpretation of his somewhat inchoate utterances). Of comparable importance to this distinction between the basis of human knowledge and what is inferred or constructed from it is Locke's distinction of kinds of knowledge; intuitive, demonstrative and sensitive. His account of this distinction and of the proper objects of the kinds distinguished is somewhat rough and ready. Intuitive knowledge is not only of evidently analytic truths (the prime instance of his favourite 'agreement or disagreement of ideas') but also of the presence of ideas in our minds, whether or not any real object corresponds to them. Thus we have intuitive knowledge of both necessary and contingent truths. Demonstrative knowledge is the result of intuiting the logical consequences of intuitive premises (so must, it would seem, be confined to necessary truths). Finally, there is sensitive knowledge, the knowledge we have of things existing independently of us, which is really no more than 'Faith or Opinion'. The existence of God he holds to be demonstrative. But as derived from the non-analytic, non-trifling premise that there is intelligence in the universe, something that is intuitive in his second, weaker sense, is presumably contingent. Moral truth is also demonstrative, but he hardly explains how.

A great deal of the apparatus of contemporary theory of knowledge is to be found here. No serious attention is given to memory and testimony, although there is a glancing reference to the latter in his discussion of probability and a similar reference to the former in his chapter on 'our knowledge of the existence of other things'. And, surprisingly for a compatriot of Bacon, he nowhere explicitly refers to induction. But most of the familiar furniture is set out in a recognizable way. Furthermore, despite his belief that natural science is at least ideally, demonstrative, he shows unprecedented cognitive modesty in admitting that all the substantial beliefs about the world that are really worth having are not matters of certain knowledge but are no more than probable.

Leibniz examined Locke's *Essay* at length. Berkeley and Hume, agreeing with Locke as to what the central problems of philosophy are, criticized him with great force but failed to undermine his authority in his own epoch. Because of the absurdity of their positive conclusions (material things are collections of ideas in God's Mind, partially and fitfully downloaded into ours, and we have no reason to believe in the existence of anything but what is currently present to our senses) they were little read and not taken seriously when they were. Locke was quickly established as the principal object of study for university students in the British Isles and as essential reading for intellectually serious people everywhere (most influentially, of course, Voltaire). Aristotle's Metaphysics was pushed out towards the margin of the syllabus. The eighteenth century philosophers other than Locke who were widely read in Britain were Clarke and Butler, Bolingbroke and the Desists; philosophers of religion and morality. In theory of knowledge Locke was without serious challenge.

Kant made no deep inroads into British thought until long after his death, in the 1870s and after, and then only in thick Hegelian disguise. Where Descartes was a metaphysician taken to be an epistemologist, Kant underwent the opposite experience. His German successors turned his attack on metaphysics into metaphysics of a new kind. The first principles of human knowledge which he had tried to demonstrate with the dizzying complexities of his transcendental and metaphysical deductions were more economically affirmed as principles of common sense or human belief by Thomas Reid and Dugald Stewart, who, in effect, grounded them on intuition. Mill was the chief critic of the culminating philosophers of the Scottish school, Hamilton and Mansel. But he shared their Lockean conception of what the main problems of philosophy are. By-passing the idealist interlude of the late nineteenth century, the same conception is to be found in Russell, from *The Problems of Philosophy* to *Human Knowledge* getting on for half a century later. It is also the evident organizing formula for two comprehensive surveys, published in the Russellian age; Laird's *Knowledge, Belief and Opinion* (1930) and Hamlyn's *Theory of Knowledge* (1970).

Not only does most subsequent theory of knowledge stem from Locke, there is very little of it in his post-medieval predecessors.

Anthony Quinton

Bacon, living in an intensely sceptical age, made short and superficial work of scepticism of the senses and confined himself to the topic of induction, which, he took for granted, could be vindicated only if it established its conclusions with certainty. Hobbes took even less notice of scepticism. Bacon at least went to the length of arguing that if one of our senses deceived us we could apply the others to correct it. Hobbes just breezily assumed an uncritical naturalistic account of perception. Going further back, in the early middle ages an Augustinian, and so broadly neo-Platonic, view of knowledge as the result of divine illumination prevailed; after the recovery of Aristotle, his comparative indifference to epistemology set the standard.

A possible reason for this neglect of the subject in the middle ages is the fact that all but the most disreputably subversive thinkers proceeded from the unquestionable (and, indeed, unquestioned) assumption that a benevolent God would not have created us with radically defective intellectual equipment. Theory of knowledge, however, flourished in the ancient world where there were no religious obstructions to it. Plato was provoked by the Sophists into the work of refutation, in the *Protagoras*, and to that of defining knowledge in the *Theaetetus*. The problem posed by his exemplary demonstration that there is more to knowledge than true belief is, of course, still with us today. Although resistant to scepticism Plato's response to it is at least concessive, even perhaps defeatist. We can have knowledge of mathematics and morals but only opinion about matters of natural fact. The Platonic academy after his death developed the sceptical side of his thought which was a persisting philosophical tradition into Roman times. Both Cicero and Augustine wrote treaties 'against the academics', i.e. sceptics.

The sceptical philosophy of the ancient world was summed up in the writings of Sextus Empiricus (mid 3rd century A.D.). Their rediscovery in the 16th century and publication in the 1560s met the religious doubts of the period, excited on the one hand by the protestant reformation and on the other by the worldly humanism of Italy. Erasmus and Montaigne in the domain of general literature are the most conspicuous of those who received its influence. Descartes brilliantly, but insecurely, turned it on its head. But its staying-power was evinced by the dominance of Locke. That dominance, I have suggested, continued until comparatively recent times, about 1960. But one notable interruption must be acknowledged, that of absolute, or Hegelian idealism. After some small, premonitory rumblings that vast intellectual contraption burst on the British philosophical scene with the publication of T. H.

Green's huge introduction to his edition (with T. H. Grose) of the works of Hume (1874) and F. H. Bradley's *Ethical Studies* (1876).

Neither Green nor Bradley was in any recognizable sense an epistemologist. This was very much in the spirit of their joint inspiration, Hegel, who had maintained, in a somewhat disputatious way, that it was an impossible undertaking. Both were, certainly, involved with epistemology from outside, as it were. Green's first major work of theoretical philosophy was his long-drawn-out critique of empiricist theories of knowledge up to and including Hume. But his critique did not attempt to revise or improve upon what it was directed on. Nowhere does Green classify the sources and objects of knowledge. Drawing on an ill-judged remark of Locke's that relations are the work of the mind, he derives from this, and the vague assertion that all judgment affirms a relation between its constituents, the conclusion that judgment is the work of the mind, and so no sort of reflection of an independent reality.

Bradley concerns himself with conceptions that figure in the theory of knowledge; substance, qualities, primary and secondary, relations, the self and so on but only to argue that since they are all one and all 'relational' they are infected with contradiction. What passes for knowledge is the work of the discursive intellect and is only of appearances. It is a kind of intellectual makeshift useful in practical life but with no claim to truth. For knowledge of the indivisible unity of the world as a whole we must turn to speculative reason, which supplies only the pretty diaphanous assurance that the Absolute is one and a flux, like but 'higher than' the flux of immediate experience, a kind of liquefied Parmenideanism.

In 1903 fatal blows were delivered at the prevailing idealism by Moore and Russell and the Lockean tradition was restored in the next two decades. By 1920 idealism was only vestigial. The German intellectual occupation of the last years of the Victorian age turned out to be as superficial as the Roman occupation that had come to an end a millennium and a half earlier. An interesting indication of this superficiality has come to light only quite recently. In the fifth volume of Russell's *Collected Papers* are to be found the essays written by Russell as an undergraduate for his tutors James Ward and G. F. Stout. They turn out to be entirely conventional in subject-matter, about themes in Locke, Berkeley and Hume, with some attention to Descartes, at one historical end, and to Kant, at the other. They are pretty good essays, as might have been expected, and Ward's comments are sensible, to the point and entirely within the Lockean tradition. His own 'panpsychism' was clearly a private matter, like a second family hidden away in a suburb.

Anthony Quinton

Although Russell had left academic life and, on the whole, philosophy by 1920 and Moore had settled down to a steady practice of repeating himself, their way of doing the subject was carried on by Broad and Ewing in Cambridge and by Prichard and Price in Oxford. Doctrinally sympathetic epistemologies appeared in the interwar years in Europe from Schlick (*General Theory of Knowledge*) and Reichenbach (*Experience and Prediction*), and in the United States, notably from C. I. Lewis.

Here, as elsewhere, Wittgenstein was the odd man out. The *Tractatus* is a work of philosophical logic for very much the most part, for all its *obiter dicta* about induction, solipsism, death and morality. It was certainly taken to be so by the members of the Vienna Circle. It appears, indeed, that they for a time persuaded him to admit their Machian interpretation of his elementary propositions as reports of immediate experience. That would have the effect of moving it in the general direction of epistemology (towards something like Carnap's *Aufbau*). But the persuasion did not last. A great deal of the *Philosophical Investigations* is a response to one particular philosophical problem, that of our knowledge of other minds. But the rest are not touched on.

Some years after his death *On Certainty* was published, which is a collection of notes on Moore's defence of common sense and his proof of an external world. Moore had said he knew for certain that there existed material things, that there were minds that were conscious of them and that people generally knew for certain that these two propositions were true. There is no question, Wittgenstein held, of our doubting these things, since they are the hard framework of all our thinking about the world and ourselves and, he concluded, there is therefore, no sense in saying, with Moore, that we know them to be true. That, one might say, is Reid, in a Viennese rather than an Aberdonian accent.

Ryle was also a non-epistemologist, even an anti-epistemologist. His only explicit comment on the subject is a rather hostile entry on it in Urmson's *Concise Encyclopedia of Philosophers and Philosophies* (unsigned but readily identifiable as his on stylistic grounds). His topics were meaning, reference (in his early days), the analysis of mental concepts, philosophical method and the philosophy of Plato. He touches on perception, but in an epistemology-dampening way, in the chapter on observation in the *Concept of Mind* and there are some enlightening *aperçus* on memory and self-knowledge elsewhere in the book. His goal was conceptual exploration, not the justification of belief. It is in keeping with this that in an essay on Locke, contributed to a French encyclopedia and to be found in his

Collected Papers, he says that Locke's main achievement is the distinction of kinds of proposition, not varieties and sources of knowledge.

Austin presents more of an epistemological appearance. *Sense and Sensibilia*, however, is not a contribution to the problem of perception (that of how belief in the existence of material objects is to be justified) but a rejection of the supposition that there is such a problem, rather than a collection of fairly loosely inter-related issues. Early in his career he advanced an account of the allegedly performative character of the verb *know* of which, rightly, nothing whatever has been heard since. Strawson abstained pretty rigidly from the theory of knowledge for a long time, breaking out only in a *festschrift* for Ayer in which he may have been guided by courteous respect for the maxim 'when in Rome ...' Ayer alone, of the major British philosophers of the middle of the century remained faithful to the Lockean tradition. His *Problem of Knowledge* of 1956 may be seen as its last gasp.

The submersion of epistemology by the philosophy of language was associated with, and is perhaps not all that clearly distinguishable from, the Americanisation of British philosophy that took place after 1960. From the end of the war until around 1960 American philosophers poured over to see what was going on in Britain. Quite soon the flow was reversed (with many of the ablest British travellers not coming back). The change has been noticed and described, by, for instance, Ayer.

> Wittgenstein was very largely responsible for diverting Western philosophy from a course which it had steadily pursued from Descartes to Russell ... The dominant tradition, inaugurated by Descartes, was one that assigned a central role to the theory of knowledge.
>
> (*Wittgenstein*, p. 142)

But the change has not been much explained, although Dummett, who welcomes it, has propounded a justification. In an essay of 1967 on Frege's philosophy, to be found in *Truth and Other Enigmas*, he says that Frege first and, in the end, most influentially, rejected the Cartesian assumption that theory of knowledge is the fundamental philosophical discipline, looking back, beyond Descartes, to Aristotle and the Scholastics.

> For Frege as for them logic was the beginning of philosophy; if we do not get logic right, we shall get nothing else right. Epistemology, on the other hand, is not prior to any other branch

of philosophy; we can get on with philosophy of mathematics, philosophy of science, metaphysics or whatever interests us without first having undertaken any epistemological inquiry at all. (op. cit., 89.)

That is pretty much of an aside and it would be unreasonable to examine it too minutely. It might just be remarked that the priority of logic to philosophy is one thing, that of *philosophical* logic, or the philosophy of language, is another. Secondly, the philosophies of mathematics and science are surely theories of mathematical and scientific knowledge for the most part, while many, perhaps most, metaphysical issues are rooted in epistemology: those, for example, of mind and body, of the reality of the past, of the existence of universals.

We must, of course, understand what the words and sentences that we hear and utter mean before we can consider claims to knowledge of the truth of the propositions they express. But we do not need to have an articulate *theory* of meaning. And that is just as well, given the absence of any sort of consensus about what kind of thing a theory of meaning ought to be.

We can, however, ask why Frege's and Wittgenstein's shift of the centre of philosophy from knowledge to meaning proved so influential. In the first place, by 1960 epistemology seemed somewhat exhausted. The project of reductively analysing all other knowledge into immediate, infallible knowledge of sense-data had collapsed and so had the sense-data into which the analysis was supposed to terminate. Today sense-data are more or less a philosophical heritage site. The realization that memory is a store, not a source of knowledge, not some kind of retrocognition, seemed to exempt it from epistemological examination, wrongly, since things can go bad in store as well as be polluted at the source. The passionately affirmed but by no means universally persuasive, private language argument seemed to have dissolved the problem of our knowledge of other minds. A general air of fatigue and exhaustion hung over the theory of knowledge. It seemed time to move on from its over-cropped soil to some more promisingly fertile region.

The new ground proved fertile enough but not of intellectually edible material. Even if the move to new ground had been more successful, there is a practical consideration to be taken into account. A part, perhaps a very large part of the importance of philosophy (and that it has some is clear from a look at its history and its influence on the whole universe of thought) is that it is taught to, and studied by people the vast majority of whom are not going in the rest of their lives to be philosophers at all, in any but the most marginal way. Are they going to benefit from being lowered into the whirlpool of sophisticated controversy that makes up contemporary philosophy of language, of: linguistic holism, the rejection of a substantive distinction between sense and reference, the causal theory of reference, possible world semantics, all of which says Dummett seem to him mistaken? (op. cit., 441) Quantum electrodynamics is in a significant way prior to, or more fundamental than, classical mechanics, but classical mechanics is the place to start.

Given the chaotic state of the philosophy of language and its own long tradition it is not surprising that the theory of knowledge should show signs of revival. Inside the circle of the old field of problems a small, bright flame was ignited in 1963 by Gettier, illuminating the long dormant problem of Plato's *Theaetetus*: what more is there to knowledge, as there must be, than truth and belief? The ingenious counter-examples with which he undermined the conventional proposal of justification as the third condition released a violent flow of more or less ad hoc repairs to the challenged definition. It soon seemed more promising to drop justification altogether and replace it, as Goldman did in 1967, with the requirement that a true belief counts as knowledge only if it is caused by the state of affairs which make it true. Another proposal was that a true belief is knowledge only if it has been arrived at by a reliable method. These larger proposals introduce an interesting innovation in epistemology, namely *externalism*, the doctrine that there can be conditions of knowledge which the subject satisfies without being aware of the fact.

As the concept of justification was being extruded from the definition of knowledge it was still crucial for something that could well be seen as more important than knowledge strictly so called: reasonable or justifiable belief. The abandonment of sense-data cleared the way for a revised, more moderate foundationalism, one that did not require infallible foundations. Such a position goes some way to meet the claims of the supporters of coherence as the prime, or sole, provider of justification and knowledge. Haack, who set out a moderate, fallibilist compound of foundationaism and coherentism in her *Evidence and Inquiry* (1963) uses as an image of the rapprochement a crossword puzzle. Answers based simply on the clues are foundational, fitting in with existing letters is the element of coherence. That allows a certain priority to foundations; until they have supplied something there is nothing for coherence to work on.

Just how far coherence must be admitted to determine justification, now that old-style infallibilist foundationalism has been rejected is perhaps the most lively area in theory of knowledge at the present time. It certainly bulks large in the best recent textbook of the subject known to me: Dancy's *Introduction to Contemporary Epistemology* (1985). I shall not attempt to explore it further here but shall turn to other innvovations—the serious study of what has hitherto been a very marginal interest of theorists of knowledge and the confrontation of a new, less playful, sceptical challenge to the possibility of knowledge.

Most studies of the subject that aim to be at all comprehensive make some reference to the role of testimony in our stock of knowledge or belief. There is something about it in Russell's *Outline of Philosophy* (1926), a longer, and more penetrating, treatment in Price's *Belief* (1964). But the first full-length philosophical study of the topic is that of Coady (1992). What is really under consideration here is the social character of knowledge, the fact that nearly everything we claim to know or reasonably believe we have acquired from other people. Popper's theory of objective knowledge puts the point dramatically, although not in an epistemologically relevant way. The most substantial contribution here has been Goldman, the proponent of the causal theory of knowledge, in his large *Knowledge in a Social World* (1999).

Old-style, Cartesian, subjectivist theory of knowledge represented the individual knower as completely self-made epistemically speaking. Relying on the usual sources—perception, memory and inference—he identifies belief-producing organisms in his environment and, after checking their reliability against his own findings, takes over beliefs that have passed his test. No-one ever said anything as weird as this explicitly but it is implied as an account of how we get knowledge and beliefs from others by the labelling of that procedure as 'testimony'. The natural habitat of testimony is in a law court. There witnesses are sworn in, their evidence is presented, it is subjected to critical scrutiny. This picture has no place for the primordial fact that it is other people who teach us how to speak, to express our beliefs and to understand the utterances of other people in general.

The conception of the individual knower as a kind of Robinson Crusoe should be replaced by one in which he is placed from the outset in a belief-supplying community, in which vast tracts of information, good and bad, lie about and between which he has to navigate. Conventional epistemology describes and evaluates the acquisition of first-hand knowledge. But philosophers do not reflect on the social aspect of knowledge. Nor, I suspect, do they know anything about the work that has been done—by non-philosophers

—in this field. How many know the work of Patrick Wilson, a librarian, who describes his *Second-Hand Knowledge* as 'an inquiry into cognitive authority'? It is not mentioned by Goldman in his very widely-based book of 1999, although it came out sixteen years earlier.

The educational value of social epistemology depends on the fact that, on the whole, people are much better at managing the beliefs whose epistemic status is investigated in ordinary theory of knowledge than they are at dealing with second-hand information: what is brought to their notice by advertisers, politicians, newspapers, radio and TV. Belief is a little like strong drink; taking too little is not a problem, taking too much is. Credulity needs to be guarded against, primarily to sources of belief like those enumerated above, all of which are self-regardingly motivated. But we need to be critical as well about beliefs emanating, or purporting to emanate, from respectable, institutional sources, notably 'science' and 'experts', both of which embrace a multitude of levels of justified credibility.

There might be something to be said in favour of a private knowledge argument, parallel to its private language correlate. Popper argued that knowledge, particularly scientific knowledge, requires a community of investigators to keep a check on each others' reasoning. (The correctness of that view is not undermined by his own conspicuous hostility to criticism and impermeability by it.) It would probably prove quite as difficult to formulate it precisely enough for it to be worth discussing as its Wittgensteinian predecessor. But just as it is quite clear that language is in fact social, whether or not it demonstrably has to be, it is equally clear that knowledge is, in a very deep-seated way, a social phenomenon.

I have welcomed the emergence of social epistemology for its educational merits, as well as its more narrowly intellectual virtues and interestingness. There is another, broadly educational task which theory of knowledge is currently much needed to perform. That is to offer systematic and coherent resistance to the prevailing tides of irrationalism. From all directions the champions of various 'victim groups'—women, homosexuals, non-white people—proclaim that there is no such thing as objective truth. This does rather excite such responses as 'is that so?', 'do you expect me to believe that?', 'how do you know that?', 'what reason have you for believing that?'.

Since generalized irrationalism is evidently self-refuting and yet is passionately affirmed, since it tries to get something across at the same time as it invites us to pay no attention to it, one should, perhaps, look around for a consistency-preserving re-interpretation, as we do with such less dramatic absurdities as 'well, he is and he isn't'. A prime source for irrationalism is the Nietzschean proposition that all belief is motivated, interested, an instrument for the exercise of power. No doubt some belief is motivated but much is not, at least discernibly, such as my belief that at the moment of writing it is Monday and that the sun is shining. But two points should be noticed. First, it must be asked what is the status of the proposition in the common-sense social psychology of belief that belief is interested? Either it is true (or nearly true or probably true) or there is no reason to pay any direct, non-diagnostic attention to it. The second is that it does not follow from the fact that a belief is strongly motivated that it is false or unreasonable. Certainly, where the connection between belief and desire is very close and direct suspicion may be aroused. The beliefs irrationalists use their doctrine to protect are much closer to their ideological preferences than that between a belief in objective truth and scientific method are to a desire to dominate the lower orders.

People in the more intellectual professions need some sort of training in resistance to irrationalism. They need to be clear that it does not follow from the fact that knowledge is a 'social construction', which indeed it is, that it is therefore some kind of imposture nor that the reality it purports to be knowledge of is some sort of fantasy.

Theory of knowledge, I have contended, has had a long and distinguished career. In Britain, at any rate, it has been the central philosophical discipline since Locke, apart from a short interruption in the late nineteenth century and from its demotion to a subordinate role since about 1960. I have argued that it does not deserve this subordination, that there are signs that it is still alive and well and that it has recently developed in a socially valuable way.

The Intelligibility of the Universe

MICHAEL REDHEAD

'I do not believe in things, I believe only in their relations'—
Georges Braque

1. Introduction

Hume famously warned us that the '[The] ultimate springs and
principles are totally shut up from human curiosity and enquiry'.[1]
Or, again, Newton: 'Hitherto I have not been able to discover the
cause of these properties of gravity ... and I frame no hypotheses.'[2]
Aristotelian science was concerned with just such questions, the
specification of occult qualities, the real essences that answer the
question What is matter, etc?, the preoccupation with circular definitions such as dormative virtues, and so on. The rise of modern
science is usually seen as a break with the sterility of
Aristotelianism, so what exactly is it that modern science does discover, if it is not the essential nature of matter, of force, of energy,
of space and time? A famous answer was provided by Poincaré:
'The true relations between these real objects are the only reality we
can attain.'[3] This is often regarded as the manifesto of so-called
structural realism, as espoused in recent years by John Worrall, for
example (cp. his (1989)).[4] In response to the arguments of Larry
Laudan (1982) against convergent realism, Worrall points to the
continuity in the formal relations between elements of reality
expressed by mathematical equations, while the intrinsic nature of
these elements of reality gets constantly revised. Thus notions like
phlogiston and ether get discarded but the mathematical relationships involving such entities survive in Lavoisier's oxygen chemistry (crudely combustion results in an increase in weight because

[1] Hume (1777) p. 30 in the Selby-Bigge edition.
[2] Newton (1713) p. 547 of the Cajori edition.
[3] Poincaré (1902) p. 161 of 1952 translation. A similar position is implicit
in the distinction made by Duhem (1906) between representative and
explanatory components of theories.
[4] For more recent discussions of structural realism reference may be
made to Zahar (1994), Redhead (1995), Ladyman (1998) and Chakravartty
(1998).

Michael Redhead

subtracting the negative weight of phlogiston is mathematically equivalent to adding the positive weight of oxygen) or in the modern theory of the electromagnetic field, which simply dispenses with the underpinning of stresses and strains in a mechanical ether.

Popper is another philosopher who attacked what he called methodological essentialism, the thesis that it is the task of science 'to discover and to describe the true nature of things'. Rather he advocated methodological nominalism which aims at 'describing how a thing behaves in various circumstances, and especially whether there are any regularities in its behaviour'.[5]

If we follow these lines of thought we will be led to a more limited, but in many ways more defensible, account of what we might want to mean by the intelligibility of the universe.

In this paper I want to explore the structuralist approach to the nature of scientific theorizing, but first we need to be a little more precise as to how exactly the structuralist thesis should be formulated.

2. Structuralism

Structuralism is a buzz-word in many areas of modern thought, in continental (particularly French) philosophy (or are they all post-structuralists now!), in linguistics, in anthropology, in the development of modern art (cp. the quotation from the cubist Braque which I chose as the motto for this paper), in philosophy of mathematics, and in philosophy of science.

Informally a structure is a system of related elements, and structuralism is a point of view which focuses attention on the relations between the elements as distinct from the elements themselves.

So think of a pile of bricks, timbers and slates, which are then 'fitted together' to make a house, or brush strokes which 'relate' to form a picture, or words which string together into meaningful sentences.

All these are are examples of *concrete* structures. But to define an *abstract* structure we can imagine collecting structures into

---

[5] See Popper (1945) pp. 31–32. It may be objected that the nature-structure distinction is not easy to draw with any precision. How something behaves in response to external factors may well be part of what we mean by the intrinsic nature of the entity in question. In my view nothing really hinges on these semantic issues. For further discussion compare Psillos (1995).

isomorphism classes, where two concrete structures in the same isomorphism class are related by a bijective correspondence which preserves its system of relations in the sense that if in the one structure the elements $x_1 \, x_2 \, ... \, x_n$ satisfy the n-ary relation R then in the second structure the corresponding elements $y_1 \, y_2 \, ... \, y_n$ satisfy R' $(y_1 \, ... \, y_n)$ if and only if R $(x_1 \, ... \, x_n)$, where R' is the n-ary relation in the second structure which corresponds to R in the first structure.

The concept of abstract structure can now be thought of in an *ante rem* Platonistic sense as the second-order Form which is shared by all the concrete relational structures in a given isomorphism class, or if this is considered, following Dummett (1991) as too 'mystical', then the more 'hardheaded' approach, as Dummett calls it, is to conceive of the abstract structure just as the isomorphism class itself, which can be *represented* by any arbitrarily selected member of that class. In particular mathematical structures involving, for example, natural numbers or real numbers can be used to represent the abstract structure associated with a physical system if they belong to the same isomorphism class. Our claim will be that it is this abstract structure associated with physical reality that science aims, and to some extent succeeds, to uncover, rather than the 'true relations' referred to by Poincaré. The abstract structure can be thought of as a second-order property of the 'true relations' rather than the true relations themselves.[6]

[6] The notion of abstract structure in the way we have introduced it was prominent in early writings in the logical empiricist tradition. See, for example, Russell (1927) or Carnap (1929). Wittgenstein's *Tractatus* can also arguably be given a structuralist reading. See Caws (1988) for further discussion of the history of structuralism. It has often been argued (see, for example, Maxwell (1970a), (1970b)) that structuralism should be rendered via the Ramsey sentence 'there exists a relation R with structure S', but as pointed out long ago by Newman in his (1928) $\exists$ R (S(R)) is a logical truth, modulo the specification of the cardinality of the domain over which the relation is defined. However $S(\bar{R})$ where $\bar{R}$ refers to a *specific* relation having the structure S is logically stronger than the Ramsey sentence, and is by no means a logical truth. But this means that the reference of $\bar{R}$ must be 'picked out' in non-structural terms. Our claim is merely that $\bar{R}$ is hypothesized in some explanatory theoretical context so it exists as an ontological posit, but that all we have epistemic warrant for is the second-order structure S. So we are arguing for a clear distinction between an ontological account of reference, and our epistemic access to it. These remarks are also relevant to the English (1973) critique of the Ramsey sentence approach to structural realism. For further discussion see Demopoulos and Friedman (1985) and Solomon (1989).

Michael Redhead

I have talked here of mathematical structures as examples of concrete structures involving mathematical objects as opposed to physical objects. Of course, there is much debate in the philosophy of mathematics as to the status of mathematical objects, and in particular whether mathematical objects can be given a purely structuralist interpretation, for example as positions or place-holders in a mathematical pattern which itself constitutes an abstract structure! (see Resnick (1997) and Shapiro (1997) for detailed discussion of these issues).

For purposes of exposition I shall follow mathematical practice in distinguishing concrete mathematical structures which are specified categorically,[7] i.e. as belonging to a unique isomorphism class, from what Shapiro (1997) calls algebraic structures, which involve many isomorphism classes. (The concrete structures involving for example the natural numbers and the real numbers are then called by Shapiro nonalgebraic.) A paradigm example of an algebraic structure would be that of a group, since there are many non-isomorphic groups. But a group with a *specified* multiplication table would be a nonalgebraic or concrete structure in my terminology. Algebraic structures are of course widely employed in pure mathematics for investigating the properties of concrete structures, and indeed in many modern developments are studied in their own right independently of concrete instantiations. However, for our purposes, when I refer to mathematical structures without qualification I intend this to refer to concrete (nonalgebraic) structures. I am sufficiently a Platonist about mathematical objects not to feel the need to *identify* mathematical structures belonging to the same isomorphism class, for example to identify natural numbers with some isomorphic set theoretic

---

[7] In a formal axiomatic presentation categoricity can in general only be achieved in the framework of second-order logic. It is possible for a second-order theory to have all its principal models isomorphic, but of course the formal theory cannot distinguish between isomorphic models, and is also syntactically incomplete, since the underlying logic is incomplete in the sense that all the second-order logical truths cannot be captured by any recursive set of axioms. While first-order axiomatizations of an infinite structure can exhibit completeness, they cannot be categorical, since the models of a complete first-order theory are only elementarily equivalent, which of course is a weaker notion than isomorphism in the case of infinite models.

So, the question of what is meant by specifying a 'mathematical structure' is formally problematic. For the purposes of the present paper I shall not discuss these issues further, but rely on an intuitive Platonic conception of concrete mathematical structures.

constructions. But this prejudice will play no part in the concerns of this paper.

Of course, we can collect up concrete structures, as the *objects* of more comprehensive structures such as are studied in category theory, for example all the concrete groups are objects in the category GROUP, and mathematicians go on to collect categories themselves as objects in categories of categories. The classes of objects involved in these developments may be too 'large' to comprise sets in the technical sense, but in the present work we shall make no attempt to delve further into such mathematical niceties.

Let us turn instead to a simple example of how mathematical structures can be used to represent physical structures, in the context of scales of measurement.

For example, there are ordinal scales such as Moh's scale of hardness of minerals which maps the physical ordering of minerals in respect of 'scratchability' isomorphically onto the total ordering of a small finite subset of the natural numbers. There is of course a range of possible selections of natural numbers which can represent such an ordinal scale. This flexibility is typical for the representation of physical structures by mathematical structures. Consider the case of ratio scales for extensive quantities such as mass. Such quantities map onto a one-dimensional vector space spanned for example by the unit of mass. Given the choice of unit (base vector) the measure, i.e. the ratio between the quantity and the unit, is specified by a dimensionless number which represents the physical mass relative to the choice of unit. But again the representation is not unique. Changing the unit by a factor α rescales the measure by a factor α^{-1}. Or, as a final example, consider interval scales such as are used to measure temperature. Both the unit and the zero of the scale are arbitrary and hence the numerical representation is unique only up to a linear transformation, for example, converting temperature T_c on the Centigrade scale to T_f on the Fahrenheit scale by the transformation $T_c = 5/9\,(T_f - 32)$.

Another very familiar example of the underdetermination of mathematical representations is the variety in the choice of coordinate maps or charts for the (local) representation of a physical manifold, such as phase space in mechanics or the space-time manifold. The choice of chart is a matter of convention, and is to be decided by pragmatic considerations of convenience, simplicity and so on.

But what has the conventional choice of mathematical representation of a physical structure got to do with physics? To answer this question we need to discuss the idea of changing or transforming a concrete structure, but in a way which preserves the abstract structure.

Michael Redhead

3. Transformation of Structures—the Notion of Symmetry

We have already considered the notion of isomorphism between structures. We now want to consider a bijective structure-preserving map of a structure *onto itself* This is what mathematicians refer to as an automorphism of the structure. In physics it is known as an (actively interpreted) symmetry of the structure. The original structure and the transformed structure cannot be distinguished structurally!

Consider then a physical structure P and a mathematical structure M that represents the abstract structure of P in the way we have described and suppose there are two distinct isomorphic maps call them x and y, from P onto M (see Fig. 1).

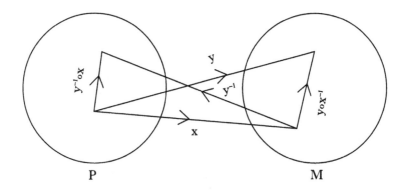

Fig. 1 x: P → M and y: P → M are distinct isomorphisms between a physical structure P and a mathematical structure M. y∘x⁻¹: M → M is a coordinate transformation, while y⁻¹∘x: P → P is a symmetry of P.

Then y∘x⁻¹ (or equally its inverse x∘y⁻¹ are clearly structure preserving maps from M onto itself, i.e. they are automorphisms of M. If we define the maps x and y as 'coordinatizing' the structure P in a general sense, then the maps such as y∘x⁻¹ or x∘y⁻¹ are what physicists call coordinate transformations—they relate different ways of using M to represent P. But notice now that to any coordinate transformation such as y∘x⁻¹ there corresponds a symmetry of P specified by the structure preserving map y⁻¹∘x of P onto itself. So the existence of coordinate transformations, different ways of using M to represent P, generate symmetries of P, and such symmetries are a very important feature of the physical structure P itself. The result is not really at all surprising. After all, M has the same structure as P, so it has the same symmetries. Coordinate transformations as we have seen are automorphisms, i.e. symmetries, of M. There must then be corresponding symmetries of P, which we have just exhibited.

We want now to prove the following

Lemma: *Any* symmetry of P can always be factorised in the form $y^{-1} \circ x$ for suitable choice of the maps x and y.

Proof Denote the symmetry of P by the map ϕ: P → P. Now form the map $y \circ \phi$: P → M, where y is any given isomorphism of P onto M. This is clearly also an isomorphism, call it x

so $y \circ \phi = x$, or $\phi = y^{-1} \circ x$ QED

Hence *any* symmetry of P is associated with a coordinate transformation (viz. $y \circ x^{-1}$). Similarly *any* symmetry of M can be factorized in the form $y \circ x^{-1}$ for any given y and a suitable choice of x, and is associated with a symmetry $y^{-1} \circ x$ of P. So if we denote by Sym (P) the group of all symmetries of P and similarly for Sym (M) then Sym (P) and Sym (M) are abstractly one and the same group represented in distinct ways by Sym (P) and Sym (M).

There is another important point to note. Apart from the possible ambiguity of representing P by a *given* mathematical structure M, there is also the ambiguity of representing P by *different* mathematical structures M and M'. This of itself does *not* lead to symmetries of P and is exemplified by the example of the finite ordinal scales of measurement discussed above. There are no symmetries of the physical structure in this case.

So it is not ambiguity of representation as such which has physical content, only the ambiguity within a *given* mathematical structure.

4. Surplus Structure

So far we have considered bijective maps such as x of P *onto* M. We now want to consider another important case where M is itself a substructure of a larger structure M', and the map x is now to be considered as an *injection* of P *into* M', or what mathematicians call an embedding of P in M' (see Fig. 2). The relative complement of M in M' we refer to as the *surplus structure* in the representation of P by M'.

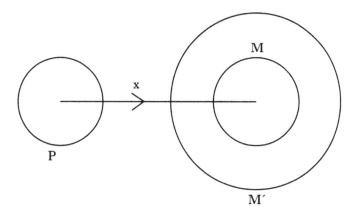

Fig. 2 Embedding of a physical structure P in a mathematical structure M'.

A simple example would be the use of complex currents and impedances in alternating current theory, where the physical quantities are embedded in the wider mathematical structure of complex numbers.

The properties of analytic functions of a complex variable along the real axis depend in a crucial way on the location of singularities in the complex plane. During the 1960s the theory of elementary particles was formulated in terms of so-called S-matrix theory in which scattering amplitudes considered as functions of real-valued energy and momentum transfer were continued analytically into the complex plane, and axioms introduced concerning the location of singularities of these functions in the complex plane were used to set up systems of equations controlling the behaviour of scattering amplitudes considered as functions of the real *physical* variables. This is an extreme example of the role of surplus structure in formulating a physical theory, where there was no question of identifying any physical correlate with the surplus structure.

In other examples, as we shall now discuss, the situation is not so clear. What starts as surplus structure may come to be seen as invested with physical reality.

A striking example is the case of energy in 19th century physics. The sum of kinetic and potential energy, T + V, was originally introduced into mechanics as an auxiliary, purely mathematical entity, arising as a first integral of the Newtonian equations of motion for systems subject to conservative forces. But as a result of the formulation of the general principle of the conservation of energy and its incorporation in the science of thermodynamics (the First Law) it came to be regarded as possessing ontological significance in its own right.

Moreover, its role in the Hamiltonian formulation of mechanics, promoted its fundamental significance, although not perhaps in an ontological sense. Here one should compare the Hamiltonian (T + V) with the Lagrangian (T − V) which provided a quite different route to the general formulation of mechanical principles.[8] Suffice it to say that different mathematical formulations of a given physical theory generally involve a role for surplus structure in the way we have introduced the term, but the ontological significance may be difficult to determine.[9]

A very interesting example of the role of surplus structure is the case of gauge theories in modern particle physics. We consider the case of the (first-quantized) Schrödinger field to bring out the points at issue. The field amplitude $\psi(x)$ (for simplicity we consider just one spatial dimension) is a complex number, but quantities like the charge density $\rho = e\psi^*\psi$ and the current density $j = \frac{1}{2} ie(\psi^* \, d/dx\psi - \psi(d/dx\psi)^*)$ are real quantities and can represent physical magnitudes. Consider now phase transformations of the form $\psi \rightarrow \psi e^{i\alpha}$. These are known as gauge transformations of the first kind, or global gauge transformations since the phase factor α does not depend on x. If we now demand invariance of physical magnitudes under gauge transformations then ρ and j satisfy this requirement. But suppose we impose *local* gauge invariance, i.e. allow the phase factor α to be a function $\alpha(x)$ of x. (This is also known as gauge invariance of the second kind.) ρ remains invariant but j does not. In order to obtain a gauge invariant current we must replace d/dx by $d/dx - i A(x)$ where A transforms according to $A \rightarrow A + d/dx\alpha(x)$ so the modified current $j(x) = \frac{1}{2} ie (\psi^* (d/dx - i A)\psi - \psi (d/dx + i A) \psi^*)$ is gauge invariant, but this has been achieved by introducing a new field $A(x)$ as a necessary concomitant of the original field $\psi(x)$. Reverting to three spatial dimensions, the A field can be identified (modulo the electronic charge e) with the magnetic vector potential, and the requirement of local gauge invariance can be seen as requiring the introduction of a magnetic interaction for the ψ field.

Again we have an example here of physical structure being controlled by requirements imposed on surplus mathematical structure.

[8] The identification of the Hamiltonian with T + V and the Lagrangian with T − V is true of many mechanical systems. For a discussion of the conditions under which these identifications can be made see, for example, Goldstein (1980).

[9] For further discussion of this important issue cp. Jones (1991).

Michael Redhead

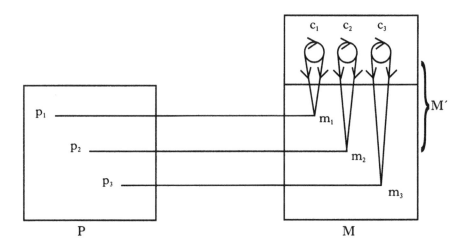

Fig. 3. Gauge transformations and surplus structure.

The situation is illustrated schematically in Fig. 3.

p_1, p_2, p_3 are three physical magnitudes, for example the charge or current at three different spatial locations. They are mapped onto m_1, m_2, m_3 in the mathematical structure M, which is a substructure in the larger structure M′. The circles c_1, c_2, c_3 in the surplus structure represent possible phase angles associated with m_1, m_2, m_3 in a many-one fashion as represented by the arrows projecting c_1, c_2, c_3 onto m_1, m_2, m_3. Local gauge transformations represented by the arrows on the circles act independently at different spatial locations. They correspond to the identity transformations on M and correlatively on P. The A field establishes what mathematicians call a connection correlating phases on the different circles c_1, c_2, c_3. The gauge transformations alter the connection as well as the individual phases in such a way as to maintain the gauge invariance of the corrected 'derivative' $d/dx - iA$.

Two ways of dealing with the surplus structure inherent in gauge theories suggest themselves. Firstly, we might just fix the gauge by some arbitrary convention, but then we have lost the possibility of expressing gauge transformations which lead from one gauge to another. Alternatively, we might try to formulate the theory in terms of gauge-invariant quantities, which are the physically 'real' quantities in the theory. Thus instead of the gauge potentials, the **A** field in electromagnetism, we should employ the magnetic induction **B**, specified by the equation **B** = curl **A**.

However, this manoeuvre has the serious disadvantage of rendering the theory non-local! This is most clearly seen in the Aharonov-Bohm effect in which a phase shift occurs between electron waves propagating above and below a long (in principle infinitely long) solenoid. The magnetic induction is confined to the interior of the solenoid, so if it is regarded as responsible for the phase shift, it must be regarded as acting nonlocally. On the other hand the vector potential extends to everywhere outside the solenoid, so if invested with physical reality its effect on the electron phases can be understood as occurring locally. This is an argument for extending physical reality to elements which originated as elements of surplus structure.[10]

Another example of this change in status of surplus structure is Dirac's hole theory of the positron, allowing a physical interpretation for the negative-energy solutions of the Dirac equation.

Another, rather different, application of the role of surplus structure, arises in considering the issue of idealization in the mathematical representation of physical structures. Consider the representation of physical magnitudes by real numbers with the order type of the linear continuum. This is not only a dense ordering, so that between any two real numbers there always exists another (indeed an infinity of others). But, moreover, it is a complete ordering, in the sense that there are no 'gaps' that could be filled by Dedekind cuts. But all these properties are far beyond any possible experimental check. It is entirely possible that all physical magnitudes are actually discrete, with the order type of the natural numbers, which are then embedded in the real number system. In this sense idealization adds (surplus) structure to the physics rather than stripping it away, as in an alternative sense of idealization involved in considering frictionless planes, point molecules and so on.

5. Expanding and Contracting Structures

So far we have considered the structural characterization of given physical theories. We now want to consider what light the structural approach can throw on the progress of science, i.e. to consider to what extent structure is preserved across scientific revolutions.

---

[10] Gauge theories, even after gauge fixing, exhibit a very important symmetry, the so-called BRST symmetry involving unphysical 'ghost' fields, which are crucial to maintaining the unitarity of the non-Abelian gauge theories, and the proof of their renormalizability via the Taylor-Slavnov identities. The move in the BRST formalism is thus to *augment* the surplus structure via the introduction of the ghost fields, again emphasizing its crucial role in modern theoretical physics.

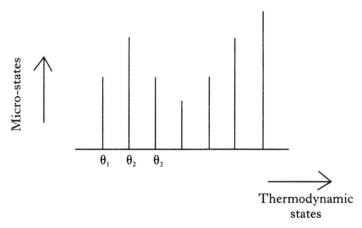

Fig. 4. Thermodynamic states and their micro-constituents

Let us consider schematically the relation between thermodynamics and statistical mechanics. Let us represent possible macroscopic thermodynamic states by points on a horizontal line (see Fig. 4), different points such as θ_1, θ_2, θ_3 ... correspond to the different thermodynamic states.

Through each point such as θ_1, θ_2, θ_3 we draw vertical lines to represent the microstates associated with the indicated thermodynamic states. The lines are of different lengths, representing the fact that different thermodynamic states are associated with different numbers of microstates. Each thermodynamic state can be thought of as 'expanded' or exploded if you like into the collection of its associated microstates. Conversely each vertical line can be 'contracted' or projected if you like onto the corresponding thermodynamic state. The transformation between the expanded and contracted structure is a many-one map. It is singular in the sense that it does not possess an inverse. The inverse *images* of points in the contracted structure produce a partition of the expanded structure into equivalence classes of elements that all map onto the same element in the contracted structure. We have already met the situation in Fig. 3 when discussing surplus structure. The points m_1, m_2, m_3 in M were expanded into the circles c_1, c_2, c_3, or conversely the circles can be considered as contracted onto the points. In the case of surplus structure we have already discussed the problematic ontological status of the expanded structure, but in the case we are now considering, the microstates of the individual atoms or molecules are to be considered just as physically real as the macroscopic thermodynamic states.

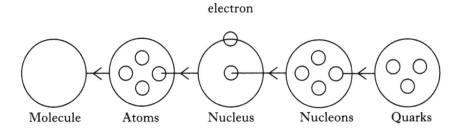

Fig. 5 Successive layers of microreduction. The arrows represent successive contractions of structure reading from right to left in the diagram.

Similar relationships obtain as we uncover successive layers of structure, molecules composed of atoms, atoms of nucleons and electrons, the nucleus of protons and neutrons, nucleons of quarks. This is what might be called the 'Chinese boxes' schema of scientific microreduction. Each box can be seen as a contraction of the next one inside it, so successive contractions 'forget' successive layers of internal structure. So the more primitive analysis represented by the outer boxes survive the more detailed microanalysis in the form of contractions of the more detailed microstructure (see Fig. 5).

We are dealing here with a case of what Heinz Post calls consistent correspondence in his (1971). The more primitive structures survive intact under a suitable scheme of translation represented by the contraction map. Other examples of consistent correspondence in which structure is preserved across theory change would include the extension of electrostatics to electromagnetic phenomena involving the interdependence of electric and magnetic phenomena as expressed in Maxwell's equations, or the case cited by Worrall in his (1989) of the preservation of Fresnel's equations for the intensity of reflected and refracted light at the interface between different dispersive media, when the phenomena are interpreted in terms of electromagnetic theory rather than the elastic solid ether theory of Fresnel.

These types of example illustrate continuity of structure across scientific theory change, and hence serve to defuse the arguments against realism arising from the apparent lack of ontological convergence as science progresses.

But we must now consider the case of inconsistent correspondence in Post's terminology, where qualitatively new structure arises.

Michael Redhead

The prime examples of this state of affairs are relativity theory and quantum theory.

6. The Development of New Structure

Consider a one-parameter family of structures $\{S_p\}$ where the parameter p is a continuously variable real number. Let us suppose for values of p unequal to zero the structures S_p are all qualitatively the same, as p varies the structure changes, but in a continuous way. But suppose the change in structure suffers a discontinuity at the point $p = 0$, so S_0 is qualitatively distinct from all the S_p with $p \neq 0$. We may say that the family of structures is *stable* for $p \neq 0$, but exhibits a *singularity* at $p = 0$.

To make these ideas precise we must provide a mode of comparison between structures S_p and $S_{p'}$, typically provided by an element $t_{p'p}$ of a group of transformations T which characterize the deformation of S_p to $S_{p'}$, so symbolically $S_{p'} = t_{p'p}S_p$. If there exists $t_{p'p} \in T$, which effects the transformation from S_p to $S_{p'}$, we say that S_p is qualitatively the same as $S_{p'}$ and write $S_p \sim S_{p'}$ according to the mode of comparison provided by the group T. If no such $t_{p'p}$ exists we say that S_p and $S_{p'}$ are qualitatively different. So for our family $\{S_p\}$ and an appropriate choice of T, we are claiming $S_p \sim S_{p'}$, $\forall$ p, $p' \neq 0$, but $S_p \nsim S_0$, $\forall$ $p \neq 0$. What do we mean by an appropriate choice of T? This will depend on those features of S_p which we regard as not really essential to the general qualitative type of structure, but just differing in 'quantitative' detail.

So think of a simple geometrical structure such as a circle drawn in the Euclidean plane. It can be deformed in a continuous way (technically a homeomorphism of the plane onto itself), so as to transform into any other closed curve. But it cannot be transformed into a straight line, which would involve 'cutting' the circle. So the straight line is topologically distinct from the circle under the mode of comparison provided by the group H of homeomorphisms of the plane. All the simple closed curves are qualitatively the same since they can be transformed into each other by the action of elements of H. We can say that they are quantitatively different in respect of shape and size but going to the straight line is not just a further quantitative change, it is in a very natural sense a *qualitative* change. The situation is illustrated in Fig.6.

Let us now apply these ideas to the case of special relativity, showing how Minkowski space-time develops from Galilean space-time. The crucial feature of the former is that it admits a non-

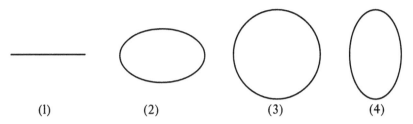

(1)   (2)   (3)   (4)

Fig. 6. Stability of structures (2), (3) and (4) are structurally stable relative to the group of homeomorphisms of the plane. Structure (1) is singular. (For more on stability of structures cp. Rickart (1995) ch. 9.)

singular metric represented relative to a Lorentz chart by the matrix diag $(1, - 1/c^2, - 1/c^2, - 1/c^2)$ where c is the speed of light in vacuo. The non-singularity of the metric corresponds to the fact that this matrix has an inverse, viz. diag $(1, - c^2, - c^2, - c^2)$. $1/c$ plays the role of our parameter p in the previous discussion. For $c = \infty$, i.e. $1/c = 0$, the metric abruptly and discontinuously becomes singular, since diag (1, 0, 0, 0) clearly has no inverse. Physically this singular behaviour at $1/c = 0$ translates into the all-or-nothing disappearance of the relativity of simultaneity at the singular value $1/c = 0$. For $1/c \neq 0$, the space-times are all qualitatively similar, they all exhibit the relativity of simultaneity, but to a different quantitative degree represented by the increasing departure of the light-cone from a horizontal plane, as $1/c$ increases. This is illustrated in Fig. 7.

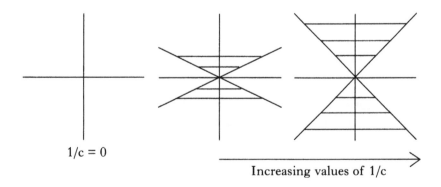

$1/c = 0$

Increasing values of $1/c$

Fig. 7. The discontinuous appearance of the light-cone as $1/c$ increases from the value zero. $1/c = 0$ corresponds to Galilean space-time, where the light-cone has degenerated into a plane. $1/c \neq 0$ corresponds to a family of Minkowski space-times with a continuously decreasing 'flatness' of the light-cone.

Michael Redhead

For sufficiently small values of the dimensionless parameter v/c where v is the velocity of the moving frame, the relativity of simultaneity may not be empirically detectable, but it only disappears in an ontological sense for v = 0, when there is no relative motion of the frames anyway, or 1/c = 0 which is the classical singular limit.

Turning to the case of quantum mechanics, the distinguishing feature of the mathematical structure is non-commutativity. The relation to the classical limit h = 0 is most clearly seen via the Moyal bracket formulation of quantum mechanics which generalizes the Poisson bracket of classical mechanics by introducing a non-commutative multiplication for functions defined over a phase space, or equivalently a non-commutative geometry of phase space in the style of Alain Connes (cp. his (1990)).

Again there is a qualitative discontinuity as the Moyal bracket degenerates into the commutative case of the Poisson bracket. The loss of commutativity in the structure is again an 'all-or-nothing' matter, while once lost the degree of 'non-commutativity' is controlled in a quantitative fashion by the numerical value of h. So, just as in the relativity example, we have a case of inconsistent correspondence between the structure with finite h (however small) and the structure with h actually equal to zero.

In both cases, we do not have continuous transformation of structure as we move away from the classical structure characterized by 1/c = 0 in the case of relativity, and h = 0 in the case of quantum mechanics to the new structures with non-zero values of 1/c or h. Qualitatively new structures emerge, but there is a definite sense in which the new structures grow naturally, although discontinuously, out of the old structures. To the mathematician introducing a metric in geometry, or non-commutativity in algebra are very natural moves. So looked at from the right perspective, the new structures do seem to arise in a natural, if not inescapable, way out of the old structures.

So revolutions in physics, understood from the structural standpoint, can be understood progressively, as compared with the U-turns in non-structural ontology emphasized by Laudan, for example.

7. Conclusion

An irregular area of unrelated shapes is meaningless. It is only when we see the eyes each side of the nose, and the mouth and chin below that we recognize a face. It is the same with the universe. Nothing

The Intelligibility of the Universe

is intelligible standing in isolation. Intelligibility is conferred by relationships, the *concrete structure* of reality. But even this is too ambitious for science to achieve. The aspect of reality that is amenable to scientific investigation is the *abstract structure* as *represented* for us by the mathematical structures of theoretical physics.

References

Carnap, R. (1929) *Der Logisches Aufbau der Welt* (Berlin: Schlachtensee Weltbreis-Verlag).
Caws, P. (1988) *Structuralism: The Art of the Intelligible* (New Jersey and London: Humanities Press International).
Chakravartty, A. (1998) 'Semirealism', *Studies in History and Philosophy of Science*, **29**, 391–408.
Connes, A. (1990) Géométrie Non-Commutative, (Paris: Inter Editions).
Demopoulos, W. and Friedman, M. (1985) 'Critical Notice: Bertrand Russell's *The Analysis of Matter*: Its Historical Context and Contemporary Interest', *Philosophy of Science*, **52**, 621–39.
Duhem, P. (1906) *La Théorie Physique: Son Objet, Sa Structure* (Paris: Chevalier et Rivière).
Dummett, M. (1991) *Frege: Philosophy of Mathematics* (Cambridge, Mass.: Harvard University Press).
English, J. (1973) 'Underdetermination: Craig and Ramsey', *Journal of Philosophy*, **70**, 453–62.
Goldstein, J. (1980) *Classical Mechanics*, 2nd edition, (Reading, Mass: AddisonWesley).
Hume, D. (1777) *An Enquiry concerning Human Understanding*, posthumous edition, Selby-Bigge edition (1902), (Oxford: Clarendon Press).
Jones, R. (1991) 'Realism about What?', *Philosophy of Science*, **58**, 185–202.
Ladyman, J. (1998) 'What is Structural Realism?', *Studies in History and Philosophy of Science*, **29**, 409–24.
Laudan, L. (1982) 'A Confutation of Convergent Realism', *Philosophy of Science*, **48**, 19–49.
Maxwell, G. (1970a) 'Structural Realism and the Meaning of Theoretical Terms', in S. Winokur and M. Radner (eds) *Analyses of Theories, and Methods of Physics and Psychology* (Minneapolis: University of Minnesota Press), pp. 181–92.
Maxwell, G. (1970b) 'Theories, Perception and Structural Realism'in R. Colodny (ed.) *Nature and Function of Scientific Theories*, (Pittsburgh: University of Pittsburgh Press), pp.3–34.
Poincaré, H. (1902) *La Science et l'Hypothèse* (Paris: Flammarion, English translation (1952) New York: Dover).
Newton, I. (1713) *Philosophiae Naturalis Principia Mathematica* 2nd edition, The 1929 Motte translation edited by Florian Cajori (1934), (Berkeley and Los Angeles: University of California Press).

Michael Redhead

Post, H. R. (1971) 'Correspondence, Invariance and Heuristics: In Praise of Conservative Induction', *Studies in History and Philosophy of Science*, **2**, 213–55.

Newman, M. H. A. (1928) 'Mr. Russell's Causal Theory of Perception', *Mind*, **37**, 137–48.

Popper, K. R. (1945) *The Open Society and Its Enemies*, Volume 1, *The Spell of Plato* (London: Routledge and Kegan Paul).

Psillos, P. (1995): 'Is Structural Realism the Best of Both Worlds?', *Dialectica*, **49**, 15–46.

Redhead, M. L. G. (1995) *From Physics to Metaphysics* (Cambridge: Cambridge University Press).

Resnick, M. D. (1997) *Mathematics as a Science of Patterns* (Oxford: Clarendon Press).

Rickart, C. E. (1995) *Structuralism and Structures: A Mathematical Perspective* (Singapore: World Scientific).

Russell, B. (1927) *The Analysis of Matter* (London: Allen and Unwin).

Shapiro, S. (1997) *Philosophy of Mathematics: Structure and Ontology* (Oxford: Oxford University Press).

Solomon (1989) 'Discussion: An Addendum to Demopoulos and Friedman (1985)' *Philosophy of Science*, **56**, 497–501.

Worrall, J. (1989) 'Structural Realism: The Best of Both Worlds?', *Dialectica*, **43**, 99–124.

Zahar, E. G. (1994) 'Poincaré's Structural Realism and his Logic of Discovery', in G. Heinzmann *et. al.* (eds), *Henri Poincaré: Akten Des Internationale Congresses, Nancy, 1994* (Berlin: Academie Verlag), pp. 45–68.

Active Powers and Powerful Actors

ROM HARRÉ

Introduction

The usual context for raising the issue of 'agent-causation' is that of human action. Cf. the excellent recent book by Fred Vollmer (1999). And a long list of articles. The motivation for mounting a defence of the propriety of agent causation might be to restore moral concepts to a place in human life, via responsibility of actors for their actions, threatened by event (internal or external) causality explanation formats.

The performing of an action is treated as an event. Taken as an effect it becomes tied to another event or set of events as its cause. The very idea of people being responsible for their actions presupposes that at least some of the actions that someone does are not wholly the product of antecedent causal conditions. Whether the determining conditions of human actions are in the environment or in the person is irrelevant to the issue. There are two problems with maintaining that people are responsible for some of what they do.

> The Leibniz problem: if God foresees everything that will happen then all events, including human actions, are necessary, that is they could not be otherwise if God is both omniscient and immutable.

> The Laplace problem: if all events are produced by deterministic causal mechanisms and the universe is always in some determinate state, then all events, including human actions, are necessary, that is they could not be otherwise if causal processes remain the same.

In either case there must be indefinitely prolonged chains of cause/effect sequences, initiated at the moment of creation.

These cosmic characteristics seem to run counter to the widespread intuition that people can freely choose some at least of their actions. The free action of a person as agent would introduce a novel event into the otherwise indefinitely extended chain of cause/effect event sequences. Unless the 'problems' can be surmounted the concept of 'responsibility' seems to lose its usual force.

The clash between the intuitive conviction that some actions are

Rom Harré

freely chosen and the rational conviction that all events, including human actions, are determined by past events, troubled Islamic philosophers as deeply as it has troubled philosophers in the Christian tradition. Profound problems call for heroic solutions. For example Islamic philosophers were responsible for the doctrine of 'occasionalism', revived in the seventeenth century in the Christian West. The occurrence of an event, singled out as an effect, is not capable of generating anything. It is simply an occasion for God to create an appropriate consequence, according to his plan for the Universe. All causal activity is reserved to God as the only *active* being. When a material situation arises in the sense organs of the human body, God creates the appropriate thought in the mind. There is no place for human freedom to act otherwise than as the evolution of the world determines, if the determining agent is God. Al-Ghazālī argues:

> neither the existence nor the non-existence of the one is implied in the affirmation, negation, existence and non-existence of the other—... Nor burning contact with fire, nor light sunrise,... For the connection of these things is based on a prior power of God to create them in a successive order (from the *Incoherence of the Philosophers,* Nasr & Leaman, 1996, p. 316).

In this paper I take a broadly similar tack, but in defence of agency in this world. I want to try to establish the viability of the concept of agent-causation in the natural sciences and other material contexts. I agree with the occasionalists that events are incapable of generating successor events. However, I believe that agents can be found in this world. This will involve the attempt to show that there are natural agents, that is causally efficacious material particulars, which exemplify the concept I wish to defend. Given the existence of such beings, their characteristics can be drawn upon to establish the general form of the concept of agent-causation in non-human contexts. My project then is to bring out the root-ideas in the concept of a causally efficacious material particular. Among these are 'tendency' (Cartwright, 1989), 'disposition' (Mumford, 1998) and 'power' (Reid, 1778). Having sketched the 'grammar' of the relevant cluster of concepts, the next step will be to try to establish priorities between event-causality and agent-causality. Does the possibility of applying the concept of 'event-causality' to a situation presuppose the applicability of the concept of 'agent-causality'? Could the concept of 'agent-causality' be properly used in a situation in which the concept of 'event-causality' would have no application? By exploring these questions the priority between the concepts could be established.

Agent-causality covers both enduring particulars like magnetic poles and enduring stuffs like caustic soda. Both belong to the general category of substances. To ensure that the agent-causality to be discussed in this paper is clearly distinguishable from event-causality, I prefer to use the phrase 'substance-causality' rather than 'agent-causality' to bring out the contrast in modes of causation.

Once the viability of the concept of 'substance-causality' has been established we will be in a position to provide provisional answers to some specific questions. The two to be tackled in this paper are:

a. What concept of causality shall we choose for the content of fundamental or rock-bottom explanations in the natural sciences, substance-causality or event-causality?

b. Could the same general 'shape' of substance-causality based explanations be dominant in both the physical sciences and the human sciences? If so what are the powerful particulars that define the ultimate level of explanation in human contexts?

Concepts of causality

A family of causal concepts

Among the repertoire of concepts already in use we can readily find examples of event-causality and substance-causality. There are ephemeral events cited as causes, for example 'The tap on the egg cracked it'. And there are enduring things cited as causes, for example 'The hot stove burned her finger'. The same diversity can be found in the natural sciences. The slippage of the tectonic plates which caused the earthquake is an ephemeral event, while the magnet which drew the nail out of the wood is an enduring thing. Why should one mode be preferred to the other?

The distinction between bringing about enduring states and bringing about ephemeral events is not tied neatly to the mode of causation. The burned finger is an enduring state, but so is the crack in the egg-shell. The extraction of the nail is an event, but so is the earthquake. There seem to be four patterns:

Active substance brings about ephemeral effect or enduring state.
Ephemeral event brings about ephemeral effect or enduring state.

Given that these patterns are in everyday use in ordinary life and in the laboratories where the sciences are practised, why have philosophers not been content to acknowledge that there is a family of causal concepts?

Rom Harré

In many cases actual explanatory formats seem to involve both event-causality and substance-causality. For instance in answering the question: 'What tripped the circuit breaker?' the answer 'Turning on the stove and the toaster at once' looks like the citation of an event as cause. But the event citation is plausible only if there is a current in the circuit. That looks like the citation of a substance as cause. Similarly in answering the question 'How did you get out?' with 'I gave the door a shove!' a strong enough person, an enduring substance, is presupposed in accepting the plausibility of an answer which cites an ephemeral event. Event-causality and substance-causality seem to go together. Explanations based exclusively on either seem to be incomplete. Is the intuition of what is to count as a complete explanation well grounded? If so, in what is it grounded?

One candidate might be the syllogism. The major premise describes an enduring and potent substance while the minor premise describes the ephemeral situation in which its powers are exercised.

All acids are corrosive
This piece of copper is in contact with an acid
This piece of copper is corroded.

Here we have a valid syllogism in A I I, 'datisi' in the 3rd figure.

This pattern of explanation is widely employed. It would follow from the above analysis that its force lies not so much in logical form, but in the content, namely the citation of a powerful particular in the major premise which is actively productive in the circumstances described in the minor premise.

Epistemological scruples

Generally discussions of causality since Hume's criticisms of the propriety of both the concept of 'efficacy' and the concept of 'substance' have confined the causal relation to concomitant pairs of events. Substances have been relegated to standing conditions. Why?

Hume's search for appropriate impressions in which the ideas of causal efficacy and of material substance could be grounded and from which they came, failed, so he said. However, when I try the test for meaningfulness I succeed. I feel the pressure of a heavy object in the earth's gravitational field, and my world is full of enduring things. How does it come about the Hume and I differ on so fundamental a matter?

It might seem that this difference in what we take to be intuitively obvious simply reflects a prior decision about the scope of the concept of causality, namely, for Hume, that it should comprehend only events. Events are ephemeral and so could not exercise causal potency.

Hume uses a general principle, that that which cannot be known directly, should not be admitted among the kinds of beings we think exist. Epistemology rules ontology. In the following passage he brings this weapon to bear upon admitting causal powers when the causal relation is between events.

> But when one species of event has always, in all instances, been conjoined with another, we make no longer any scruple of fore-telling one upon the appearance of the other, and of employing that reasoning, which alone can assure us of any matter of fact or existence. We then call the one object, Cause; the other, Effect. We suppose that there is some connection between them; some power in the one, by which it infallibly produces the other, and operates with the greatest certainty and strongest necessity. ... But there is nothing in a number of instances... except only, that after a repetition of similar instances, the mind is carried by habit, upon the appearance of one event to expect its usual attendant, and to believe that it will exist. This connection, therefore, which we feel in the mind, this customary transition of the imagination from one object to its usual attendant, is the sentiment or impression from which we form the idea of power or necessary connection (Hume, 1777: Sect VII, Part II, p. 59).

There is no need for him to develop a similar argument against active substances, since in the next quotation we find him giving the concept of 'substance' in general a similar treatment. If the idea of 'substance' is not supported by an impression then it must be expunged from our repertoire and so 'active substance' goes with it.

> The idea of a substance ... is nothing but a collection of simple ideas, that are united by the imagination, and have a particular name assigned to them, by which we are able to recall, either to ourselves or others, that collection ... the particular qualities that form a substance, are commonly referred to an unknown something, in which they are supposed to inhere (Hume, 1739: Part One, Section VI).

Simple ideas do endure, but their union into a subject of which they might be properties is, like the relation of causality, rooted only in something psychological. It was expectation that was the real source of the idea of causal efficacy in the one case, and imagination that was the real source of the idea of substances in the other. In short neither 'efficacious event' nor 'active substance' are allowable, since neither concept is legitimated by a suitable impression. The two pillars of the science of physics, substance and causal efficacy are demolished, according to Hume.

If one is unimpressed by Hume's positivistic criterion for the legitimacy of concepts, perhaps the best strategy for rehabilitating genuine causality is to characterize the concept of 'causally active substance' as it is used in some commonplace contexts. The next step will be to abstract some general features of the concepts in question from the examples discussed in the section above.

Causally active substances: characterization

From the point of view of substance-causality a causally active substance is one which has a certain kind of property, namely a causal power, native tendency or inherent capacity to act in certain ways in the appropriate circumstances. We will need to take account of two classes of properties, observable and transcendental. A powerful particular or extended substance must be able to be identified at any time, at least provisionally. It must, therefore, have some properties which it always displays some of which are characteristic of the type of entity which it is while others are idiosyncratic.

These points can be expressed in the well-established seventeenth century terminology of nominal and real essences. The set of observable properties which are used to pick out an individual as an instance of a type or a member of a class is the nominal essence. This could be conjunctive or disjunctive. The properties which contribute to the real essence of an individual as an instance of a type etc., may be imperceptible.

Observable Properties

Again, making use of a well known distinction, the observable properties of a potent individual entity or material stuff fall into two groups. The occurrent properties of an entity are there to be observed whenever an organism with the appropriate sensory systems attends to it. Such a property does not depend on circumstances since it is displayed in all circumstances. Dispositional properties are usually contrasted with occurrent, in that they are manifested only in certain circumstances, though they are ascribable at all times.

It is worth emphasizing that dispositional properties are amongst the observable properties of an entity. In the usual conditional form in which a dispositional property is ascribed, 'If X (certain conditions) then Y (a display)', both X and Y must be observable. Dispositional properties are distinguished by the grammatical form of the means by which they are ascribed, not by the epistemic status of their content. The difference between occurrent and dispositional properties is simply that between unconditional (continuous) and conditional (discontinuous) displays to a suitably endowed observer.

The conditions involved have to do with the display of the property rather than with its existence. What is it that is permanently possessed by a material individual, and which produces the display when the conditions are satisfied? This is the relevant causal power, potent but imperceptible, known to a human being only through its manifestation in dipositional displays.

Transcendental Properties

A causal power is a property continuously possessed by an active substance, that produces the dispositional phenomena observed to be characteristic of the being in question. Kant's term 'transcendental' seems an appropriate way to characterize such properties in general.

There are at least five major characteristics that distinguish causal powers from all other properties of material substances be they individual like electric charges or mass like magnetic fields.

1. A causal power is continuously possessed by a material particular, whether it is currently being exercised or not. A magnet's poles exist whether they are actually interacting with other poles or with fragments of magnetically sensitive elements and so on.

2. A causal power is continuously active, not in need of stimulation. It will produce the relevant phenomena unless its action is blocked. The force of gravity is continuously exercised on a material body, which accelerates towards the centre of the earth only when released into free fall.

3. A determinable causal power, like electric charge, comprises determinates which differ not only in magnitude but also in valency. There are positive and negative electric charges. Some Leyden jars can be more highly charged than others. Any given Leyden jar can be more highly charged on some occasions that on others.

4. The observable 'signature' of the existence of a causal power as a property of a material particular is spontaneity. A causal

sequence begins with the release of the potency of the active particular. An electron does not have to be activated to interact with a magnetic field.

5. The manifestation of a type of power as an observable disposition is context sensitive. For example the power of water as a solvent is manifested in the disposition to dissolve all the common salt in the dish, but hardly any of the chalk.

Causal powers were popular among physicists and philosophers in the eighteenth century. Kant (1778[1970]) built his philosophy of physics on the notion, while Greene (1727) developed a post Lockean metaphysics based on a generalization of the notion of a causal power. The most systematic treatment is to be found in the writings of Thomas Reid. Here is a précis of his account of the concept of a causal power.

Power is not an object of our external senses, nor even an object of consciousness. There are some things of which we have a direct, and others of which we have only a relative conception, power belongs to the latter class. ... power is a quality, and cannot exist without a subject to which it belongs. We cannot conclude the want of a power from its not being exerted; nor from the exertion of a less degree of power, can we conclude that there is no greater degree of power (Reid, 1788: Ch. 1).

It is important to bear in mind that Hume's critical attack on the two major concepts for referring to transcendental beings, causal powers and substances, was in the face of an almost universal enthusiasm for their use in the interpretation of physics. Agency had an equally important place in psychology and moral philosophy as is evident in Kant's concept of the noumenal self and Joseph Priestley's concept of the cognitive powers of matter (Priestley, 1777).

Hierarchical explanation formats

The above account of the concept of a causal power as a property of a material entity invites hierarchical explanations of natural phenomena. The observable phenomena are to be accounted for by the activity of the material particulars in question, that is by their causal powers. Leibniz, for instance, set up explanatory hierarchies in his physics, which terminated in a basic level of primitive active and primitive passive forces (Gale, 1970). This way of building physics invites not only a hierarchical form of explanation, but also a realist interpretation of its deeper levels. Causal powers are real properties of material particulars, as real as the perceptible properties.

Realist explanation formats

The link between event-causality and positivism follows directly from Hume's strictures on ascribing any reality to that which is supposed to link cause-events and effect-events in one of the regular sequences that give rise to the idea of causality, via the impress of repetitions. Yet the natural sciences have been very much engaged in investigating just such links. In general they are constituted by material systems which exist continuously through the temporal sequence of concomitant events of the appropriate types. The violin bow is scraped across the strings. The audience hears a sound. There is an ontological tie, namely the vibrations in the air, the mechanism of the ear and the processes in the auditory systems of the brain. The means by which the intervening mechanism is known are different from those by which the original event sequence is known. In short the account is hierarchical. Diagrammatically it might look something like this

Cause-event → Generative Mechanism → Effect-event.

The generative mechanism of molecules, ear drum, stapes etc. provides the ontological glue that counters Hume's presumption that events are wholly independent of one another, so that either can occur without the occurrence of the other.

Realist explanations are hierarchical, since the generative mechanisms at the first level can be redescribed as sequences of cause/effect *events*. However these, in their turn, must be ontologically glued by a new level generative mechanisms, and so on. In this paper I shall not pause to defend a realist reading of the hypotheses by which we are able to think about imperceptible entities, structures and processes. Taking that for granted allows me to proceed directly to reflections on the character of the hierarchy so created.

A foundational dilemma

Reflecting on the character of such hierarchies raises the fundamental question to be addressed in this paper: which concept of causality has priority, event-causality or substance-causality? If we give event-causality priority, that is construe every case of substantival-causality as reducible to a case of event-causality, then we can

Rom Harré

hardly avoid accepting, in principle, the indefinite openness of hierarchical explanations. Each time a scientist underpins a claim to have found a sequence of events that are related as cause and effect by developing a hypothesis about the enduring mechanism generating the sequence the functioning of the mechanism can be described wholly in terms of regular sequences of relatively micro-events.

If we give priority to substance-causality then we make available the possibility of a closure to the hierarchy. The lowest level generative mechanism could simply be a system of powerful particulars. This move seems to be typical of physics. Not so long ago the hierarchy of causes in physics and chemistry was closed by the hypothesis of three categories of subatomic particles, protons, electrons and neutrons, characterized by their causal powers. In this and similar ways giving priority to substance-causality opens the way for a rational closure to any hierarchy that emerges in the development of the physical sciences.

Put this way the issue between those who advocate causal powers as real properties and those who do not turns on the contrast between event-causality and substance-causality, the contrast with which this paper began. The next step will be to present arguments to support the claim that substance-causality is ontologically prior to event-causality, in that the existence of the former is a necessary condition for the possibility of the latter. Nevertheless, both *concepts* are required in everyday life and the natural sciences, since we know of causal powers only by having observed occurrent and dispositional displays. The latter will typically take the form of regular sequences of pairs of events of the same type.

An example of the disposition/causal power scheme from physics

Part of my case in support of substance-causality is its role in the physical sciences. A striking instance of the use of this scheme is the common 'charge/field' scheme found throughout physics. A charge is a property of an enduring entity. Associated with each charge and with each pair of magnetic poles there are fields. A field is an array of dispositions distributed in space and lawfully related to the charge or pole that is their origin. Field dispositions are complex in that they usually involve both magnitude effects and directional effects. So a test body, if released at a certain point in a field will have a tendency to accelerate at a certain rate in a certain direction. Charges are specified in terms of scalars, undirected magnitudes, and fields in terms of vectors, directed magnitudes.

100

Active Powers and Powerful Actors

Enriching the concept of a disposition: Bohr and affordances

Enough has been said, one hopes, to make the further exploration of the disposition/causal power scheme worth undertaking. The discussion has focused on the philosophy of physics and it is in that context that one finds examples of the enrichment of the scheme.

Though he did not use both Kantian terms, Nils Bohr did work with a distinction between phenomena and noumena. The former were able to be fully described with the concepts of classical physics, since they were observable states of macro-apparatus. The latter were not able to be described by such concepts and were susceptible only of a mathematical representation. It made no sense to try to find an interpretation of the mathematical formulae of quantum mechanics by any use of the concepts of classical mechanics. That would have tied noumena to phenomena conceptually. Phenomena were brought into being in pieces of apparatus which were actively attached to the world. Qualitatively similar states of the world interactively combined with different kinds of apparatus brought into being different and incompatible phenomena. By 'incompatible' here is meant phenomena which required different kinds of apparatus to be constructed at the same place at the same time. Particle-engendering apparatus cannot be combined with wave-detecting apparatus, in such a way as to co-produce particle phenomena and wave phenomena. To describe this situation clearly was beyond Bohr's capacity and he was much misunderstood. However, a refinement of the concept of a disposition has been developed in the psychology of perception, for just those cases in which the human means by which phenomena are brought into being cannot be eliminated from the account of what has happened. This is the concept of an 'affordance' (Gibson, 1979). It is used in this way: a sharp knife affords clean cut slices of apple. Such a type of slice only exists because of the existence of the human artefact, a sharp knife.

Phenomena that are brought into existence by the use of human artefacts, experimental apparatus in the case of physics, enable the physicist to display some of what *the world plus the apparatus* affords. The dispositions that are manifested in phenomena are affordances of the set-up. The causal powers of the world that underlie these affordances can be described only in mathematics, for instance in the Schrödinger equation. It is a serious mistake to try to create an imaginable, that is classically expressible, model for those aspects of the world that the equation describes.

Rom Harré

Following the format established in this paper, the demonstration of dispositions as conditionally linked phenomena, in this case affordances, requires the postulation of one or more powerful particulars, perceptible or imperceptible as substances, as sources of activity in the system being explored. There seem to be three sources of activity in a Bohrian experimental set-up. There is the world, the manifestation of some aspect of which is facilitated by the apparatus. There is the apparatus which in most cases is itself a source of activity, and there is the human experimenter managing the apparatus/world complex. Further developments of this analysis are beyond the scope of this paper. However, the direction in which they must go should be clear.

Some arguments to establish the priority of substance-causality over event-causality

If it could be shown that the necessary conditions for the differential application of the concept of event-causality to an event sequence include the presumption of substance-causality, but not vice versa then we have established the substance-causality has priority over event-causality. We can take an event sequence to be a causal sequence only if we have some confidence in the hypotheses which establish the character and ontological plausibility of properly sited generative mechanisms.

Events as releasers

Since they are ephemeral, events can have no generative power, and cannot be the 'glue' which holds the members of an event sequence together as a causal process. At best an event can stimulate a quiescent mechanism into action. There is another and more important way that an event can be causally efficacious. A powerful particular has a tendency to act unless it is constrained or blocked. An event which releases a blocked tendency, or removes a condition that was frustrating the action of such a tendency will appear as a cause of the events that come about through the exercise of the tendency. But if the same type of event occurred elsewhere, in a situation in which there was no pre-existing tendency or active force, then nothing will subsequently occur. That an event is a cause is dependent on the existence of the tendency. For example the removal of support under something poised in the earth's gravitational field will be followed by a fall. Interposing a sheet of paper between a charged body and that which it might act upon shields the action and prevents the exercising of the power of the charge by activating the disposition to act at the relevant place in the field.

Here we have a criterion for distinguishing between event-pairs which are related as cause and effect, from those which are merely concomitant by coincidence. Genuine cause-effect pairs will be related by a generative mechanism, which, in the case of fundamental causal processes will consist of one or more powerful particulars such as charges or poles.

Arguments from the 'passivity of events'

In a 'Cartesian' cosmology there are no genuinely active beings. An original quantity of motion, imparted by the Creator, is conserved by redistribution through the interactions of passive material corpuscles. God is the only originating powerful particular. Descartes' cosmology is dogmatically set out, for instance in *The World*. He makes use of his cosmological principle of God's immutability and his conserving power as follows:

> This rule ... [a law of mechanics] depends solely on God's preserving each thing by a continuous action, and consequently on his preserving it not as it may have been some time earlier but precisely as it is at the very instant that he preserves it (Descartes, 1633 [published, 1664]).

Berkeley (1719) arrived at the necessity of postulating a transcendental source of activity through his analysis of the nature of the world as we human beings perceive it. Having abolished the distinction between primary and secondary qualities he was able to abolish the broader distinction between qualities that inhered in matter and ideas, qualities as we perceive them. Perceptual qualities, he argues, are inert. Ideas could not cause ideas. There is no good ground for the hypothesis of an imperceptible material substance, taken in Lockean fashion to be constituted out of primary qualities, as the cause of the ideas we experience. Nevertheless ideas are caused, so that cause must be transcendental, a spirit, a being not to be found in the world as perceived.

Kant's philosophy of physics was thoroughly dynamic. In his *Metaphysical Foundations of Natural Science* (Kant, 1778 [1970]) he used the Leibnizian foundational principle of paired active and passive forces to give an account of material stuff in dispositional terms. The boundary of a material thing was the locus of all points at which the forces of attraction and repulsion were equal. The tendency of a test body to move towards the centre of a material thing was exactly balanced by the tendency to recede from it. The shapes and quantities of matter are phenomena, the transcendental conditions for their existence are active force fields.

In short sensory qualities are products, not producers. Something active must be bringing about our perceptions. *A fortiori* the active being or beings is not amongst those beings we can perceive. The prior member of a perceived pair of events, even when they satisfy a type to type condition, that is exemplify a pattern that has regularly been perceived, could not be the active cause. Once again these arguments should lead us to admit the necessity of the postulation of transcendental powerful particulars as the sources of observed patterns of events, if we are to allow for explanations at all.

An argument from continuity

A process is a sequence of events, each coming into being and passing away. The continuity of a process cannot be accounted for in an ontology which admits only events. Only substances are continuous in time, and so capable of grounding a naturally necessarily coherent causal process, rather than a contingent sequence. Russell's argument in *Logical Atomism* (Russell, 1924) that material things are logical constructions out of sense data, that is simply classes of sense data, begs the question. If that is what material things are they are infected by the same passivity as the sense data (Lockean ideas) of which they are constituted. The same objection could be raised to Mach's rather similar claim that words for substances are just compendious devices for referring to stable groups of sensory elements (Mach, 1883).

Either one abandons the project of explaining the patterns of phenomena we perceive, or one admits causally active but transcendental beings, described in the formal terms of mathematical physics, for example Maxwell's laws of electromagnetism.

Philosophical support can be given to the case for adopting the second horn of the dilemma by reflecting on the conditions for the identity of causally active substances. Contrary to the reductive analyses of the sense datum theorists and their predecessors we do routinely identify some material things and stuffs as causally active. The red wine *stains* the white table cloth. The chlorine solution *kills* the bugs. The magnet *attracts* the iron filings, and so on. The identity conditions for active beings include their power to produce the required event sequences, *ceteris paribus*. If it does not stain the cloth it is not red wine, however it may look. If it does not attract little bits of iron it is not a magnet. If it does not dissolve paint it is not a brush cleaner.

The Humean argument against including causal efficacy among the perceptibles, an argument which would undercut the use of simple household products as exemplars of active causality, conflates dispositions and powers. Dispositions, as I have argued above, are observables, since the whole content of the conditional form consists of perceptible conditions and perceptible manifestations. The powers that are cited to account for the existence of dispositional properties are not perceptible. So Hume's failure to perceive them is one with his failure to perceive his 'self' by introspection. That is just what you would expect of beings which are transcendental in the sense of this paper, that is imperceptible but necessary conditions for the intelligibility of phenomena.

Of course, no argument can stop Hume, Mach and Russell resting content with a world which in the end is unintelligible. The project of physics is to render the world intelligible, and to achieve that end active beings, on the model of those everyday materials mentioned above, must be postulated.

The argument for the priority of substance-causality to event-causality boils down to the claim that in order to identify an event sequence as a cause-effect sequence we must use the presence or absence of a powerful particular as a criterion. However, whether there is or is not such a particular there and working is not an empirical question. It has to do with the role of postulating such beings in creating a plausible foundation for an intelligible world.

The Kantian Argument for Transcendental Agency

Kant's conception of the person is built around two transcendental unities. There is the transcendental unity of apperception that binds all one person's items of experience into a single consciousness. There is the self as agent, the person as capable of acting from reason independently of material conditions and psychological promptings. The latter is relevant to the project of this paper. How did Kant support his claim for the existence of such a transcendental being?

I believe I can identify four steps in his account of the necessity to postulate a transcendental ego as a powerful particular.

1. Freedom: 'the power to begin a state on one's own ...[must be] a pure transcendental idea ... [because it] contains nothing borrowed from experience ... [it] cannot be given determinately in experience ... [because the very possibility of experience requires a cause for every happening] (Kant, 1787 [1996]: 535).

2. The basis of our practical idea of freedom is a certain intuition, namely 'the independence of our power of choice from coercion by impulses of sensibility'(Kant, 1787 [1996]: 533). We experience spontaneity.

3. What conditions must the subject as actor satisfy? Causality is intelligible 'according to its action as a thing in itself'. It has an 'intelligible character'. [In order to be outside the reign of causes and effects it] 'would not stand under any conditions of time' ... thus 'not subject to the law of time determination' [which requires the sequencing of events, and thus cause and effect] ... [As such it is] 'free from any influence of sensibility and determination by appearances' and in so far as 'the subject is noumenon nothing occurs in it ... this active being would to this extent be independent and free in its action from all natural necessity' (Kant, 1787 [1996]: 539/540).

4. A human being is 'on the one hand phenomenon, but on the other hand—viz in regard to certain powers—a merely intelligible subject, because his action cannot be classed at all with the receptivity of sensibility' (Kant, 1787 [1996]: 544).

In offering this an account of how freedom is possible in a world of causally related *events* Kant does not add any more categories of events to those already identified. For example there are additional spontaneous events, events with no antecedents just appearing from nowhere. Rather a person realises that at a certain moment in the chain of events he or she is able to give reasons for what happens. Reasons are logically related to their topics, and so the relation is timeless. Causes are materially related to events and so their relation is temporal The difference between the two accounts turns wholly on the central place of persons as powerful particulars in one account and their absence in favour of events in the dominant place in the other. The transcendental ego is free from time determination. Transcendental agency is 'outside' the pattern of event sequences. Like the powerful particulars of the physical science it is *as if* it were stable and continuous, since it is outside the flux of time determinations.

Kant may or may not have solved the age-old conundrum of how there can be free choice in a world in which the future is fixed in some way, either by Divine foreknowledge or by natural necessity or both. However, he has developed a version of the substance-causality scheme, in that the transcendental ego, though imperceptible, mimics the attributes of the kinds of material substances that play the part of powerful particulars in scientific accounts of the causality of regular patterns of perceptible phenomena.

The Kantian solution to this problem illustrates the *general shape* of substance-causality. However, the 'location' of the active agent in the transcendental realm is unsatisfactory. Is there any another possibility?

People as agents

What would a contemporary version of the Kantian way look like? What would play the role of the transcendental ego, stable and continuous, but nevertheless in time? To come anywhere near an answer a substance-causality account must be defended against event-causality.

Event-causality as the standard model for the domain of human action

A start can be made by setting out examples of each in which it is entirely clear that the sort of causality invoked is appropriate. Taking these as paradigm cases will enable a comparison between them and the sorts of examples which have seemed problematic since Avicenna struggled with the problem a millennium ago (Ibn Sīnā (Avicenna) (c. 1020 [1973]) *Metaphysica* trans. P. Morwedge, New York: Columbia University Press).

If we follow the lead of event-causality to explain human actions we are led to the following kinds of examples as paradigm cases:

Occurrences in the environment cause reactions in the human organism. For example a sudden noise and the startle response would be a model case. A generative mechanism is ready to hand to provide the link between cause and effect. It consists of material structures in the nervous system, the muscles and so on.

Occurrences in the nervous system, one part of the human organism, cause reactions in other parts. An epileptic fit occurs as the result of a discharge in the brain would be a model case. In this case there is also a non-causal event sequence, the pattern of the occurrence of an experienced aura followed by the seizure. There is no difficulty, in this case either, of providing a detailed account of the material mechanism that links discharge and fit.

In neither case is there a hint of the presence or role of an active agent. Does it make sense to offer a generalisation of these formats as the standard case? So long as event-causality is the only causal concept in play it seems that the act of choosing, with some difficulty and agony of mind, between a slice of Tin Roof Fudge Pie and The Healthy Alternative would be an event in an event

Rom Harré

sequence in the prior elements of which the cause event would be found. Events, as Kant knew very well, are in the material realm and 'glued' by the enduring stuff of some material mechanism.

It seems to me that much that has been written in recent years in defence of agent-causality, starting with Taylor (1966), and which has been elegantly summed up by Vollmer, (1999), is undercut by taking event-causality as the standard model, and trying to fit agent-causality into it. Not surprisingly this has proved to be difficult. An alternative is to hand in the natural sciences, which are shot through with examples of substance-causality. Taking that as the standard model changes the philosophical project. In such a setting the project becomes: what is the type of powerful particular that is characteristic of the human domain?

Substance-causality as the standard model for the domain of human action

My purpose in this paper is to develop a prolegomenon to a defence of 'person' as the relevant powerful particular that grounds all that happens in the world of human action, that world in which the criteria of identity for actions are based on meanings. If we follow the lead of substance-causality we are led to persons as powerful particulars, embodied agents enduring in time. Arguments for this choice of ontological category as that of the basic particulars for the human world have been given by Strawson (1959: Ch. 3) and others. His arguments do not include a defence of the category of person as causally fundamental. It has yet to be shown that persons are the basic category of powerful particulars. Strawson's account leaves open the question of the sources of human behaviour. Persons could be fundamental ontologically, and yet not agents. By defending the fundamental and prior role of substance-causality in the material context a 'space' has been made for it in the human case.

References
Berkeley, G. (1719) [1985] *Principles of Human Knowledge* (London: Fontana).
Cartwright, N. (1989) *Nature's Capacities and their Measurement* (Oxford: Oxford University Press).
Gale, G. (1970) 'The physical theory of Leibniz' *Studia Leibnitiana* 2 117.
Gibson, J. J. (1979) *The Ecological Approach to Visual Perception* (Boston, Mass.: Houghton Mifflin).
Greene, R (1727) *The Principles of the Philosophy of the Expansive and Contractive Forces* (Cambridge: Cambridge University Press).

Hume, D. (1739) [1965] *A Treatise of Human Nature* (Oxford: Clarendon Press).

Hume, D. (1777) [1963] *Enquiries concerning the Human Understanding and the Principles of Morals* (Oxford: Clarendon Press).

Ibn Sīnā (Avicenna) (c. 1020 [1973]) *Metaphysica* trans. P. Morwedge, (New York: Columbia University Press).

Kant, I. (1787 [1996]) *Critique of Pure Reason* trans. W. S. Pluhar, (Indianapolis: Hackett).

Kant, I. (1778 [1970] *The Metaphysical Foundations of Natural Science* trans, J. Ellington, (Indianapolis: Bobbs-Merrill).

Mach, E. (1883) [1914] *The Analysis of Sensations* (Chicago: Open Court).

Mumford, S. (1998) *Dispositions* (Oxford: Clarendon Press).

Nasr, S. H. & Leaman, O. (1996) *History of Islamic Philosophy Part II* vols. I and II (London: Routledge).

Reid, T. (1788) [1969] *Essays on the Intellectual Powers of Man [the Human Mind]* (Cambridge, Mass.: M.I.T. Press).

Russell, B. A. W. (1924) 'Logical atomism' *Collected Papers of Bertrand Russell* I, (London: George Allen & Unwin).

Strawson, P. F. (1959) *Individuals* (London: Methuen).

Taylor, R. (1966) *Action and Purpose* (Englewood Cliffs: Prentice-Hall).

Vollmer, F. (1999) *Agent Causality* (Dordrecht: Kluwer)

The Foundations of Morality

MARY WARNOCK

I might have entitled this lecture 'The origins of morality' or, 'Where does morality come from?'. These titles sound vaguely historical, and would therefore have been misleading; whereas I suppose 'The Foundations of Morality' sounds in some sense analytic, and therefore more familiarly, perhaps painfully, philosophical. But I do not think that these different titles would mark a substantial difference in what I aim to explore, albeit superficially, in what follows. What interests me is the question how, or on what, is the moral sense of any individual founded?

If one were to believe, like G. E. Moore, or Franz Brentano, that there exist intrinsically good things in the world, things which, to take Brentano's formulation, it is Right to Love, and that these good things include certain kinds of behaviour (as well as, for example, objects of natural beauty, or works of art); and if one further believed that one could know without possibility of error when the love one felt for something was Right, then my question would be quite easily answered. What would be required would be to present a person, perhaps a child, with examples of such intrinsically good things, and encourage him to love them. And this would not preclude him from discovering other intrinsically good things for himself, and loving and pursuing them as well. He would come to know what he ought to love and pursue, what, on the other hand, he ought to hate and avoid, and this knowledge would constitute his moral sense or conscience.

Such a belief in objective values is, however, far from philosophically respectable, indeed may seem barely intelligible, whether like Moore you hold that intrinsic goodness is not capable of being further analysed, only recognizable at sight, or whether it is the rightness of your love of something which is so recognizable, as Brentano suggests. In contrast, J. L. Mackie's book, *Ethics: Inventing Right and Wrong* (Penguin Books, 1977) starts with the words 'There are no objective values'. Mackie concedes that in ordinary discourse words denoting values are used as if they were objective descriptions, but this, he argues, is simply a mistake. Thus he refers to his own sceptical or subjectivist theory of morals as an Error Theory. I do not believe that the dichotomy 'Subjective/Objective' is helpful in this context. For, at least in Mackie's use, it suggests a sharp dis-

111

tinction between what is and what is not a 'hard fact', none but 'hard facts' being objective. He says (p16) 'The kinds of behaviour to which moral values and disvalues are ascribed are indeed parts of the furniture of the world and so are the natural, descriptive, differences between them; but not ... their differences in value. It is a hard fact that cruel actions differ from kind ones, and hence that we can learn ... to distinguish them in practice, and to use the words 'cruel' and 'kind' with fairly clear descriptive meanings; but is it an equally hard fact that actions which are cruel in such a descriptive sense are to be condemned?' And to this question, he suggests the answer 'no'. But it is surely a mistake to suppose that we can use words such as 'cruel' or 'kind' without already implying in their use some sort of moral approbation or disapprobation. We would not be motivated to draw a distinction between the two kinds of acts except in the context of our own or another's moral sensibility. A 'hard fact' in Mackie's use seems to mean a fact which could be thought to exist in a world where there were no people making judgements, as one might think of the waves breaking on the rocky shore, without anyone to observe them. Without entering on the thorny subject of what counts as a fact, hard or otherwise, it seems clear that the difference between cruel and kind acts cannot be thought of as analogous to the difference between calm and rough sea in a landscape without humans.

I shall argue that Mackie is right to think of morality as an invention, a system developed over the years, and still developing, rather than something given from the beginnings of the world; but that to believe this is different from believing that, insofar as its language suggests 'objectivity', it is a fiction. For this is what his theory amounts to: we make use of a language of morals and of other values which demands agreement, or which may be absolutely demonstrated to be correct (for that is what 'objectivity' entails) while all the time those of us who are philosophers or sceptics or other know-alls, recognize that demonstrability of correctness is not to be had, and agreement is impossible, or at best unlikely. The existence of fixed or absolute values, which everyone can be brought to recognize, is a myth, even if a useful myth for the propping up of society. Such a theory is akin to Thrasymachus's theory in Plato's *Republic*, that justice, or morality, is really no more than the interest of the stronger; or to Nietzsche's *Genealogy of Morals*, in which the people who understand are distinguished from the suckers.

Obviously, if morality is an invention, it is a human invention, and therefore could not exist in a world inhabited only by animals other than humans, or by no animals at all. And this manifest truth has consequences for the answering of my question, how is morality founded, for the individual? I shall return to this point in due course. There are also consequences with regard to the variability of morality, or ethics, over the human race as a whole, and within one group of the human race over time. It is one thing to say that only humans can develop ethical systems, quite another to suggest that all their systems must be the same. And they manifestly are not, in detail, the same. It is a fact of which everyone is aware, however anxious they may be to believe in absolute standards, that not only do different races and different groups have different moral standards, but moral standards change within a single group from generation to generation, sometimes quite dramatically. Any theory which presupposes strict uniformity and stability can soon be bedevilled by counterexamples. Nevertheless, in my view, the variability and instability of morals, used by Mackie and many others to support the non-objectivity of morality, is something which can easily be made too much of. Aristotle seems to me to have got it about right: he is pretty laid back about the certain and invariable truth of any pronouncement about ethics. The subject-matter of ethics, he says (*Nicomachean Ethics* I.3) admits of much variation and fluctuation of opinion, to the extent that some people think it is all a matter of convention, rather than of nature ... so we must be content with answers to our questions (about what is the good for man) that are for the most part true. It is the mark of an educated man, he goes on, to look only for the amount of precision, or proof, that the subject admits. It is equally foolish to accept probable reasoning from a mathematician and demand scientific proof from a rhetorician. Following Aristotle, then, we can be content to say things which are for the most part true about the development of morality, both among people in general and within individuals, as indeed about the human condition in general.

There is enormous pressure these days to acknowledge the differences that exist between moral beliefs. This is partly the result of an on the whole benign belief in tolerance. Never a day goes by but we are reminded that we are a multi-racial society, and it is assumed that different races have different moralities, as, by and large, they may be supposed to practise different religions. Thus school teachers, for example, are encouraged not to be, as they say, 'judgmental', and not to put forward any moral beliefs or precepts of their own. If they are permitted to express any moral opinion, they must preface it with that most maddening of phrases 'I happen to believe...'. And this rather incoherent unwillingness to express definite moral opinions is reinforced by the general relativism roughly referred to

Mary Warnock

as Postmodernism. This group of doctrines, originally a tool of aesthetic criticism, has trickled slowly, but pervasively, through the universities and teacher-training colleges and thus into the schools. It suggests that any point of view is as valid as any other, and that there is no limit to the different viewpoints from which things may be seen (but some viewpoints have been unduly neglected ... those of women, say, or black people). No one is entitled to impose a particular view on anyone else. In the reading of a text, any interpretation is worth considering; indeed there is no 'proper' interpretation, for there is no true fixed meaning to be found, referring to a common 'outside world'. The text refers to nothing but itself. In this riot of relativism it is not surprising that any thought of objectivity in morals should be completely ruled out.

However, with regard to morality, I believe such relativism is grossly exaggerated. I do not, of course, want to deny that there are substantial differences between the way in which different cultures think of, let us say, the proper relation that should hold between men and women, or the respect that should be paid to the aged or the justification of female circumcision. I could not possibly deny either that even within one culture there are diametrically opposed views about the ethics of abortion or bringing about the early death of the terminally ill, or switching off a life-support machine where a baby has no hope of independent survival. All these are issues which give rise to deeply felt disagreements Nevertheless it is possible to discover large areas within which moral values are shared, and there is an important sense in which they must be shared in a civil society. Moreover it seems to me that the greatest gap that exists between people is the gap between those who have some moral sensibility, who understand, that is, what morality feels like, and those who have none. To pursue this further will be to come close to the heart of my original question, How is morality founded?

But first there is a further point to be made about the different values implied by multi-culturalism in society. It is important here to distinguish moral values from the moral teachings of a particular religion. This is a distinction very often overlooked, but of the greatest importance. A hundred years ago most articulate people in this country, asked where morality comes from, would have given an answer which implied a strong connection between morality and religion. And if asked about the motives which made people wish to behave well rather than badly they would have been even more likely to reply in terms of obedience to the will of God, following the teachings of Christ or other such direct references to Christianity. The same would have been true no doubt of people of

114

other religious faiths. In the *Euthyphro*, Plato raised the question whether the gods commanded things because they were good, or whether things were good because the gods commanded them. On the whole I suggest that the Christians of a hundred years ago would have answered the *Euthyphro* question by saying that God, being good himself, commanded only those things that were good. Yet obedience to God's commands also had a value of its own, as is shown by the Jewish legend, incorporated into the Old Testament, of Abraham preparing to sacrifice Isaac, in obedience to an apparently unjustifiable command. But in any case the thought that God was owed obedience, because he was great and good, was a familiar one within the Christian churches, as is evidenced by innumerable hymns; and even if not many people believed whole-heartedly in hellfire, or in heavenly singing with the Angels, it was certainly held that obedience to God's laws brought reward of some kind, and even that bad behaviour would somehow be punished in the end.

When the growth of Darwinism, and the new understanding of history and of mythology swept the western world, and society became gradually secularised, it was natural that the status of morality should be brought into question, because of the close connections there had always been between religion and morality. Atheists had, after all, been thought not to be just cognitively mistaken, but positively wicked. And the fear that if God is dead all things are permitted became a real fear. Yet if, as I have suggested, most people had always believed that God's commands were not simply whimsical or arbitrary, but were based on what was in some prior sense good, (that is, that it made sense to say that God himself was good) then such fears were really baseless. It should have been possible to peel off religion from morality and leave intact a concept of right and wrong, good and evil. And I would argue that the further secularisation develops, in all areas of life and thought, the more necessary it is to effect this separation. For one of the difficulties in the way of founding a moral sensibility in a secular society is the confused thinking which supposes that if you speak of morality you must in some sense be speaking of religion; and, conversely, if you abandon religion, you must be abandoning the morality that had seemed so closely interwoven with it.

This is not to say that to be religious is no longer possible; nor to suggest that for an individual who holds a religious faith there is no connection between that faith and morality. The ideals and inspiration of morality may well, for any individual be directly derived from religious faith and experience. Nevertheless (and hereby I declare an interest) it seems to me important to enable ourselves to

Mary Warnock

root morality in a secular world; because the consequences of an erosion in morality are to my frightened eyes becoming ever more manifest. At this point I revert to something I said before. It is not so much differences between conflicting moralities that is alarming; it is the vast difference between the possession of some moral sensibility and none. There is all the difference in the world between two people who hold different views about abortion, both their opposing views couched in moral terms, concerned with say, the value of a woman's being allowed freely to choose a termination and, on the other side, the greater value that ought to be accorded to an embryonic human life, and different views of, let us say, mugging an old woman for her savings, where one of the disputants is morally outraged, the other indifferent altogether to morality. It is the latter dispute that urgently raises the question where moral sensibility can be dredged up from; and in order to answer it in a practical way, it must be separated from any connection with religious belief. Philosophers have, since the Age of Enlightenment been accustomed to such a separation when considering theories of morality. It is non-philosophers, and especially those such as priests and bishops who are professionally believers who must be shown how to effect the separation (and the former Bishop of Edinburgh, Richard Holloway has set an example, in his recently published book *Godless Morality*.)

As I have said already, if Franz Brentano or G. E. Moore were to be believed, and there exist things manifestly good in themselves, such that merely to contemplate them is to perceive their goodness, or their fitness to be loved, (and equally I suppose if there were things the contemplation of which made it obvious that they were unfit to be loved) then producing examples of such things, offering them for contemplation would set a person on the road to a life where morality, doing good and avoiding evil, would have a place. But the implausibility of such a solution is manifest. There is obviously an epistemological problem; How do we know when we have found such an object of intrinsic goodness? But even if we could be satisfied with a roughly Platonic answer to this problem, namely that if once you are acquainted with such goodness (the Form of the good) you could not doubt that this is what you were acquainted with: you would be overwhelmed with love and desire for it, there would remain the further problem of whether such acquaintance would affect your conduct. As Hume said 'Tis one thing to know virtue, another to conform the will to it'. And Aristotle had no doubt that the subject matter of ethics, as opposed to other more lofty subjects was the distinctively practical reason, concerned with getting people, or people getting themselves, to make good choices and act on them. The form of the good, or the idea of goodness in itself, he argued, was an empty and useless concept: what is needed to be a good bridle maker is an idea of what constitutes a good *bridle*. What is needed is not an abstract idea of goodness, but something that can be valued as good or as bad in the world.

Let us consider, then, what it is to value something, high or low, in the world. Something which is actually within our experience, day to day, and is not an ideal or an abstraction. The noun 'value' is a noun from which many people, including myself for many years, instinctively shy away. It sounds portentous. It is beloved of politicians who exhort us to embrace 'family values', or not so long ago, 'Victorian values'. Yet it stands for a concept which is central to the understanding of both humans and other animals. It stands for that which those animals pursue and avoid, whether instinctively, because they are genetically programmed to do so, or because they have learned. That to which we ascribe value, high or low, comprises everything that we believe to be good or bad, nice or nasty, pleasurable or painful, great or mean, and so forth. If there were no assurance of the permanence of such values (not only of the continuing ability of humans to make value-judgments, but of at least some continuity in the actual values they ascribe to things), then we should have no assurance of understanding the meaning or significance that people ascribe to things in the present, let alone the significance to be perceived in the past or projected into the future. That we claim, at least sometimes, to be capable of such understanding rests on a conviction that, more or less, humans remain the same, intelligible to one another through their common likes and dislikes, and bound together by possible sympathy throughout time. We are aware of continuity through time, not merely in our own lives (making us feel that there is a connection in memory between us in the past and us now) but in the life of humanity as a whole. We could not have such a concept of general, human continuity without imagination; and it would almost certainly be true to say that human beings, alone among animals are possessed of imagination in this sense: the ability to think of past present and future, and to think of their species as a whole, spreading both temporally and geographically beyond what can be immediately perceived. And with imagination, which allows us to think of others as members of the same species, goes that particular form of the imagination, sympathy, upon which Hume, rightly as it seems to me, based our moral sensibility.

To illustrate this human, (probably uniquely human, at the pre-

Mary Warnock

sent state of evolution), capacity for imagination and sympathy, let us consider our ability to understand stories, historical or fictitious. The story is perhaps the most important vehicle through which values, the nice and the nasty, the terrifying or the cosy, are conveyed. C. S. Lewis in his essay *'On Stories'* (*Of this and Other Worlds*, ed. W. Hooper, Collins 1982, pp. 25–45) argued that, for example, the story of Jack the Giant-Killer conveyed a central value, namely a particular kind of fear, the fear of the monstrous, which cannot be conveyed otherwise than in concrete terms, and which is immediately intelligible. He himself conveyed exactly this kind of fear in one of his children's books, *The Silver Chair*, where the huge rocks beside the path along which the children walk are sleeping giants. The narrative has a point, a significance, which cannot be conveyed otherwise than through the idea of giants. It is not that we, grown-up sophisticated people, actually fear giants in our real lives. It is that we know this kind of fear which may come upon us imaginatively, perhaps among huge, uncouth lumpy mountain, or in forests of huge trees. Here we have an example of values (albeit non-moral values) in the real world. We ascribe significance to our experience by imagination, always seeing in things more than the naked eye alone could perceive.

To say that a story may speak of these or any other kind of intelligible values must not, of course, be taken to imply that there exist fixed entities, separate from the ordinary world, everlasting and unchanging, with names attached to them, which are value-names. This was the demand of Plato and of Moore and Brentano. Of course there must be some connection between our various uses of a value word, 'terrifying' for example or 'honest', so that we can recognize instances of the concept and understand the situations in which the word is intelligibly used. But this does not entail the prior possession of a fixed and immutable value. It is rather that individual occasions and instances exemplify for us an instance of the value. We evaluate the instance, in the context of the historical use of the word. It is the function of imagination to see this general concept in the particular instance. And this entails further that to use and understand a value word, such as 'terrifying' or 'honest' is to make use of a shared concept. To write or tell a story, whether Jack the Giant-Killer or Anna Karenina is to show that you assume an understanding of its 'point', the significance it contains; or at least that you believe that in telling the story you will cause your readers to understand the point through sympathy with the characters, though the point may never have been presented to them thus before. Wittgenstein's argument against the coherence of the concept of a private language, containing descriptive words understood, and intended to be understood by one person alone, a concept he held to be contradictory, could be used with as great or greater force in the context of a language of values. The background of a language which ascribes values to things is a shared humanity, a shared 'form of life'. This does not entail total conservatism with regard to values. But it does entail continuity. In the moral revolution of the 1960s, with the new acquisition of the contraceptive pill, surely one of the most dramatic revolutions of our time, the old values of care for the female by the male were not thrown away; they were changed, as the facts of contraception changed. (And of course there were many people who had no idea of such values anyway, and continued as exploitative as before.)

It follows that it is part of the form of life we lead, where what is regarded as nice or nasty, good or bad is to a large extent shared, that it is important to hand on to the next generation the value judgments, value assumptions of the past. Granted that what we like and dislike may change, and the reasons we give for liking or disliking things may change, still we are the same species as we were, and what is pleasurable or painful, agreeable or disagreeable remains to a certain extent constant. It may be, for example, that one of the great pleasures of life, one of the things which bound civilized society together, used to be the writing of letters. Even in my childhood and adolescence the exchange of letters between friends was a factor of enormous importance, causing pleasure, and sometimes pain that was serious, and of significance for life as a whole. This is no longer so; nevertheless human communication, by whatever means, remains a value that is central, and so we can still understand stories that turn on letters delayed or never written or which convey the transition from hope to despair or the reverse.

It is essentially by the fact that, over time and over distance human animals can exercise their imagination and share their likes and dislikes, sorrows, pleasures with other humans, sympathising, and taking in the fact that there exist people other than themselves or those they can see and hear, that moral sensibility is made possible. The huge merit of Hume's theory of morality is that he sees not only that it is founded on sympathy and our ability to be moved by the pleasures and pains of other people, but that dependent as our moral sense is on our own sentiments of pleasure and pain in the contemplation of actions, it is not just any sentiment of pleasure or pain which 'denominates an action virtuous or vicious'. 'Nor is every sentiment of pleasure or pain which arises from characters or actions of that peculiar kind which makes us praise or condemn.

119

Mary Warnock

The good qualities of an enemy are hurtful to us; but may still command our esteem and respect. 'Tis only when a character is considered in general, without reference to our particular interest that it causes such a feeling or sentiment as denominates it morally good or evil.'

Hume is here accurate about the nature of moral judgments at the expense of his general epistemology. For he is, in general, committed to the view that we have no access, in perceiving or judging, to anything except our own feelings, coming one by one like images on a screen, and made up by us, through imagination, into objects independent of us in the outside world. But here, in talking about morals, he supposes that we are able to consider the world apart from our immediate, unfocused feelings, and distinguish those that are based on a general judgment of the world and those that are not. But this internal inconsistency is not my concern here.

The crucial words in the passage I have quoted are 'without reference to our particular interest'. What I may want for myself is irrelevant to my judgement, if that judgment is to be properly described as moral. John Stuart Mill, though he recognized that children were naturally selfish, even if affectionate, and had to be taught to adopt a moral point of view, never really explained how this could be done. He attempted to show that if each person wants his own happiness this somehow entails that all would want the happiness of all. Nothing could be further from the truth, even if we accept the theory that maximizing happiness is the end of morality. The fact is that if people are to be taught to develop a specifically moral sensibility, they must necessarily, as Hume says, consider their own or other people's actions without reference to their own particular interest. To say this is to suggest that self-denial or self-sacrifice, of which Mill did not approve, lies at the heart of personal morality.

It is necessary here briefly, and as a digression, to distinguish between our personal or private morality and public morality, or, as I should prefer to call it, morally based public policy. Plainly if I am a member of a Government Committee set up to advise ministers about how to deal, let us say, with juvenile offenders, I am concerned with public policy, and am interested that this policy should not be in breach of generally accepted moral values. And the fact, for it is a fact, that there are common, shared values is all-important in this context. Because it is possible to identify ways of treating children that virtually everyone would agree were cruel, we on the Committee need have no difficulty in condemning some of the secure centres where children are currently locked up. They are not only inefficient, but inhuman and pay no attention to the needs, both educational and recreational of children, however they have offended. And a disregard of other people's needs is a shared disvalue. But in condemning this kind of institution, or suggesting some positive alternatives, though the Committee is concerned with recommending something morally acceptable, there is no question of personal sacrifice, altruism, or putting aside one's own interests. These requirements are requirements of private morality. And private morality is where the concept of the moral must first take root. Moral sensibility, the wish to do what is right, or avoid what is wrong must stem first from the individual in his dealing with other individuals. Only so can there be any certainty that in matters of public policy an awareness of what is or is not morally tolerable will be maintained. But this is by the way.

To return to the individual: if, as I have suggested, values are those things which human beings like, or dislike, love or hate, then it is essential to recognize, if there are to be moral values, that human beings are very like one another, will like and dislike, broadly the same sorts of things, and, being possessed of imagination can share, understand and take seriously the likes and dislikes of people other than themselves. But it is also necessary to face the fact that human beings, though possessed of these unique gifts of imagination and sympathy are naturally prone to selfishness and greed, to seeking goods and power for themselves at the expense of others. The development of a moral sense in an individual, or the invention of a moral system for a society is the founding of systems, institutions and sentiments which will mitigate human selfishness, by which every individual in the world is likely to be tempted. It is not just greed which is a human temptation; everyone is capable of being a bully, of exercising power to make other people suffer.

And so children from the youngest age should be taught both that, being human, they are subject to temptations to treat other people badly, and that they are capable, being human, of overcoming these temptations, and behaving well or at least better than they would have if they followed all their selfish instincts. Such teaching requires that those who teach, parents or school-teachers, should be prepared to assert the common values which we have seen to exist, to be perceived in events and actions in the everyday world. And in these cases there is no need to be pussy-footing about cultural relativism. We are not concerned with different cultures, still less with different systems of religion. The values to be invoked are general human values. No one in the world likes to be bullied; no one in the world likes to have his property stolen; no one in the world likes to

121

Mary Warnock

be deceived, or treated unjustly or exploited. It is essential, if individuals are to develop moral sensibility that these values should be shown to be universal and serious, and should be the matter for imagination and sympathy whenever they are seen. When such non-self-regarding sympathy has been established as a form of consciousness, then there is time enough to debate about public issues such as abortion, arranged marriages, the conservation of rain-forests.

The only way, it seems to me that such general human values can be taught is that they should be referred to in specifically moral terms, without fear of causing offence. The names of the virtues and vices should be freely used, greedy, generous, kind, cruel, deceitful, brave. Such words are both descriptive and already contain within them the Aristotelian concept of what it is to be a good specimen of a human being. The notion of the good life, or the good for man, is encapsulated in them, as is the central idea of morality, that it exists as a way of regulating our behaviour one towards another. Humans alone among animals can recognize that they are, in some sense all in the same boat, and, besides that, that their likenesses are far greater than their differences. It is this fact that makes it possible to found their morality on shared values, without pretending that there are absolute values to be perceived by some supernatural sense or divine revelation. In his essay 'A Sensible Subjectivism?' (in *Needs, Values, Truths* (Third Edition), Oxford 1998, p. 210) David Wiggins concludes thus:

> In 1960, Bertrand Russell wrote 'I cannot see how to refute arguments for the subjectivity of moral values, but I find myself incapable of believing that all that is wrong with wanton cruelty is that I don't like it' … [But] we can drop the first person. What is wrong with cruelty is not even for Bertrand Russell that Bertrand Russell does not like it, but that it is not such as to call forth liking given our *actual* collectively scrutinized responses. Those responses are directed at cruelty and at what cruelty itself consists in on the level of motive, intention and outcome…. To be sure … these things would not impinge as they do upon us if our responses were not there to be called upon. In the presence of a good reason to call them in question we should not be able to trust them or to take too much for granted about the well-foundedness of the properties they are keyed to. But in the total absence of such a reason, it will not be at all question-begging for Russell simply to remind himself as thoroughly and vividly as he can of just what it is that he dislikes, abhors, detests … about cruelty and its ancient and hideous marks.

This seems to me to express admirably the fact that there are shared values, and that the foundation of morality, for any individual must be to understand and grasp these values, as affecting both himself and those with whom he is sharing the human boat, within which everyone has a duty to everyone else.

This notion of the human boat, the human predicament, is the very same as the idea that it is possible coherently to talk about 'the common good'. Alasdair MacIntyre (*Dependent Rational Animals* 1999, p. 119) says this 'If we need to act for the sake of such common good in order to achieve our flourishing as rational animals, then we also need to have transformed our ... desires in a way that enables us to recognize the inadequacy of any simple classification of desires as either egoistic or altruistic'. And this seems to me to be true.

But even this cannot be the last word. Once again I must revert to Hume:

> 'Tis one thing to know virtue and another to conform the will to it.

For those who have no moral sensibility, who are not interested in morality, it is necessary, if they are to acquire it that they should come to want to be good rather than bad, and should be interested in being so, however far they are from always succeeding. And this is the most difficult lesson to teach. At the end of his book *The Object of Morality* G. J. Warnock wrote this:

> ... It is possible for a person to want to be moral; and a person is moral, by and large, exactly in proportion as he really wants to be so. We may thus say that, just as the need for morality, its having a point derives from very general facts about human beings and their predicaments, so also it is a fact about human beings that they are capable of morality; the disease and its remedy, so to speak, have a common source. But the essence of the remedy is not reason. It is non-indifference.

Whether these are comforting words or not I do not know. But it seems to me that they are true. Non-indifference is the foundation of morality.

Cutting Philosophy of Language Down to Size

RUTH GARRETT MILLIKAN

When asked to contribute to this lecture series, my first thought was to talk about philosophy of biology, a new and increasingly influential field in philosophy, surely destined to have great impact in the coming years. But when a preliminary schedule for the series was circulated, I noticed that no one was speaking on language. Given the hegemony of philosophy of language at mid-century, after 'the linguistic turn', this seemed to require comment. How did philosophy of language achieve such status at mid-century, and why is it losing it now? Has the Anglo-American tradition really begun to put the philosophy of language in better perspective? I hope so. Indeed, I will end with suggestions for how to keep it more securely in its proper place.

William Alston is one of the most respected and well-balanced philosophers of language from the period of its heyday, and we are blessed with a characteristically lucid article of his on philosophy of language written for the 1967 edition of *The Encyclopedia of Philosophy* in which he explains why this subject is so central (volume 4, pp. 386–90). 'Whenever philosophers turn their attention to any subject matter ... one thing they try to do is to clarify the concept of that subject matter'. Accordingly, he says, a view that many philosophers came to hold was that the primary job of the philosopher is 'conceptual analysis'. Alston then claims that a 'shift in the centre of gravity of philosophy' took place with a shift in understanding of what 'conceptual analysis' is. Rather than being understood as an attempt directly to analyse the nature of its subject matters, for example, of *causality* or *knowledge*, or as an attempt directly to explore these concepts as psychological phenomena, the conceptual analyst was now understood as 'trying to make explicit what it is one is saying when he says ...', this or that pertaining to *causality* or *knowledge*. Although Alston doesn't remark on it, that, of course, was how this tradition of philosophy managed to continue to understand itself as an *a priori* discipline after the demise of rationalism. Otherwise, it was thought unclear why philosophers wouldn't need to turn to data or to experimental work in order to carry out their tasks.

125

Ruth Garrett Millikan

Alston proceeds

> In so far as conceptual analysis takes the centre of the stage the pursuit of the philosophy of language receives a powerful impetus ... the analytic philosopher will spend a great deal of his time in trying to decide what a given expression means, whether two expressions mean the same thing, how a given expression is used, and so on.

Thus

> ... the need arises to develop an explicit theory about what it is for a linguistic expression to have a certain meaning, what it is for two expressions to have the same meaning, and what it is for a sentence to be used in order to do so-and-so ... it follows that in so far as philosophy consists of conceptual analysis it always deals with language in one way or another. This might be taken to imply that philosophy of language is the whole of philosophy and one might choose to use the term 'philosophy of language' in such a way that this would follow.

Alston does not recommend this usage. But it is clear that the conclusion could easily be drawn that philosophy of language has something like the status of first philosophy, since in an important way all other philosophy depends on it. Moreover it seems to follow, paradoxically, that by underpinning all of philosophy it also underpins itself. For what is the methodology of the philosophy of language itself to be? Presumably it too will proceed by 'trying to make explicit what it is one is saying when he says...', say, that a word has a certain referent or is synonymous with another word.

To appropriate the methodology of conceptual analysis as basic is, I believe, implicitly to make certain very strong assumptions about the nature of language, which assumptions cannot, in principle, be questioned by use of the method. Then it is by begging the question that the philosophy of language promotes itself to become the foundation for the entire philosophical enterprise. These two strong assumptions concern referential or extensional meaning. (I will just say 'referential', terminologically counting properties and relations as 'referents'.) They are assumptions that externalist theories of thought content and direct reference accounts of word meaning have been trying to challenge for some years. But neither of these latter two programmes can be carried through, I believe, without a fundamental shift in methodology, a shift that amounts in the end to abandonment of the position that philosophy is always, at root, an *a priori* discipline.

The first assumption I call the 'seed assumption'. Unlike the act of *knowing* an empirical fact, which act can be successfully completed only through co-operation of the external world, the act of *referentially meaning* something, though perhaps not of actually referring to something (recall Frege's empty descriptions) is completed within the mind itself. The intentional nature of the act of referring has its source or is given its shape by the mind. The mind, or its contents, alone determines the *criteria* in accordance with which a reference succeeds or fails to be made. The seeds of reference, if not the flower, are always entirely within the mind.

The second assumption I call the 'one-to-one assumption'. A univocal term in a public language is associated with one psychological state common to all competent users. For referential terms, typically the idea has been that the same seed of reference or criterion for successful reference must be grasped by all of its competent users. The paradigm here is the Fregean view that an unambiguous word or sentence corresponds to a single *Sinn* that is grasped by all who understand it.

The one-to-one assumption explains why conceptual analysis can be applied to referential terms in a public language. If there is something common to the psychological states of all who grasp the meaning of a public term, then there will be some single correct description that captures this common element, and any competent user should be able to recognize that description. The one-to-one assumption taken with the seed assumption leads to the view that the various types of referring or denoting expressions—proper names, common names, names of properties and relations, definite descriptions, indexicals—are mirrored in distinct types of mental structures. Then there is a one-to-one relation not only between referential linguistic meanings and inner seeds of meaning, but also between types of referring expressions and types of meaning seeds. These two assumptions are independent. The one-to-one assumption can be held without the seed assumption, for example, by taking linguistic meanings to be stereotypes that don't determine extensions. And the seed assumption can be held without the one-to-one assumption. There might be such things as inner seeds of referential meaning and yet public communication might characteristically rest only on shared reference. This last position has tempted some, for example, in the case of proper names.

The program of conceptual analysis is most agreeable when coupled with some form of linguistic idealism. If our language determines our concepts and categories and these in turn determine the forms we use to mould and measure our world, then to explore the

Ruth Garrett Millikan

structure of our concepts and categories will be to explore the structure of our world. To project the same conceptual schemes as one another will be to live in the same world. Thus, for example, the idea that we are the authors of the criteria of identity used to individuate various kinds of objects—that terms such as 'apple' and 'rabbit' 'possess built-in modes, however arbitrary, of dividing their reference'[1]—clearly entails that the referents of our words and thoughts are determined to fit structures that we project. An examination of our peculiar cognitive ways will reveal the structures that our referents are necessarily determined to have. Assume that these structures are acquired by internalizing the rules of a public language and the result is an extreme form of linguistic idealism. Our language constitutes our world. But then it must also constitute *itself* within that world since, of course, it is part of the world. Philosophy of language is called on to support itself as well as the rest of philosophy.

Less radically, concepts may be understood to be nodes in a net of response and inference dispositions, their references determined by their positions in the net plus, perhaps, their dispositional causal relations to objects and properties in the world—their 'causal roles'. (The classical notion that concepts correspond to sets of necessary and sufficient conditions for application and also the view that concepts are organized around prototypical instances are, of course, merely simple variations of this theme.) Then to analyze the position of the concept in the net will be to trace out central requirements on the nature of its referent. Assume, again, that these inference dispositions are acquired by internalizing the rules of a public language, and it again follows that the meanings of referential terms can be traced by conceptual analyses. The principle is the same, of course, if the rules or habits of language are conceived as governing rich 'forms of life' and not merely perceptual judgments and inferences. Quine, Wittgenstein, Sellars, and so forth, all look very much alike when considered in these general terms, as do nearly all contemporary psychologists studying concepts. All make both the seed assumption and the one-to-one assumption.

Two important challenges to these assumptions are familiar to us all. First is the effort to evict 'meaning' from the 'head' along with the defence of 'direct reference'[2] views, begun a quarter century ago

[1] W. V. Quine, *Word and Object* (Cambridge MA: MIT Press, 1960), p. 91.
[2] W. V. Quine, "Two Dogmas of Empiricism", *From a Logical Point of View* (Cambridge MA: Harvard University Press, 1953) pp. 20–46.

by Putnam and Kripke.[3] The denial that 'meaning is in the head' looks as though it should threaten the assumption that the seed of referential meaning is wholly in the mind. Second is the attack on the analytic-synthetic distinction and on the notion of linguistic meaning spearheaded half a century ago by Quine. These latter moves look as though they should threaten the assumption of a one-to-one relation between public linguistic meanings and psychological states. It looks as though no inseparable inference connections will be learned as one learns one's language. Between them these two challenges have considerably diminished the influence of runaway conceptual analysis, but neither has succeeded in extracting its roots. I would like to understand the reasons for this failure.

Because the one-to-one assumption is so commonly made, the literature is often unclear about whether it is linguistic meanings that are being examined or merely referential thoughts. I will try to keep these issues entirely separate, discussing, first, only the seed assumption. Later I will discuss the one-to-one assumption.

Putnam[4] is credited with launching the 'externalist' position that 'meaning is not in the head'. What Putnam claimed, more exactly, was that knowing the meaning of a natural kind term was not merely a matter of being in a certain psychological state. Putnam's claim, as it bears on the seed assumption, was, for example, that if the psychological state associated, for any one of us, with the term 'water' were to be realized in a person living on twinearth, this psychological state would constitute a thought not of water but of twinwater. Putnam contrasted his position with the classical one that the extensions of thoughts of natural kinds are determined via prior thoughts of their defining properties. Instead, thoughts of natural kinds are, he said, 'indexical'. Facts about the environment of the thinker help to determine the thought's extension. Putnam's position has been considered a kind of 'externalism' concerning content for natural kind terms, 'externalism' being touted as new and quite radical. Putnam himself compared his position to Kripke's position, also taken to be new and radical. He said that natural kind terms, like Kripke's proper names, were rigid designators, not standing in each possible world for whatever extension certain properties have in that

[3] H. Putnam, 'Realism and Reason', *Meaning and the Moral Sciences* (London: Routledge and Kegan Paul, 1978); S. Kripke, *Naming and Necessity* (Cambridge MA: Harvard University Press, 1972).

[4] H. Putnam, 'The Meaning of Meaning', *Minnesota Studies in the Philosophy of Science* **VII**, Keith Gunderson (Ed) (Minneapolis: University of Minnesota Press, 1975). Also in Putnam, *Mind, Language and Reality* (ibid.).

world, but always standing for the same kind, determined by its disposition relative to the thinker in *this* world. But I'd like to compare Putnam's move with one made much earlier in the century by Bertrand Russell concerning thoughts of individuals.

F. H. Bradley had worried that to make a judgment about a particular individual, one would have to grasp its entire complex individual nature, so as to distinguish it in thought from all other possible individuals. But Russell said no. All you need is to distinguish the individual from other *actual* individuals with a true definite description. However, such a description would usually have to begin with a reference to the individuals' relation to some prior individual or individuals, for example, to Socrates or to Greece or to this earth, the threatened regress ending with a final reference to oneself. For example, I might end by making references to the causes of various of my current sense data—*this* one, *that* one—thus locating the object of my thought in relation to me in the historical (the causal/spatio-temporal) order. Or I might think of James as whoever bears the relation 'same person' to whatever causes the characteristic such and such (Jamesish) looking and such and such (Jamesish) sounding sense data around here.[5]

The important point is that, on this sort of analysis, you have to be in the same world as the individual you are judging about, existentially[6] related to it in the right way. The possibility of having thoughts of individuals rests on the actual historical relations they bear to you, or, putting this broadly, on the actual-world context of your thinking. To my knowledge, no one after Russell has questioned this view. What individual my thought is about is determined by existential relations external to my mind. Another person in exactly the same psychological state might well be thinking of a different individual.

[5] Of course Russell took definite descriptions to express disguised judgments, so that this way of judging about an individual did not involve a thought whose referent was that individual. The judgement really concerned the contents of the world entire—that given the world entire, certain propositional functions were or were not always true. The disagreement between Frege and Russell whether judging about individuals is done with an existence claim or with a truly referential thought but that might not have a referent is trivial in this context. When we consider thoughts rather than the functions of language forms, what is the difference between a presupposition of existence and a belief in existence? The difference seems merely a matter of what one is psychologically prepared at the moment to bring into question.

[6] By 'existential' I mean within the historical order. 'Existential relations' are spatial, temporal, or causal relations.

Cutting Philosophy of Language Down to Size

Does it follow that meaning has not been thought to be 'in the head' in the case of thoughts of *individuals* for nearly a century?

Surely it was not meaning, but merely extension, that Russell discharged from the head in this way. Whether we separate the meaning from the denotation (Russell's way) or the *Sinn* from the *Bedeutung* (Frege's way) or the intension from the extension (Carnap's way) or the meaning from the reference (Quine's way) makes little difference. The division has always been between what was fully determined within or before the mind, and what was partly determined by (in a broad sense) the external context of the mind. Meaning has been whatever is left in the head after you carve off those parts of the completed act of referring that lie outside. And it has always been meaning alone that determines what properties or relations confirm a certain extension as the one referred to. What's inside determines how things must be outside for the reference to be successful. No matter how much external world involvement there is in reference, the seeds of referential meaning remain in the mind. That is the classical position.

So now Putnam tells us that there are mind-independent natural kinds out in the world waiting to be named by us just as there are individuals. And just as with individuals, you don't have to think of them by knowing their essences. You need not distinguish them in thought from all other logically possible kinds, but only from the other actual kinds in this world. Just as with individuals, you can point to them in thought with descriptions containing indexicals, your thoughts completed through existential relations to them. Water is whatever bears the relation 'same liquid' to the stuff in the lakes and streams *around here*, or whatever bears the relation 'same liquid' to the stuff causing and such (the waterish) surface properties *around here*. Nothing is new from the standpoint of the philosophy of language and mind. Meaning remains as much in the head as it was. Only the realist ontology is new, the (re)introduction of kinds that are not merely nominal. And even here, Putnam did not argue that the criterion of sameness for 'same liquid' is nature-given rather than nominal. The conceptual analysts' move then is perfectly obvious. Treat Putnam's analysis as introducing definite descriptions in place of definitions or graspings of essences. Nor has there been a shortage of variations on this theme.[7] Certainly Putnam was

[7] The very clear essay on this theme is R. Fumerton, "Russelling Causal Theories", *Rereading Russell: Essays in Bertrand Russell's Metaphysics and Epistemology, Minnesota Studies in the Philosophy of Science* **12**, C. W. Savage and C. A. Anderson (eds), (Minneapolis: University of Minnesota Press, 1989), pp. 108–18.

never clear on why this obvious move would not be possible, on why meaning needed to be pushed out of the head.

Similarly, Putnam's theory of the 'Division of Linguistic Labor',[8] reduces to the claim that some people think of some kinds by way of descriptions such as 'the substance the chemists have in mind when they say "molybdenum"'. What is threatened here is not the assumption that meanings are in the head, but rather the one-to-one assumption, the assumption that everyone who understands the linguistic meaning of a public referential term must think of its referent in the same way. Burge's claim[9] that what a person means may depend on the habits of the surrounding language community can be trivialized in a similar manner. Kripke's suggestion on the reference of proper names becomes just (here I am caricaturing) that people not present at Aristotle's baptismal ceremony describe him to themselves as 'the person at the beginning of a chain of "Aristotle" tokens, certain more recent members of which chain are *this* token and *that* token'.

To clinch this deflationary account, we call attention to the method by which philosophers have arrived at their so called externalist theories of thought content. They have used the method of conceptual analysis. They have brought forward examples and counter examples to be judged for their conformity with our intuitive notions of what the referent of a person's thought would be, given this or that circumstance.

Some externalists have tried trading in descriptions for indexical 'characters', in Kaplan's sense. Rather than containing a description of the relation its referent must bear to the thinker, the referential thought is purely indexical. It inarticulately points to that which bears a certain existential relation to it. Compare a token of the word 'I'. It refers to whoever has produced it, but it does not describe this relation. It does not mean 'the person who produced this token'. But indexicals are semantic elements too. They have meaning only by a prior assignment of character. What then gives a mental indexical its character? What determines which particular existential relation its referent must bear to it? The obvious answer is given by Ned Block.[10] The rules determining the values of mental indexicals must be implicit in the cognitive dispositions of the thinker, in what the thinker would ultimately be disposed to identify

[8] Putnam, 'The Meaning of "Meaning"'.

[9] T. Burge, 'Individualism and the Mental', *Studies in Metaphysics, Midwest Studies in Philosophy, IV*, **4** (1979), 73–121.

[10] N. Block, 'Advertisement for a Semantics for Psychology', *Midwest Studies in Philosophy*, **10** (1986), 615–78.

as her referent given these or those, perhaps unexpected, circumstances. The seed of referential meaning remains in the head.

The boldest externalists are 'direct reference' theorists, holding that some or all of our referential thoughts are 'Millian'. No semantic analysis can be given of a Millian thought beyond saying what referent it brutely names. But then a theory is needed telling what *constitutes* that one thought brutely has one referent while another thought brutely has another. Various theories of thought content have aspired to this, such as Dretske's informational theory, Fodor's asymmetrical dependency theory, Papineau's or my teleological theories. Each tells its own story about the sort of existential relation that cements a mental representation to its referent. But how do we prove that one of these relations rather than another is the reference relation? If asymmetrical dependency were the reference relation, for example, then of course referential meaning would be fully external. Similarly, if being the last thing you stepped on before that thought occurred to you were the reference relation, again, referential meaning would be fully external. If you think the former more plausible than the latter (marginally!), how can you prove it?—unless, as Putnam put it,[11] you can show that the former is more like the 'intended' relation of reference, more in accord with what we mean by 'reference'? Philosophy of language supports itself again! Putnam called it 'internal realism'.

Think of the matter this way. How could something be the criterion determining the referent of my own term or thought, if what I actually use is another criterion? Of course, I may have in reserve some more ultimate criteria that would prompt me to readjust my current criterion, for example, if I should find out more about the inner nature of the liquid I call 'water', or if I should find out how certain experts distinguish molybdenum. But these adjusted criteria would still be *my* criteria, set by my criteria for setting criteria. My meaning remains in my head. If the externalist proposes that something is 'reference' that we do not recognize by our own lights as reference, then he is just changing the subject. No way, it seems, can we defend any fully externalist view of referential meaning.

How do we exit this loop? This is what I think is needed. First, construct an externalist theory of reference that portrays it playing an indispensable role in the uses of both language and thought. Second, given this theory, make plausible that reasonable people should have come to the reasonable but mistaken conclusion that references/extensions are determined by criteria projected by

[11] H. Putnam, 'Realism and Reason', *Meaning and the Moral Sciences*, (London: Routledge and Kegan Paul, 1978).

individual minds. Third, make plausible that, despite their corresponding to different conceptions, the reference described by the theory is the same as the reference of our ordinary term 'reference'.

These can all be accomplished, I believe, though only the briefest sketch is possible here.

The inner seed assumption, expressed in Putnam's terms, is that the referent of a thought must always be something 'intended' by the thinker. Put this a slightly different way: It must have been a purpose of the thought to grasp that referent. Stated this second way, I believe the assumption is correct. The shift is from a purpose of the thinker, a psychological purpose, to a purpose of the thought, a biological purpose. The purposes of my thought need not be purposes of *mine*. But it is certainly understandable that classical theories of reference should have confused these two kinds of purposes. This is why thoroughly reasonable people have been lead to adopt the seed assumption.

Consider, for example, the purpose of my breathing. The purpose of my breathing is not a purpose of mine, not determined by an intention of mine. A frog's breathing has exactly the same purpose as mine, determined in the same way—certainly not by the frogs intentions. Similarly, neither the purposes of the frog's vision and hearing nor the purposes of mine are determined by anyone's intentions. Why then should the purpose of my thoughts, in particular, of my referential thoughts, be determined by my intentions? More plausibly, the purposes of all of these are biological, not psychological purposes.

Now, whatever gloss you put on the notion 'biological purpose', or 'biological function', one thing is clear. Biological purposes are not always achieved. In the biological world, failure in the particular case may even be the rule rather than the exception. The vast majority of individual animals die before reproducing. It would be very surprising if the biological purposes of human thought were invariably achieved. It is plausible that the various mechanisms designed to aid in forming empirical concepts are more successful sometimes than others. However, just as it may be perfectly clear what the goal was of the cat that pounced but missed the mouse, sometimes it may be perfectly clear what the goal of the concept forming mechanisms is, even though they are not currently dead on target.

The central task of empirical concept formation, I have argued, is learning to recognize what is objectively the same through enormous diversity of appearances, a wide variety of proximal stimulations (Millikan, 2000). The cognitive systems succeed or fail in the performance of quite specific tasks, such as the task of learning to recognize Mama reliably, or dogs, or orange juice, or doorknobs. These specific tasks get set as goals by the system when it is placed in a certain environment and supplied with a certain history of experience. Just as a dog that is tracking a rabbit is tracking some *particular* rabbit, though, of course it may sometimes lose the scent, when the cognitive systems attempt reidentification of something, perhaps using certain marks or criteria as a guide, whether they are successful or not, usually there is something entirely definite and real it is their current purpose to be tracking and to be learning better ways to track. Thus reference can remain stable while ways of identifying change, both during individual cognitive development and during the history of science.[12]

So it is possible coherently to question the inner seeds of reference assumption, the first assumption underlying the method of conceptual analysis. The second or one-to-one assumption, that the linguistic meanings of referential terms correspond to particular psychological states is seldom discussed, even though numerous difficulties resulting from it are well known.

Starting with Russell, indeed, even with Frege, it was recognized that if proper names abbreviated descriptions, still, nothing seemed to prevent different speakers from using different descriptions to back the same name. Nor is the problem specifically with description theories. In so far as thinking of an individual depends on a unique existential relation one has to that individual, each of us will think of the same individual in a different way. Suppose, for example, that for each of us—by description, or indexically, or causally—Aristotle is the man at the beginning of a causal chain issuing finally in this particular token and that particular token having the shape or sound 'Aristotle'. Still, each of us will begin by confronting different tokens of 'Aristotle', or if the same token, then it will be related to us in different ways. If we focus instead on nondescriptive ways of recognizing, the scattering is even more obvious. I can recognize my daughters Aino Millikan and Natasha Millikan in hundreds of different ways. Now that you've heard of them, you can use their names too, but are you able to recognize them any of my ways? True, both of us now know them as my daughters. But many of their acquaintances, who surely mean the same as we do when using their names, have no idea who their mother is. That there must be some inner psychological state common to all who

[12] For much fuller detail, see Millikan, *On Clear and Confused Ideas: An Essay About Substance Concepts* (Cambridge: Cambridge University Press 2000).

Ruth Garrett Millikan

comprehendingly use a proper name seems entirely out of the question.

Turning to names for kinds or properties, the valid conclusion of Putnam's arguments for division of linguistic labour, and also Burge's arguments against 'individualism', are not that meaning is not in the head. Meaning-in-the-head can always be saved by putting more complicated descriptions in the head. What these arguments *do* show is that people who use a natural kind term such as 'molybdenum' or 'arthritis' think of the same natural kind using different methods, some relying on experts, some not. And difference in method goes much deeper. Suppose in the case of the familiar stuff water, for example, that we all think of it, simply, as the watery liquid around here. Still, why suppose that the property *watery is* recognized in the same way by all speakers of English? Might it be that Helen Keller actually *understood* the word 'water' that Annie Sullivan spelled into her hand? Putnam says that the ways people recognized water prior to discovering that water is H_2O did not determine the extension of their thoughts of water, but were subject to replacement by more accurate measures. Do today's children fail to understand the contemporary term 'water' before they have learned chemistry? What in the conception of water has to remain the same to prevent the word 'water' from changing its meaning?

If there were, indeed, something in common among the psychological states—the methods of recognition, inference patterns or whatever—of all who understood a univocal referential term, how would these states be uniformly acquired in the course of language learning? Quine's arguments in *Word and Object* quite effectively showed,[13] I believe, that for the most part there could not be such a thing as THE inner rules of a language, THE correct criteria for application or methods of recognition, THE correct entailments, and so forth, that constitute public linguistic meanings. For the most part, everyone has his own private 'sentence associations', his own private application and inference procedures. Each follows his own causal pathways. There is no way to enforce any particular ones of these to be constitutive of the language being learned. Again: Helen Keller both wrote and spoke English.

Wittgenstein suggested that the criterion for meaning the same was agreement in judgments. *Why* do we think that Helen Keller spoke English? Because of agreement in judgments. Those around her acknowledged, for the most part, the same mundane truths that she did. She merely discovered these truths in a different way. But

---

[13] Ibid.

agreement in judgments gives evidence only of agreement in reference. It tells nothing about the private methods by which those judgments were reached. Yet agreement in judgments, for the most part, is the only evidence we have when trying to coordinate our language use with others. This is not incompatible with there being *some* judgments you can learn to agree on only by following a specific pattern of recognition. If you are going to manage to agree in judgments about bachelors you must begin by having some way of recognizing incoming information that concerns men as such, and a way of recognizing incoming information that concerns marriage. That this is the only way to manage agreement in the case of judgments about bachelors is not a matter of the rules of English. It is a matter of the constitution of bachelorhood. There just aren't any other reliable signs of this state to go on (Millikan, 2000, §3.4).

Yet there has been a dogged persistence in the view that a univocal linguistic meaning corresponds to a single psychological state. Thus Quine, rather than conclude that the public meaning of referential terms might be, simply, their referring, proclaimed the 'indeterminacy of translation'. He *trashed* linguistic meaning! Putnam's reaction was equally bizarre. After concluding that linguistic meaning is in part a function of reference, he anxiously offered a substitute internal sort of meaning that competent speakers of a language were to be required to share:[14]

> Speakers are required to know something about (stereotypical) tigers in order to count as having acquired the word 'tiger'. ... After all we do not permit people to drive on the highways without first passing some tests to determine that they have a *minimum* level of competence ... English speakers are required by their linguistic community to be able to tell tigers from leopards ... this could easily have been different ...[15]

A more flimsy fantasy has never been concocted, I submit, by a competent philosopher.

There are, of course, classical arguments—four of them—that referential terms must have, besides public reference, also a public sense. One concerns assertions of identity, the second, assertions of existence, the third, interchangeability in intensional contexts, and the fourth, psychological explanation.

First, if only reference is shared by everyone for a referential term, how can an assertion of identity be informative? Peter

---

[14] True, he uneasily speaks here of 'acquiring words' rather than of learning their meanings, but the shift in terminology is not material.

[15] 'The Meaning of "Meaning"', p. 168.

Strawson provided the answer in 1975.[16] He explained that what an identity sentence, A=B, does to your head is, as Michael Lockwood rephrased it,[17] to merge the contents of two information folders, one of which formerly had been accessed with the word 'A', the other with the word 'B', so that all the information can now be accessed with either word. Why wasn't this the end of the matter'?[18]

Second, if a referential term, 'A', has no univocal public sense, what meaning will the assertion 'A exists' have, or the assertion 'A doesn't exist'? In the same spirit as Strawson, we answer that what 'A doesn't exist' does to your head is remove your mental folder of virtual information about A to an inactive file, such that it does not engage in the normal way with perception or action. 'A' will now be treated as only a pretend name. 'A exists' reverses this effect.[19]

Third, if 'A' and 'B' name the same, why is 'x believes that A is A' not always equivalent to 'x believes that A is B'? Because, very occasionally, in a context that makes this clear, using a certain word to describe the content of a person's belief carries the implication that the person himself would accept this word as helping to express this belief. But a person might believe that A is A without knowing that A is called 'B'.

Fourth, we describe the contents of people's beliefs and desires using embedded sentences, and having captured their contents in this way, we successfully predict their behaviours. How is this possible if the embedded sentences don't correspond to determinate psychological states? The answer is that this whole image of how behaviours are predicted is quite wrong. Comparative psychologists learned long ago that only the distal and not the proximal behaviours of an animal are predictable. You can predict that the cat will move the correct lever in the right direction to let itself out of the experimental box, but you can't predict whether it will use the left paw or the right, or perhaps lean with its tail. Having learned which way the lever needs to be pushed, it will do this different ways different times. Similarly, you can predict that Sam, who sincerely said he would arrive at seven, probably will, in one way or another—by bus, by subway, by car, on foot or bicycle—arrive around seven. And if he says he will take the 6 o'clock bus, you can predict that he will

---

[16] P. F. Strawson, *Subject and Predicate in Logic and Grammar* (London: Methuen and Co. Ltd., 1974).

[17] M. Lockwood, 'Identity and Reference', *Identity and Individuation*, M. K. Munitz (ed.) (New York University Press, 1971), 199–211.

[18] See R. G. Millikan, *Language, Thought and Other Biological Categories* (Cambridge: MIT Press, 1984), chapter 12.

[19] See R. G. Millikan (ibid.).

probably manage to identify the 6 o'clock bus. There is no need for concern with his methods of recognition. True, occasionally it is helpful to know something about the ways a person can or can't identify a certain referent. If you wish to know why Sam didn't even attempt to speak to his favourite author who was at the same party he was, it may help to know that Sam doesn't know what she looks like. But if he does know what she looks like, it is not likely to be useful to know whether it's the line of the nose or the chin that cues him. Similarly, when you order basil with your groceries, you are not concerned whether the grocer recognizes basil by the smell, or the shape of the leaf, or the label on the box, so long as it's basil that he brings.

Notice that the attempt to understand the meanings of words and the reference of thought in this way, without the seed assumption and without the one-to-one assumption, besides requiring development of certain broad aspects of a realist ontology, also implicates broad issues in theoretical cognitive psychology, child development, and, indeed, the history of science. Understanding what reference is is not conceived as a wholly *a priori* project. The aim is to help create the framework for an empirical theory of human cognition. Indeed, if the nature of reference is at all as I have suggested, then to investigate any of our empirical concepts is to investigate the nature of the world, not merely of what's in our heads. This is consonant, I believe, with the actual role philosophy has always played in relation to the sciences. The philosophies of mind and of language, for example, have provided the foundation for much that has happened in modern empirical psychology and linguistics. Large parts of philosophy have traditionally operated as theoretical empirical sciences. There is also a long tradition, including, for example, Russell, that has explicitly endorsed this kind of role for philosophy.

Dropping the seed assumption and the one-to-one assumption puts a very different face on both the appropriate methods in philosophy of language and its status relative to other parts of philosophy and science. I hope this is the face it will wear in the coming century.[20]

---

[20] It will surely have been noticed that this essay has presupposed a heavy duty realist ontology throughout. The ontology is discussed at length in R. G. Millikan, Language, *Thought and Other Biological Categories* (ibid.), chapters 16–17; R. G. Millikan, *On Clear and Confused Ideas* (ibid.) chapters 2–3.

Ruth Garrett Millikan

References

N. Block, 'Advertisement for a Semantics for Psychology', *Midwest Studies in Philosophy* **10** (1986), 615–78.

T. Burge, 'Individualism and the Mental', *Studies in Metaphysics, Midwest Studies in Philosophy IV* **4** (1979), 73–121.

R. Fumerton, 'Russelling Causal Theories' *Rereading Russell: Essays in Bertrand Russell's Metaphysics and Epistemology, Minnesota Studies in the Philosophy of Science* **12**, C. W. Savage and C. A. Anderson (eds), (Minneapolis: University of Minnesota Press, 1989), 108–18.

C. G. Hempel, 1950, 1965. 'Empiricist Criteria of Cognitive Significance: Problems and Changes', reprinted in *Aspects of Scientific Explanation and Other Essays in the Philosophy of Science* (New York: The Free Press, Macmillan Co., 1965), 101–22.

S. Kripke, *Naming and Necessity* (Cambridge: Harvard University Press, 1972).

M. Lockwood, 'Identity and Reference', *Identity and Individuation,* M. K. Munitz (ed.) (New York University Press 1971), 199–211.

R. G. Millikan, *On Clear and Confused Ideas,* (Cambridge University Press, 2000).

H. Putnam, *Language and Reality: Philosophical Papers* **i,** (Cambridge: Cambridge University Press, 1975).

H. Putnam, 'The Meaning of "Meaning"', *Minnesota Studies in the Philosophy of Science VII*, Keith Gunderson (ed.) (Minneapolis: University of Minnesota Press, 1975). Also in Putnam, *Mind Language and Reality* (ibid.)

H. Putnam, 1978a. *Meaning and the Moral Sciences* (London, Hently and Boston: Routledge and Kegan Paul, 1978).

H. Putnam, 'Realism and Reason', *Meaning and the Moral Sciences* (London: Routledge and Kegan Paul, 1978).

W. V. Quine, 'Two Dogmas of Empiricism', *From a Logical Point of View*, (Cambridge MA: Harvard University Press, 1953) 20–46.

W. V. Quine, *Word and Object*, (Cambridge MA: MIT Press, 1960).

P. F. Strawson, *Subject and Predicate in Logic and Grammar* (London: Methuen and Co. Ltd., 1974).

Philosophy, Environment and Technology

DAVID E. COOPER

I

A striking feature of philosophy in the century just passed is the scale of attention paid to questions concerning the natural environment and technology—a scale so large that any brief survey of the development, current state and possible future of such attention would degenerate into telegrammatic reportage. I shall indeed address the question why philosophical concern with environment and technology has 'taken off', and with some confidence that its answer will enable a reasonable estimate of the central issues which deserve continuing reflection. But that question, too, is unmanageably large as it stands. So I need to do something to restrict it.

On a familiar view, the philosophies of environment and technology are, and should be, *applied* philosophy, the bringing to bear upon 'special area[s] of interest' of the skills which students of philosophy are supposed to have acquired, such as sensitivity to conceptual distinctions or fallacious reasoning.[1] On another conception, however, these philosophies of ... are less a matter of applying skills refined in 'core' disciplines, such as logic, than of reflection on the place of environment and technology within that global understanding of humanity's relation to the world to which philosophy has traditionally aspired. I do not want to impugn the piecemeal analyses of concepts and arguments which crop up in environmental and technological debate, and anyway there is no sharp distinction between that enterprise and addressing the 'big', 'metaphysical', issue of man's place in the order of things. Still, my emphasis will be on the engagement of the philosophies of environment and technology with that 'big' issue—not least, because that is the issue which has done most to inspire their emergence and shape their programmes.

[1] Frederick Ferré, *Philosophy of Technology* (Englewood Cliffs: Prentice Hall, 1988), p. 9. See also R. M. Hare, 'Moral reasoning about the environment', in B. Almond & D. Hill (eds), *Applied Philosophy* (London: Routledge, 1991), for a similar conception of philosophy's contribution to environmental thinking.

David E. Cooper

One way to approach the question about the 'take off' of philosophical concerns with environment and technology is first to consider why it is that these concerns have 'taken off' *together?* Why, so to speak, does 'environment and technology' trip off the tongue as lightly as 'bacon and eggs'? That question suggests not only a taxonomy of possible approaches to the initial one, but a convenient way of locating some of the principal issues and positions to be found in a very wide literature.

But doesn't the question have an obvious answer? Surely, it is the increasing 'devastation of the earth', to cite Heidegger, and the increasingly 'technological texture to life', to cite another philosopher,[2] which are responsible for the 'take off' of environmental and technological concerns. They have 'taken off' together because, plainly, environmental devastation is a product of technology, of what the Luddites called 'engines of mischief'. One has only to recite the familiar litany: global warming, acid rain, deforestation, nuclear waste, factory farming, and so on. The two philosophies of ... go in tandem, then, because of historical, contingent connections between technology's impact and environmental crises.

One problem with this answer is the apparent assumption that philosophy has little momentum of its own, but stands at the beck and call of events and trends in the wider world. This assumption makes it hard to explain why, say, disease and war have never been the subjects of thriving philosophies of ..., despite their having, during many periods, woven the 'texture to life'. It makes it difficult to explain, as well, why individual philosophers, from Chuang Tsu to Marx, should have been preoccupied with people's proper relationship to technology and the natural environment—well before any devastating impact of the one on the other had become visible.

There is another problem. According to the 'obvious' answer, philosophical interests in environment and technology go together only for contingent reasons. This implies that, had history taken a different turn, those interests would have been no more intimately connected than, say, ones in environment and music, or in technology and sex—occasionally meeting, but only tangentially. We can at least imagine a world whose environmental ills are due, not to technology's impact, but only, say, to uncontrollable population growth, and where technology, despite its massive impact on human life, is, like IT for the most part, 'environmentally clean'. The implication of the 'obvious' answer is that, in such a world, there would be no 'take off' of philosophical attention to environment and technology in tandem.

[2] Don Ihde, *Existential Technics*, quoted in Ferré, op. cit., p. 9.

II

The above remarks suggest a division among attempts to explain 'take off' into those which do and those which don't imply that environmental and technological concerns are only contingently connected. I begin with two examples of the first sort. Consider, to begin with, the explanation of the upsurge in environmental concern implicit in the familiar image of 'the expanding moral circle'. According to devotees of this image, the history of moral sensibility is a progressive one in which, step-by-step, moral concern has expanded to encompass ever larger constituencies. This has been rational progress since, at each step, some arbitrary discrimination has been removed. In one popular version, from a baseline where only one's fellow white males were morally 'considerable', we have progressed to include first women, then non-white people, then animals, and eventually the living world at large within the circle of moral concern. Environmental ethics has 'taken off', on this story, because it was only recently, in the wake of earlier expansions of the circle, that the arbitrariness of drawing a moral line between animals and non-sentient nature could be appreciated. Appreciated, for example, by Aldo Leopold, whose 'land ethic' invites a perception of the natural environment as an extended 'community' to which people are ethically bound in the way they are to their respective human communities.[3] If this story were true, then environmentalist attention to technology is required only for the contingent reason that technology has been a main engine of damage to that enlarged community, the 'land', to which, Leopold writes, we owe respect and moral regard.

Among some promoters of the 'expanding circle' image, Leopold's is a step too far. His insistence that something is right if and only if it tends to the good of the 'biotic community' has been accused of encouraging an 'eco-fascism' which, like its political relative, is too ready to sacrifice individuals for the sake of a whole. And the moral line between sentient and non-sentient beings which he erases is, for some critics, not an arbitrary one like that between whites and blacks.[4] Debates over such issues—between 'individual-

---

[3] *A Sand County Almanac*, partially reprinted in L. Pojman (ed.), *Environmental Ethics: readings in theory and application* (Boston: Jones & Bartlett, 1994), pp. 84ff.

[4] Both for the charge of 'eco-fascism' and the refusal to delete the boundary between sentient and non-sentient nature, see Tom Regan, *The Case for Animal Rights* (Berkeley: University of California Press, 1983).

David E. Cooper

ists' and 'holists', or 'sentientists' and 'non-sentientists'—fill many pages in the literature of environmental ethics. Those debates are genuine and interesting, and can be detached from the context of the 'expanding circle' story in which they are often set. That is just as well, for the story is a myth. Even when attention is confined to the West, the idea that there has been a uniform, step-by-step widening of the moral constituency up to the inclusions of animals and the living world at large is a distorting one. There have been communities which afforded to their animals a moral respect not extended to human beings outside those communities,[5] just as there have been ones which regarded nature as something that can be wrongfully violated. The suggestion that philosophical preoccupations with the environment owe to a sudden recognition—the latest episode in the progressive repudiation of arbitrary discrimination—that non-human life, too, is morally 'considerable', is therefore implausible.

Let me briefly turn to another explanation, this time focused on technology, on which it is, again, only for contingent reasons that the two philosophies of ... go in tandem. In today's climate of apprehension towards technology, it is not easy to recapture the technophiliac mood which prevailed among many philosophers early in the past century. But it was there. For some, the enthusiasm was founded on utilitarian considerations: the new technologies promised the eradication of disease, poverty and other ills. For others, however, it was the liberating potential of technology which was central—its enablement of men and women to master and direct their lives. Friedrich Engels had set the tone when he argued that it was not the arrival of reason or language which first separated men from animals, but 'the generation of fire by friction'. Through technical mastery of natural and social conditions, man would ascend 'from the kingdom of necessity to the kingdom of freedom'.[6] Countless twentieth century writers continued the theme—most volubly, perhaps, the inventor of the 'geodosic dome', Buckminster Fuller, for whom it was the engineer, the 'mind-over-matterist ... informed technician', who, by enabling people to dispense with unaided reliance on their own bodies, would make 'man infallible'.[7] The theme is still with us, modulated to suit the IT era.

---

[5] See James Serpell, *In the Company of Animals* (Oxford: Blackwell, 1986), for examples.

[6] *Anti-Dühring* (Moscow. Foreign Languages Publishing House, 1959), pp. 158 & 391.

[7] Quoted in Ferré, op. cit., p. 61.

'You can create your own universe!', proclaims one computer buff, by controlling and outsmarting the computer, 'You could be God!', asserts another.[8]

To the extent that the natural environment is a 'kingdom of necessity', our subjection to which is lifted by technological control, the liberationist vision induces a certain attitude towards nature. But the emphasis of Fuller and others is squarely on the potential for human self-direction which technology offers, and as such implies no particular view of the proper relation of human beings to their environment. Reflection on how we should treat the living world at large may indeed be necessary, but only because of the contingent fact that technological progress often requires vigorous intervention in that world. For the liberationist, the reason philosophy of technology 'took off' was the recognition that, in the modern age, the perennial quest for self-direction was at last nearing a successful conclusion.

This liberationist vision spawned important controversies.[9] From its early days, it was countered by dystopian scenarios—to be found in novels and films as much as sociological tomes—of technology running out its creators's control, of enslaving rather than liberating. Today, disputes couched in the vocabulary of freedom and enslavement concerning the potential of IT and genetic engineering are the stuff of Sunday broadsheets. One thinks, for example, of the difference between those who extol the control, made possible by biotechnology, which people now exert over their reproductive life—postponing the having of children, choosing their sex, and so on—and those who foresee unprecedented power over reproduction concentrated among experts enthused by the eugenic potential of genetic engineering.

Imbued as modern intellectual debate is by competing perceptions of technology's power to liberate or enslave, it is not these which have been responsible for a distinctively philosophical concern with technology. Just now, I mentioned the novelists, filmmakers, sociologists and Sunday journalists who engage in such debates. Doubtless philosophers, too, like any reflective men and women, may stick their oars in: but, to recall my initial remarks, I doubt if their contribution rises above that of refined commonsense. And this is because the issues involved are basically empirical

[8] Quoted in Steven Levy, *Hackers: Heroes of the computer revolution* (New York: Anchor, 1984).

[9] See my 'Technology: liberation or enslavement?', in R. Fellows (ed.), *Philosophy and Technology* (Cambridge: Cambridge University Press, 1995), for discussion of several such controversies.

David E. Cooper

ones. Will biotechnology empower individuals' control over their lives or deliver control into the hands of eugenicists? Will the internet, as Tony Blair and Jean-François Lyotard predict, advance democratic supervision of government, or is it a dangerous weapon in the armoury of political propagandists? Lively questions, but not ones with, so to speak, philosophical mileage to them. The significance of technology must be sought elsewhere if a distinctively philosophical engagement with its import is to be explained.

III

To continue the search, I turn to two accounts on which the connection between philosophical concerns for environment and technology is not merely contingent. On both views, those concerns would have 'taken off' together even in that imagined world where technology is environmentally clean and environmental devastation due to other factors. On both views, these concerns are treated as critical responses to what they respectively discern as the prevailing metaphysics of modernity. On the first view, an upsurge in attention to human beings' relationship to the natural world and to the place of technology in their lives manifests a critical engagement with the final stages of, to cite a famous title, the 'dialectic of Enlightenment'.[10] The modern age, it is argued, is dominated by what, in hindsight, was the implicit metaphysics of 'the Enlightenment project'. That project began benignly, in the aspirations to promote human well-being and, as a precondition of this, to exorcize irrational beliefs and superstitions, including what Marx called 'the deification of nature'. But with the increasing prestige of the natural sciences as the loci of rational thought, those benign aspirations eventually hardened into the doctrines which, for good or ill, have stamped modern thought. These were to the effect that the real, objective world is the one depicted by the natural sciences, a 'disenchanted' world devoid of significance and value. Because the world is disenchanted, the rational conduct of life cannot be a response to what the world demands of us, for it demands nothing, and can therefore consist only in the adoption of the most efficient means for satisfying our preferences. Just as theoretical science provides the one objective account of the world, so applied science—technology—furnishes the appropriate means for achieving the ends we pursue. The paradigmatically rational person has become

[10] See Max Horkheimer and Theodor Adorno, *Dialectic of Enlightenment* (London: Allen Lane, 1973).

Weber's technocrat, the expert who, having gauged people's preferences, calculates the most efficient technical means to satisfy them.

In 'the dialectic of Enlightenment', conceptions of technology
and the natural world are necessarily intertwined. As one writer
puts it, 'an instrumental conception of the relation between humanity and the "natural" world' gets 'endorsed' by the conception of a
rational person as one who, standing 'outside' a world subjected to
detached, scientific investigation, then 'harnesses' that world as a
means to his or her preferred ends.[11] Whether or not in practice the
natural world needs to be harnessed through technology is beside
the point. The important consideration is that, should this need
arise, it would be irrational not to proceed: disenchanted, de-deified
nature deserves no say in the matter.

The above account of 'the dialectic of Enlightenment' and its
culmination in technological modernity has been challenged. But
certainly it has provided the context in which many important
debates—distinctively philosophical ones, moreover—are typically
conducted. As such, a certain perception of the legacy of
Enlightenment has indeed inspired philosophical reflection on environment and technology in tandem. I have in mind, for example,
the continuing debate as to whether there are intrinsic values 'in'
nature that should constrain our efforts to harness it—or as to
whether it is not a stunted conception of rationality which pre-
scribes that people sever their emotional ties to the natural world so
as to attain to a detached, objective standpoint.[12]

I now turn to a second diagnosis of the 'take off' of our two
philosophies of ..., which also treats reflection on environment and
technology as something made imperative by a prevailing metaphysics. The metaphysics in question is not, this time, the rational-
istic, scientific realism supposedly evolved from the Enlightenment
project. Among the technophiles of the early decades of the last
century, there were figures whose enthusiasm was for technology,
not as a liberating force, or as a triumph of practical reason, but as
the latest and most authentic expression of the 'will to power'. In
their view, Nietzsche had demonstrated that it is will to power
which shapes history and that the 'higher type' of human being is
one who maximally embodies that will—a type best represented in

[11] Kate Soper, *Humanism and Anti-Humanism* (London: Hutchinson,
1986), p. 24.
[12] Most of the best-known figures in contemporary environmental
ethics—John Passmore, Arne Naess, and J. Baird Callicott, for example—
have addressed these issues. See the selection of readings in Parts II–III
of Pojman (ed.), *Environmental Ethics*, op. cit.

modern times, they hold, by the technologist. These figures included Italian 'futurists', Russian 'constructivists', and most importantly several German thinkers now referred to as 'reactionary modernists'. The two classic expressions of this brand of technophilia were Oswald Spengler's *Man and Technics* and Ernst Jünger's *The Worker*, with their respective celebrations of the 'Faustian' engineers who represent the 'victory of technical thought' in the 'pitiless ... battle of the will to power', and of those industrial 'titans' or 'cybernetic storm-troopers' at the forefront of the 'mobilization of matter'.[13] In these writers, dithyrambic celebration of technology owes not to any confidence in the utilitarian benefits of industry, but to 'belief in an activistic metaphysics'.[14]

Although Martin Heidegger—that 'Schwarzwald redneck', as Richard Rorty describes him—was no enthusiast either for an 'activistic metaphysics' or technology, he was persuaded by these writers that the prevailing metaphysical 'stamp' or *Gestalt* of the age was indeed a technological one, responsible for the enterprise of a 'total mobilization' of the earth. Indeed, in his terminology, 'technology' is less the name of certain processes and activities than of a particular 'way of revealing' or experiencing the world—as so much 'standing-reserve' or 'equipment' at the disposal of human beings. 'The earth now reveals itself as a coal-mining district, the soil as a mineral deposit', and the river Rhine as a 'water-power supplier'.[15] As such remarks make clear, the metaphysics of will to power in its latest technological version is inseparable from a certain view of the natural environment. For Heidegger, technology is, in essence, the 'equipmental' way of 'rendering things manifest', of revealing nature, as so much potential material for human control and exploitation. On this account, then, the 'take-off' of the philosophies of technology and environment in tandem is due to the appreciation that the enterprise of technology, and the 'equipmental' way of experiencing the natural world which it reflects, together bear the prevailing metaphysical 'stamp' of modernity.

[13] Spengler, *Man and Technics: a contribution to the philosophy of life* (London: Allen & Unwin, 1932), pp. 76 & 16; Jünger, quoted in Thomas Nevin, *Ernst Jünger and Germany: into the abyss 1914–1945* (London: Constable, 1997), pp. 135 & 140.

[14] Carl Schmitt, quoted in David E. Cooper, 'Reactionary modernism', in A. O'Hear (ed.), *German Philosophy Since Kant* (Cambridge.. Cambridge UniversityPress, 1999), p. 292. This article deals, in some detail, with the views of Spengler, Jünger and Heidegger.

[15] *The Question Concerning Technology (and other essays)* (New York: Harper & Row, 1977), pp. 14ff.

Heidegger's account has been immensely influential: even if the story it tells is rejected, the account itself has done much to shape contemporary debates about environment and technology. Among those sympathetic to it, the question, for example, has loomed large of people's proper response to the dominance of the technological *Gestalt*. Is it to swim with the tide of history and join in the 'Faustian' enterprise, to don the armour of the 'eco-warrior' and resist it, or— as Heidegger's own remarks suggest—patiently to await, in quietistic spirit, the demise of this particular episode in 'the history of Being'?

IV

I have presented these two latest scenarios—the 'dialectic of Enlightenment' one and the 'will to power' one—as alternative, indeed rival, attempts to account for the upsurge of our two philosophies of .... At a certain level, that is right, for the meta-physical moods, critical reflection on which is supposed, on those scenarios, to inspire that upsurge, are indeed different. Technology cannot embody the latest anthropocentric perspective or *Gestalt* in the story of mankind's imposition of will to power and, at the same time, represent the triumph of objective, disengaged reason. I suggest, however, both that elements from the two scenarios may be combined—indeed, that they feed off one another—and that it is this combination which best explains the 'take off' and subsequent course of distinctively philosophical reflection on technology and environment.

Let's recall, first, that the Enlightenment ambition to arrive at rational, objective depiction of the world, free from sentiment and prejudice, increasingly took the form of privileging a natural scientific description of the world—culminating in a 'scientism' or 'bald naturalism' according to which, as John McDowell puts it, reality has an objective 'intrinsic nature, which is captured by ... the natural sciences'.[16] On that view, a thing just *is* what physics or chemistry says it is, while other attributes we may ordinarily ascribe to it— colour, smell, and beauty, say—are 'subjective', ones which a thing can only be said to have in virtue of certain relations to *us*. Now there is reason for holding that this view owes its appeal to a background, usually ignored, of pragmatic interests. The properties attributed to things by the natural sciences are precisely those which it is most important to take into account for purposes of predicting, and hence controlling, the behaviour of things. In the absence of

[16] 'Reply to commentators', *Philosophy and Phenomenological Research*, **LVIII**, 1998, p. 420.

David E. Cooper

those purposes, there could be no reason to privilege natural scientific description—to identify a thing with the object as it figures in such description, while relegating other ways of describing it to so much subjectively smeared gloss. If that is right, then the metaphysics bequeathed by the Enlightenment project is not, after all, the 'disengaged' account of reality it purports to be: it is in hock to just those practical interests, in control and manipulation, which technology is designed to satisfy.

Consider, second, that on Heidegger's scenario 'scientism' plays an important strategic role in cementing that 'equipmental way of revealing' which is at the heart of technological metaphysics. It does this by enabling the technophile to marginalize other ways of revealing—religious, say, or aesthetic—as nothing more than passing 'subjective' perspectives. Objections to treating the Rhine as something more than a 'water-power supplier'—as the artery of German culture, the abode of the Rhine-maidens, or whatever—are met with the insistence that the river as such is simply a mass of moving H_2O, something therefore 'neutral', to be used as people find most beneficial. If so, then the technological 'way of revealing' is not merely the encountering of the natural world in its relation to human purposes, but as composed of and reducible to so much neutral 'stuff' which only 'sentiment' could invest with a significance exceeding its utilitarian potential. The 'baldly' naturalist vision of things becomes servant to the prevailing, modern, 'equipmental' form of the metaphysics of will to power.

The suggestion, then, is that the 'take-off and subsequent direction of distinctively philosophical reflection on environment and technology primarily owe to a perception that the predominant, controlling vision of human beings' relationship to the world is the joint product of a reductionist scientism and an 'equipmental way of revealing' things. That alliance is not accidental, since the former at once depends for its plausibility on the latter and, in repayment, cements the idea that no other 'way of revealing' is a serious option for hard-headed moderns. For some, this controlling vision is something to celebrate and secure; for others, a deeply distorting one responsible for the 'devastation of the earth'. Either way, it is something with which to engage, and the means of engagement are the philosophies of environment and technology.

V

To give some body to this rather abstract suggestion, I turn to the domain of mutual interest to both philosophies of ... which is, and

150

promises to remain, the prime focus of discussion—biotechnology. Underpinning claims that people's qualms about biotechnological procedures are 'sentimental' or 'irrational taboos' is the conviction that, in Richard Dawkins's words, organisms are 'merely vehicles for genes'. How, if this is so, and if 'all genetic material is the same, from worms to humans', rhetorically asks one scientist, can it not be 'legitimate to shunt genes around from one species to any other species'?[17] Such remarks illustrate the manner in which, in this domain, reductionism is deployed to brush aside, as 'ancient theological scruples' or whatever, 'ways of revealing' living things which might render the prospect of 'shunting genes' among them appalling. How could that prospect appal once it is squarely recognized that creatures are simply convenient, transitory carriers of genes? But I suspect, too, that this very 'recognition' itself owes to the recent possibility of such shunting operations. Biologists have long known that living bodies are composed of cells with a capacity to transmit genetic 'information'. Reductionist claims, of the 'Creatures are merely vehicles for genes' ilk, only gained currency, however, when biologists acquired the ability to employ that knowledge in the engineering of cells and hence of their 'vehicles'— plants, animals, people. If that's right, then genetic reductionism owes as much to the manipulative and practical applications of genetic theory as defence of those applications does to the reductionism.

We have, then, precisely the combination described earlier: a 'bald naturalism' and an 'equipmental way of revealing' things feeding off one other. It is this combination, I suggest, which is responsible for the disquiet at biotechnology that it is in the brief of philosophy to address, whether the particular focus of disquiet is GM foods, transgenic animal procedures, or cloning human beings to produce organisms whose 'spare parts' may be 'raided' by their 'parents'. To be sure, the issues most frequently aired in these areas are of a broadly utilitarian type, ones concerning potential risks and benefits. But these are not issues with, as I put it, much philosophical mileage. Clearly many people experience disquiet of another kind, even if, in deference to the prevailing tone of contemporary public debate—be it in the House of Commons or on the *Today* programme—it remains muted or gets translated into a more acceptably utilitarian idiom.

[17] Quoted in Andrew Linzey, *Animal Theology* (London: SCM Press, 1994), pp. 150–1, and Alan Holland, 'Species are dead. Long live genes!', in A. Holland and A. Johnson (eds), *Animal Biotechnology and Ethics* (London: Chapman & Hall, 1998), p. 236.

David E. Cooper

The disquiet I have in mind is often expressed by critical references to biotechnologists as 'playing God' or emulating Dr.
Frankenstein. (Readers of the novel will know that, for Mary
Shelley, what was 'supremely frightful' about the creation of the
monster had nothing to do with its, admittedly lethal, consequences.) The disquiet expressed in these ways is best diagnosed as
the sense that the integrity of things—living things, at least—is violated, indeed doubly violated, by the combination of attitudes
which lurk behind the enterprise of biotechnology. The integrity of
a living thing—what makes it the distinctive being it is—is diluted
and distorted when it is regarded only in its relationship to, its
potential place in, practical human endeavours. And it is all but
erased when the thing is pared down to the stuff—the genetic material—of which it is composed, with the result that the only distinctiveness it has is the superficial one of being a certain vehicle for this
stuff. To regard the natural world, therefore, as so much stuff con-
veniently divided up into living things which are at our disposal is
doubly to violate the integrity of things.

That there is this sense of violated integrity when the living
things happen to be human bodies is obvious. A human body is not
simply a vehicle of its genes, but the vehicle of a person's engagement with the world and other people. In a good sense, I *am* my
body—the 'lived', active body which works, plays, and is in inter-
course with other human bodies, that is, not the collection of cells
described in biology.[18] To regard the body in the reductionist-cum-
equipmental manner is to diminish persons and their distinctiveness. And that is one reason why the prospect of engineering human
or human-like bodies to serve as 'spare parts' emporia is one with
the power to appal. The sense of violated integrity is only slightly
less pronounced when the living things are non-human animals.
Advocates of transgenic procedures like to say that these procedures
are only the speedy and efficient version of breeding techniques
which go back to the dawn of husbandry. But Stephen Clark is surely right to observe a difference between 'old-style pastoralists', who
had to honour the natural ends of animals to profit from them, and
'new-style artificers', who first 'work out where the profit lies, and
mould the ends to suit them'.[19] It is one thing, for example, to
exploit the natural virility and aggression of a bull in the rearing of

[18] On the notion of the 'lived' body which a person *is*, see Maurice
Merleau-Ponty, *Phenomenology of Perception* (London: Routledge &
Kegan Paul, 1981).
[19] 'Intrinsic criticisms of biotechnological technique', in D. Oderberg,
(ed.), *Human Lives* (London: Macmillan, 1995), p. 17.

a herd, another to engineer placid bulls—ones described as having the bovine equivalent of Downs Syndrome—more convenient for the extraction of semen.

Where the living things are neither sentient nor intelligent, the sense of violated integrity—at the hands of the GM food industry, say—may be less widespread: but it is surely there—and understandably so. I am reminded of a remark by Wittgenstein. These days, he says, anyone is regarded as 'stupid' who doesn't know that water is simply H_2O: and thereby, he says, 'the most important questions are concealed'.[20] Water, he is implying, is not *just* H_2O: it is what sustains life, pounds on to the beach, what we swim in and baptise with. To reduce water to a neutral stuff at our disposal is to be blind to what it is, to its integrity. As it stands, Wittgenstein's complaint is closer to Heidegger's despair at the reduction of the Rhine to a power supplier than to qualms at GM agriculture. But, to make his point, his example could as well have been wheat, rice or—something he indeed mentions in the same passage—sugar, instead of water. They, too, are not *just* XYZ or whatever their chemical descriptions specify.

People respond differently to this talk of biotechnology's violation of the integrity of things. On the *Today* programme, it would doubtless be mauled by some terrier-like interviewer. Elsewhere it would receive a more sympathetic hearing. My argument is not that we should necessarily share that sense and so condemn biotechnology as the devil's work. It is that in the estimation of that sense, in reflection on the questions which it induces—questions, finally, of a metaphysical kind about what things are—that a distinctively philosophical contribution is to be made. The philosophies of environment and technology—especially in the domain which promises to preoccupy them in the foreseeable future—indeed turn out to belong with that global reflection on the nature of the world and our relation to it which has been the traditional calling of philosophy.

[20] *Culture and Value* (Oxford: Blackwell, 1980), 71.

Has Philosophy Made a Difference and Could it be Expected To?

JOHN HALDANE

I. Intimations of 'Undeniable Progress'

In 1989 Oxford University Press launched a new programme of monographs in moral philosophy entitled the 'Oxford Ethics Series'. Given that the series' editor is Derek Parfit it is unsurprising that the books published to date feature rigorous analysis and argumentation regarding the nature of reasons and requirements. Perhaps by way of intended commitment to this profile, the following brief statement appears on the cover of the first volume (Shelly Kagan's *The Limits of Morality*): 'The books in the series will contain philosophical arguments about morality or rationality. The aim will be to make undeniable progress'.

The second sentence is, or should be, arresting. It is, after all, a common enough complaint that philosophy is characterized by a general and marked *failure* to make progress. What was being discussed in antiquity about substance, time, identity, knowledge, value and virtue, and was discussed again in the early and late middle ages, the modern period and the enlightenment, is *still* being debated today with no incontestable sign of advance let alone of resolution. Generally, this complaint is made from outwith philosophy but it is sometimes voiced from within (particularly by those attracted to 'scientific conceptions' of the subject), and given the highly academic character of the series it is likely that Parfit had fellow philosophers in mind when boldly promising 'undeniable progress'. Interestingly, though, the claim is not repeated on subsequent volumes and nor is it printed on the paperback edition of the initial monograph.

Nonetheless, even if it gave hostages to fortune, it expressed a mood of optimism and a determination that things were going to get better. The same outlook is evident in Parfit's own book *Reasons and Persons,* published the year before the launch of the Ethics Series. Towards the end of it he writes of 'how human history, and the history of ethics may be just beginning' and then continues

Some people believe that there cannot be progress in Ethics, since

John Haldane

everything has already been said. Like Rawls and Nagel I believe
the opposite. How many people have made Non-Religious Ethics
their life's work? Before the recent past, very few. In most civiliz-
ations, most people have believed in the existence of a God, or of
several gods. ...
    ... Civilization began only a few thousand years ago. If we don't
destroy mankind, these few thousand years may be only a tiny
fraction of the whole of civilized human history. ...
    There could clearly be higher achievements in the struggle
for a wholly just world-wide community. And there could be
higher achievements in all of the Arts and Sciences. But the
progress could be greatest in what is now the least advanced of
these Arts and Sciences. This, I have claimed, is Non-Religious
Ethics. Belief in God, or in many gods, prevented the free
development of moral reasoning. Disbelief in God, openly
admitted by a majority, is a very recent event, not yet
completed. Because this event is so recent, Non-Religious
Ethics is at a very early stage.[1]

This prompts several thoughts. First, I very much doubt that the
commonly voiced worry that there cannot be progress in ethics has
much to do with the belief that everything has already been said.
Rather I take it to express the suspicion that whatever has been, is,
or *ever might be* said is rationally insufficient to resolve any significant ethical or metaethical dispute.
    Second, there is an ambiguity in the claim that progress in
moral reasoning has been inhibited by religion. One interpretation would see religion as providing an external constraint on the
range of speculation; another would see it as operating within
moral reasoning by providing part (or all) of the form and content of morality. Elizabeth Anscombe had an instance of the latter circumstance in mind when she claimed that '[i]n consequence of the dominance for many centuries of Christianity
[which derived its ethical notions from the Torah], the concepts
of being bound, permitted or excused became deeply embedded
in our language and thought'.[2] This suggestion, subsequently
developed by Alasdair MacIntyre in *After Virtue*, is certainly an
interesting one and, if correct, is likely to make the task of devel-

[1] Derek Parfit, *Reasons and Persons* (Oxford: O.U.P., 1984) 453–4.
[2] G. E. M. Anscombe, 'Modern Moral Philosophy', *Philosophy*, Vol. 33,
1958; reprinted in G. E. M. Anscombe, *Ethics, Religion and Politics:
Collected Philosophical Papers, Vol. III* (Oxford: Blackwell, 1981) the passage comes on p. 30 of the latter version.

oping a non-religious ethic more difficult than that of simply carrying on ethical thinking freed from the external constraints of religion.[3] On the other hand, of course, difficulty in constructing a secular ethic devoid of concepts historically associated with religious ideas suggests the possibility that their contribution is internal to ethical thought as we have it, and even that it might be internal to any ethical thought at all. If that last could be established then the dilemma facing the would-be secular moral philosopher is obviously fairly dramatic: *either religious ethics or no ethics at all*.[4]

For the present, however, I am interested in a third aspect of Parfit's claim, namely, the idea that we have entered an era which will see the abandonment of ancient myth-bound conceptions and the adoption of new progressive styles of thinking. There is a marked similarity between this suggestion and the attitude of Paul Churchland to the relationship between traditional styles of psychological interpretation and the new philosophical-cum-scientific psychology which has only recently begun to develop but which he believes is fast making progress. According to Churchland the former involves the application of a primitive and ancient theory of 'folk psychology', while the latter constitutes a replacement of this by a systematic causal account rooted in an understanding of neuropsychology. He writes:

The [folk psychology] of the Greeks is essentially the same FP we use today, and we are negligibly better at explaining human behaviour in its terms than was Sophocles. This is a very long period of stagnation and infertility for any theory to display,

[3] See A. MacIntyre, *After Virtue* (London: Duckworth, 1981) who writes (at p. 51): 'Thus moral utterance has throughout the period in which the theistic version of classical morality predominates both a twofold point and purpose and a double standard. To say what someone ought to do is at one and the same time to say what course of action will in these circumstances as a matter of fact lead towards a man's true end and to say what the law, ordained by God and comprehended by reason, enjoins'.

[4] In fact I doubt that an unrestricted version of this claim is true, but a qualified one, perhaps no less significant in import might be established, namely *either religious ethics or no absolutist ethics*. See in this connection Peter Geach, 'The Moral Law and the Law of God' in Geach, *God and the Soul* (London: Rouledge & Kegan Paul, 1969); reprinted in Joram Graf Haber (ed.) *Absolutism and its Consequentialist Critics* (Lanham, Maryland: Rowman & Littlefield, 1994).

especially when faced with such an enormous backlog of anom-
alies and mysteries in its own explanatory domain.[5]

More recently, in his 1998 Royal Institute of Philosophy Lecture,
Thomas Nagel, who is otherwise far removed from the eliminative
materialism of Churchland and has in the past warned against 'scientism', expresses optimism about the possibility of solving the
mind-body problem, likening the present situation in respect of it
to that previously obtaining in the sciences with regard to the physical reality of such phenomena as sound. Whereas it would once
have made no sense to suggest that sound has a physical microstructure, theoretical progress has now made that claim generally intelligible. Likewise it might be expected that progress will bring us to a
point where it is intelligible to claim that experiences are physiolog-
ical states:

> Our problem [at present] is that there is no room for a necessary
> connection with physiology in the space of possible development
> defined by the [current] concept of mind. But that does not rule
> out the possibility of a successor concept of mind which will both
> preserve the central features of the original and be open to the
> discovery of such connections. This kind of thing happens all the
> time in the course of scientific history, as with the concepts of
> sound, or element, or species, or space, or number.[6]

Parfit, Churchland and (to a lesser degree) Nagel are three prominent examples of a common feature of contemporary philosophical

[5] Paul Churchland, 'Eliminative Materialism and the Propositional
Attitudes', *Journal of Philosophy*, **78**, 1981, 73-75. Needless to say I con-
test Churchland's account of ordinary psychological expalanation. For a
debate see Paul Churchland and John Haldane 'Folk Psychology and the
Explanation of Human Behaviour' *Aristotelian Society, Supplementary
Volume*, **62**, 1988 and Paul Churchland, 'Theory, Taxonomy and
Methodology: a reply to Haldane's *Understanding Folk*', and John
Haldane, 'Theory, Realism and Common Sense: a reply to Paul
Churchland' both in *Proceedings of the Aristotelian Society*, Vol. **93**, 1993.
The more general 'progessivist assumption' in philosophy of mind is ques-
tioned in John Haldane, 'The State and Fate of Contemporary Philosophy
of Mind' *American Philosophical Quarterly*, **37**, 2000.

[6] Thomas Nagel, 'Conceiving the Impossible and the Mind-Body
Problem', *Philosophy*, **73**, 1998, 343. Elsewhere Nagel writes that 'As we
judge the results [of a few great figures of the past] to be mistaken in fundamental ways, so we must assume that even the best efforts of our own
time will come to seem blind eventually' *The View from Nowhere* (Oxford:
Oxford University Press, 1986) 10. Even here, though, the progressivist
assumption is detectable.

thinking. The issues are central, the authors are eminent and the cast of mind is clear enough: after centuries of enquiry handicapped by outmoded styles of thought we are beginning to get somewhere, and if we take real care then we can reasonably hope for 'undeniable progress'. As I hinted earlier, the model is that of scientific research, which is to say of observation, conjecture and experiment leading (*pace* general scepticism) to discovery and understanding. Characteristically, J. J. C. Smart expresses the view with a directness that not all advocates of it would find comfortable. He writes:

> [M]etaphysical theories are further removed from control by experiment and observation than are typical scientific theories even though, as I think, this is a difference in degree rather than kind.[7]

Students of the history of philosophy, particularly of the pre-modern periods, aware and appreciative of models of enquiry other than the scientific ones are likely to be suspicious of this progressivist consensus. I share that doubt, but reflecting on it leads me to the conclusion that it is not so much that one side (let us call it the *literary humanist* tradition) is right and that the other (call it the *natural scientist* one) is wrong; but rather, and more radically, that there is simply no such thing as '*the* nature of philosophical enquiry'. I do not mean to suggest, in the spirit of an 'intellectual liberation movement', that conceptions of philosophy are ideologically motivated stereotypes intended to oppress the conceptually marginalized. What I have in mind is the idea that philosophy arises out of a number of different kinds of interest which are often deeply submerged but which show themselves from time to time in responses to such issues as the nature of philosophical knowledge and its place in relation to other forms of understanding. The claims of Parfit, Churchland and Nagel are characteristic of one kind of interest which, as it happens, is prominent if not pre-eminent today. In the wider world, however, it commands only limited attention and it will never eliminate other interests even within academic philosophy; but nor by the same token will it itself ever be eliminated. I shall return to these suggestions in the concluding section.

---

[7] J. J. C. Smart, 'Why Philosophers Disagree', *Canadian Journal of Philosophy*, Supplementary **19**, 1993, 81.

John Haldane

II. Twentieth Century Philosophy and the Differences it has made

In order to reach that point, however, I need to do a certain amount of survey work. The purpose of this is to get clearer about the kinds of understanding that philosophy seeks and can hope for, and in doing so to become clearer also about why the very idea of philosophical progress is problematic.

The question 'Has philosophy (in the twentieth century) made a difference?' is multiply indeterminate: philosophy in respect of some branch or as a totality? and a difference to whom? and in what respects? Likewise with the query 'can it be expected to?'. This is ambiguous between a question of what is likely to occur, and one of what it is reasonable to require. Disambiguating these meanings and exploring all possible permutations of them would provide too large an agenda, but I shall try to cover at least the main possibilities, beginning with philosophy's impact *beyond* philosophy. This has had two forms: philosophy as midwife to science and philosophy as counsel to agents.

(a) Philosophy as midwife to science

Examples of the former influence include the births of pharmacy, biology, music and astronomy, but the most recent major delivery is that of psychology. In the *De Anima* (and in the *Parva Naturalia*) Aristotle deals fairly systematically with conceptual questions about cognition, volition and emotion—topics which also feature in his ethical writings. The medievals followed the tradition of psychic anatomy and even when the change to more scientific and empirical approaches began it was initiated in the context of retranslation of and commentary upon Aristotle's work. So far as I am aware, the first occurrences of the term 'psychology' (*psychologia*) are to be found in the late sixteenth century in the writings of two Germans: Johannes Freigius and Rudolphus Goclenius both of whom devoted considerable attention to Aristotle's writings while nonetheless moving away from scholastic apriorism. Even by the nineteenth century, however, the link between psychological theory and Aristotelianism was still in place and it is worth recalling that Brentano's *Psychology from an Empirical Standpoint* was the work of a scholastically trained neo-Aristotelian. This was published in Leipzig in 1874, the same city in which five years later Wilhelm Wundt established the world's first laboratory of experimental psychology.

In Britain, Wundt's work impressed Alexander Bain who is often described as the founder of British psychology on the basis of his two volume treatise, *The Senses and the Intellect* (1855) and *The Emotions and the Will* (1859).[8] Whatever else, however, Bain was certainly a philosopher. He was a follower of Mill and of the Scottish empiricist tradition and held the Chair of Logic at Aberdeen from 1860 to 1880. While there he founded *Mind* which from its establishment in 1876 until 1974 bore the full title *Mind, A journal of Psychology and Philosophy*. In his diary Bain records that on 27 May 1889 he attended a meeting of the Aristotelian Society to hear a paper read by George Stout then a Fellow of St John's College, Cambridge on the subject of 'The development of the distinction between the Physical and the Mental, considered from the Psychological point of view'.[9] Three years later Stout, who was also an admirer of Wundt's work, became editor of *Mind*; and in 1896 he both published *Analytic Psychology* and was appointed to a newly instituted lectureship in comparative psychology at Aberdeen. In 1899 he was elected to the first Wilde Readership in Mental Philosophy at Oxford—an event of which C. A. Mace has written that 'by appointing him to the position the University admitted that psychology might be possible; and Stout, by producing the *Manual of Psychology* [in the same year] established its existence as a fact'.[10] In 1903 Stout moved to the Chair of Logic and Metaphysics at St Andrews where he also played an active part in psychological research. In 1929 Mace himself was appointed there to a new post in logic and psychology. He left St Andrews in 1933 and Stout retired from the University in 1936 by which point the subjects were growing apart. By the centenary of his birth in 1960 the separation was complete and Stout is remembered by members of two disciplines who are each generally ignorant of his role in the history of the other.

Similar accounts could be written for the other subjects I have mentioned, and among recently developed fields of study mathematical logic and theoretical linguistics are obviously indebted to philosophy for their existence. Some have wondered whether this repeating pattern of subject emergence means that philosophy is shedding what were hitherto parts of itself and is thereby diminishing in extent. One response might be to point to the possibility that as well as losing material philosophy is also gaining it as more

[8] See T. C. Flugel, *A Hundred Years of Psychology* (London: Duckworth, 1933) pp. 79–80. On Bain in general see R. C. Cross, 'Alexander Bain', *The Aristotelian Society, Supplementary Volume* **44**, 1970.

[9] C. A. Mace, 'George Frederick Stout' *Proceedings of the British Academy*, Vol. XXXI.

[10] C. A. Mace, 'George Frederick Stout', 5.

isues are brought under within its reach. It would, however, be more apt to say that philosophical enquiry leads to the conclusion that certain issues with which it has dealt also have a formerly unappreciated empirical dimension. In this way philosophy assists the birth of a subject without necessarily letting go of those aspects of the issues that are of enduring philosophical interest. Here the example of psychology is very much to the point. Aspects of Stout's enquiry into the relation of mind and body are now properly recognized to be the concern of empirical psychology but, the question of their metaphysical relationship remains, as it has always been, a philosophical issue. Indeed philosophy of mind has grown considerably in the period since the emergence of empirical psychology.

(b) Philosophy as counsel to agents.

In contrast to its role in giving birth to new academic sciences, the influence of philosophy in its office as a counsel to agents is more pervasive, and most extensive outside the academy. Historically, questions of personal and social conduct have generally been raised and answered in relation to the requirements of prudence and of various sorts of codes. In addition to overtly religious prescriptions drawn from scripture or fashioned by religious authorities, there have been two kinds of non- (or non-directly) religious codes. On the one hand, those which are role-specific: governing particular ranges of activity appropriate say to a soldier, a teacher, a doctor, or a merchant; and on the other, those which are more general, pertaining to class or social position: for example, those governing the feelings and behaviour of a gentleman, a lady, someone in service, and so on. I cannot argue the point here, but the case can be made that in the background and implicitly widely accepted stood one or more broad versions of religious natural law theory. By this latter I mean the view which holds a) that there are objective values and requirements, b) that these are universal, c) that they can be known by natural reason, and d) that they are promulgated by God (or by some 'Cosmic Principle') so as to be known, as in c) and/or through conscience.[11]

The wars, revolutions and economic and social changes of the twentieth century unsettled, and in many cases destroyed, the hitherto relatively stable roles and conditions to which these codes were

[11] For an attempt to survey natural law, its history and its bearing on contemporary issues see John Haldane, 'Natural Law and Ethical Pluralism' in R. Madsen and T. Strong (eds.) *Attitudes to Ethical Pluralism* (Princeton, NJ.: Princeton University Press, forthcoming).

tied. Thereby they contributed to their break-down—a process which is still, and almost visibly, continuing. Additionally, the decline of religious practice and belief, first among the intelligentsia and then, in trickle-down style, among ever larger groupings has undermined confidence in the possibility of reconstructing the familiar moral order on the basis of a shared theological view. Ironically, however, sufficient has remained of common moral consciousness for it to be have been felt that new technologies are giving rise to ever more ethical problems.

Into this breach has stepped secular philosophy. The process began as the difficulties were first registered and it has increased as they have been more widely recognized. One early contributor was Bertrand Russell who produced a long line of publications in moral and social thought including *Principles of Social Reconstruction* (US title *Why Men Fight*) (1916), *Marriage and Morals* (1929), *New Hopes for a Changing World* (1951), *Common Sense and Nuclear Warfare* (1959), *The Conquest of Happiness* (1961) and *Has Man a Future?* (1961). No other significant British philosophers of his generation made anything like the same scale of contribution, but in America John Dewey was active in trying to fashion a secular philosophy of life.

More influential and less episodic than such first-order interventions, however, was philosophy's donation of moral-theoretic concepts to the thinking of the educated classes. It would not be difficult to chart the increasing prominence across the twentieth century of utilitarianism, of social contractualism, of something like Kantian respect for autonomy, and of rights-based theorising, each appealed to singly and often severally in presentations of policy proposals and in justifications for action. I am not as yet thinking of the 'applied ethics' movement which is a branch of academic philosophy, but of the practice of non-philosophers of substituting claims about welfare and rights for appeals to codes or to the natural justice recognized by heaven.

Recognition of this undirected influence has also had an effect *within* philosophy as professionals have come to see the potential for normative theorizing. In this sphere motives have been somewhat mixed. First, there is the perception of the need for clear and focused reflection of the kind which trained thinkers are able to provide. Second, there is the recognition that engaging in normative moral and social philosophy is not at odds with maintaining the highest intellectual standards. Any doubts about this possibility were properly silenced by such major works as John Rawls's *A Theory of Justice* (1971), Robert Nozick's *Anarchy, State and*

John Haldane

Utopia (1974), Thomas Nagel's collection *Mortal Questions* (1979), and books and essays by the likes of Ronald Dworkin, Alasdair MacIntyre, Charles Taylor, Michael Walzer, and Bernard Williams. Third, there has been a growing sense that philosophy has a special responsibility to address moral questions. This was felt most extensively first of all in the United States because of pressing issues of civil rights, nuclear weapons and non-defensive wars; but it quickly spread to Europe and beyond. Of course, one might observe that it is simply obvious that philosophy has this responsibility, and that it holds not by reason of some external relation between the subject and society but because of the very nature of the discipline. After all, moral and political philosophy are ancient limbs of the subject. Even so, various influences had acted to obscure these truths: the effects of scepticism, of academic professionalism, and of a particular, and happily short-lived, metaphilosophical view to the effect that it is not the business of philosophy to judge good and bad, right and wrong, but only to analyse the logic of these concepts. Something of these inluences still operates but to a far lesser degree than thirty or forty years ago, as is evidenced by the enormous growth in the various branches of applied philosophy. This last brings me to a fourth and less creditable motive: the belief, increasingly evident to anyone in the field but especially to those dealing with academic employment and grant awards, that applied ethics offers jobs and funding—indeed, and ironically from a Socratic point of view, that it might even be a honey pot.

III. Philosophy's internal development

All of this noted, I now move on to the question of whether philosophy in the twentieth century has made any significant difference to the way in which traditional philosophical problems are conceived or to their resolution. In order to provide any answer we need to recall, if only briefly, the main lines of development since the start of the century and that in turn calls for a prefatory note.

There is an issue still unresolved in the history of philosophy about the origins of modern scepticism. One very important example is that of inductive scepticism rooted in the objection that ampliative inference based on observation is essentially fallible. Though I cannot pursue it far here, I believe that some of the standard accounts of the rise of inductive scepticism cannot be right since the same conditions that are pointed to in explanation of why it arose in the modern period actually obtained five hundred years previously. So, for example, the common suggestion that it arises from the experimentalism of modern science; or that it is due, as Ian Hacking proposed, to the development of the natural/conventional sign distinction and the rise of scepticism about causal necessity;[12] or again, as others have argued, that it is the consequence of nominalism, all fail to explain it, for each and all predate the relevant period. That is not to deny that all three touch upon significant intellectual developments, but they provide at most necessary and not sufficient conditions for the rise of Hume-style inductive scepticism. The further and most important fact is that Aristotle, and the medievals who followed him, had a view of epistemology that the moderns came to reject but which has surfaced again in the twentieth century in the writings of Quine. His pragmatic suggestion is that we reject the modern notion of epistemology as the general theory of warrant for belief, and treat it instead as an explanatory project: '... Cartesian doubt is not the way to begin. [For] [r]etaining our present beliefs about nature, we can still ask how we can have arrived at them'.[13] In doing this we, like the pre-moderns simply bypass the problem of how induction could justify a belief in natural regularities and examine instead how it is that our belief in regularities might be accounted for in a theory of nature.[14]

The fact remains, however, that scepticism about induction, about outer and inner perception, about substance, causality and identity are brought together by Hume in a way that devastated naive realism. The two reactions to this—the Prussian and Scottish ones, of Kant and Thomas Reid, respectively—are often contrasted in terms of the first being transcendentalist and the second naturalistic, or in terms of the first resting on claims about what is antecedent to experience and hence *a priori*, and the second taking the form of an analysis of experience in defence of the *a posteriori*. However, a rather different account of these reactions supports the idea that each lead by stages and in the hands of successor philoso-

---

[12] See Ian Hacking, *The Emergence of Probability* (Cambridge: Cambridge University Press, 1975).
[13] See W. V. O. Quine, 'The Nature of Natural Knowledge' in S. Guttenplan (ed.), *Mind and Language* (Oxford, 1975). For Quine's view of the bearing of naturalized epistemology upon the problem of induction see his 'Natural Kinds' in N. Rescher (ed.), *Essays in Honour of Carl G. Hempel* (Dordrecht: Reidel, 1970).
[14] For an extended version of this account of the origins of inductive scepticism see John Haldane, 'Insight, Inference and Intellection' in M. Baur (ed.) *Insight and Inference: Proceedings of the American Catholic Philosophical Association*, **73**, 1999.

John Haldane

phers to versions of a common philosophy, *viz*. idealism. The fate of Kantianism in this respect is well known through the work of Hegel and others. Kant having left reality as-it-in-itself as something that cannot be a direct object of knowledge, it is unsurprising that the next generation came to the view that it therefore has no working role in the scheme of knowledge or of discussable metaphysics and may as well be dropped from them.

The fate of the Scottish Common Sense tradition is less well known and deserves to be more widely studied. Reid and his followers asserted, somewhat in the manner of medieval explanatory epistemology, that God or nature had so ordained things that causal interaction with the environment, in the form of sensation, immediately and non-inferentially gives rise to conceptions, perceptions, and beliefs concerning the world. Thomas Reid actually spoke of this as occurring 'by a natural kind of magic'.[15] It did not take long for someone to wonder whether this response to scepticism was not question-begging, or void given the possibility that the presumed connections might not in fact obtain and we would be none the wiser for it. That 'someone' was James Frederick Ferrier of St Andrews, author of the very term 'epistemology'. His solution was to substitute logically or conceptually necessary connections for causal and contingent links between subject, thought, experience, and world. In other words for Ferrier the only adequate solution to Humean scepticism is to insist that there is no gap between cognition and reality *because they are in fact one*. There is no mind-independent world. Subject and object, self and other are all aspects of the Absolute. The shadow of Hegel falls across every page of Ferrier's work serving to confirm the claim that the end point of the Prussian and Scottish reactions to Hume was the same: *idealism*.[16]

The thought that epistemology, metaphysics and logic might point in the direction of the transcendent, and even better that reality might be 'absolute spirit' was of great comfort to the intellectual classes of the middle and late nineteenth century. These troubled souls were struggling to hang on to notions of spirit and transcendence in the face of empiricism, natural science and revisionary biblical scholarship, and finding traditional Christian theology

[15] Thomas Reid, *Inquiry and Esays* (eds.) R. E. Beanblossom & K. Lehrer (Indianapolis: Hackett, 1983), *An Inquiry*: ch. 5 (*Of Touch*), section III (*Of Natuiral Signs*) pp. 43–44.
[16] See *The Philosophical Works of the late James Frederick Ferrier* (ed.) Sir Alexander Grant and E.L. Lushington (Edinburgh: Blackwood, 1975) in three volumes—shortly to be republished by Thoemmes of Bristol. Of particular interest is the *Institutes of Metaphysics* (Vol. I).

increasingly difficult to believe. Apart from providing a support (or a substitute) for Judaeo-Christianity, idealism was found on the European Continent to be particularly congenial to aesthetic interests; while in Britain it was taken to support a politics of the common good. After all, if you and I are really aspects of the one reality then the classic problem of moving from prudence to altruism cannot arise: your good *is* my good, and vice versa.[17]

While sharing appreciations of the value of the arts and of politics, Moore and Russell came to find the epistemology and metaphysics of idealism to be repugnant, and the favoured arguments for them to be presumptuous or fallacious. By careful analysis they dismantled these, for example by showing that the claim then commonly advanced by idealists such as Bradley that all relations are internal and that relata are not really distinct existences but aspects or modes of the one, is an avoidable artefact of the ways in which things are described.[18] Thus arose Cambridge analytical philosophy: (1) Moore's defence of common sense against the sceptics, thereby denying those who accepted the initial sceptical conclusion a ground for supposing that knowledge could only be re-established on an idealist basis; (2) Russell's logical analyses deployed effectively against Idealists and Platonists; and (3) Wittgenstein's exposure of logical form and later of 'grammar', collectively established a model of rigorous and effective elimination of ill-founded philosophies.

In considering these achievements and asking whether they constitute an enduring contribution—whether in that sense they have 'made a difference'—it is necessary to distinguish between methodological and substantive progress. The analytical tradition tended to have certain assumptions associated with it, including some form of distinction between the conceptual and the empirical, or between questions of meaning and of mind-independent fact. Upon reflection this distinction suggests a division of theoretical labour between the philosopher and the natural scientist, for any problem will either be clarified without residue by conceptual analysis, or any non-conceptual residue will be handed to the scientist for study.

[17] For an interesting discussion of the relation between idealist metaphysics, social philosophy and politics see Andrew Vincent and Raymond Plant, *Philosophy, Politics and Citizenship, The Life and Thought of the British Idealists* (Oxford: Blackwell, 1984).

[18] See G. E. Moore, 'The Refutation of Idealism', *Mind*, **12**, 1903, and 'External and Internal Relations', Proceedings of the Aristotelian Society, 19, 1919–20; both reprinted in *Philosophical Studies*, (London: Routledge & Kegan Paul, 1970).

John Haldane

Generalizing and simplifying, one can see in this the possibility of a covert eliminativist-cum-scientistic programme, which also implies the foreseeable end of philosophy. Contrary to the logic of its analytical methodology, however, philosophy in the twentieth century has largely gone the other way. In particular ethics and metaphysics are institutionally stronger now than in the earlier part of the century.

Here it may be worth referring to some work done by Nicholas Rescher using the *Philosophers Index* as a measure of publication in all fields recognized by the profession.[19] As founding editor of the *American Philosophical Quarterly*, the *History of Philosophy Quarterly*, and *Public Affairs Quarterly* and as the most widely published senior philosopher in the English-speaking world, Rescher has an unparalleled claim to be in a position to assess and evaluate trends in the subject. Following upon a number of essays in which he has discussed some of these developments, he recently looked at the headline topics in the *Index* for 1998 and counted by column the number of publication entries under each. From this, together with sampling of actual publications, he arrived at certain conclusions about the standing of several areas of philosophy and contrasting approaches. The number of recorded columns for the listings under various headline topics (wherever there were at least four columns), and the consequent ranking, is as follows:[20]

1. Ethics	32		11. Education	9
2. Metaphysics	24		12. Knowledge	8
3. Science	16		13. God	7
4. Logic	14		13. History	7
4. Religion	14		15. Aesthetics	6
6. Epistemology	13		16. Culture	5
6. Philosophy	13		17. Feminism	4
8. Social Philosophy	12		17. Politics	4
9. Political Philosophy	11		17. Reason	4
10. Language	10		17. Truth	4

[19] Nicholas Rescher, 'Who has Won the Big Battles of Twentieth-Century Philosophy?', *American Philosophical Quarterly*, **36**, 1999.

[20] Rescher orders the information alphabetically by headline topic and includes headings where there was at least one column of entries. There is more work to be done on the staistics available by consulting *The Philosopher's Index* (Bowling Green, OH.: Philosopher's Infornmation Center).

The ranking of philosophers by number of entries naming them in titles is as follows

1. Heidegger	153	4. Quine	48
2. Nietzsche	123	5. Russell	36
3. Derrida	55	6. Strawson	28.

Summarizing, the situation at the end of the century, as indicated by professional academic publication (mostly but not exclusively in the English-speaking world) is that traditional speculative and practical philosophy seem to be doing well, while positivism and cultural theory are lagging far behind. Of course any such verdict is open to contest on a variety of grounds, including the choice of topic headings and the selection of journals and publishers included in the *Index*. But it is *a* measure and I know of no other easily available that might be better.

The reasons that analytical philosophy (broadly construed) has not eliminated itself in favour of science are in fact not hard to find, and once pointed out are likely to be acknowledged.[21] First, the result of analysis is typically to show that there is more of philosophical substance and difficulty in an issue and not less than was initially supposed. Second, the process of isolating the core philosophical elements of an issue tends to have the effect of conserving and not of dissolving them. Third, progressive refinement in the formulation of a thesis generally serves to eliminate weaker and partial versions in favour of stronger, purer variants. Witness, for example, the situation in the philosophy of mind in which the result of half a century's work has not been to exclude most positions but to produce clearer and more robust versions of each.

Reflecting on the question of why philosophers disagree J. J. C. Smart is concerned to avoid the conclusion that the last century of extensive professional activity has achieved no advance. He writes:

> Despite intractable disagreements there does seem to be progress in philosophy. If we look at a copy of *Mind* or *The Journal of Philosophy* and compare it with one of a hundred, or fifty, or perhaps only twenty five years ago, we may sense a general increase in technique, sophistication and clarity, though not always in literary elegance or in aversion to fence sitting. ... There is also wide-spread agreement on some meta-issues; for example, that

---

[21] Here I am also drawing on Rescher's essay 'The Rise and Fall of Analytic Philosophy' in N. Rescher, *American Philosophy Today and Other Philosophical Studies* (Lanham, Maryland: Rowman & Littlefield, 1994).

John Haldane

various influential arguments by eminent philosophers of the past do not by today's lights look sound, even though there may still be controversy about the theses that these arguments were meant to establish.[22]

I agree with Smart about the increased professionalism of academic philosophy, but I think he overestimates the extent of substantive agreement even at the metaphilosophical level by concentrating on the main English-language tradition of which he is a notable member, and failing to attend to, or choosing to set aside as marginal, the work of those labouring in other traditions. Furthermore, there can be little doubt that younger generations of analytical philosophers have begun to look to other schools in search of inspiration, and in doing so have become less confident that arguments by eminent philosophers of the past may be set aside as unsound. Witness in this connection recent moves among hitherto analytical philosophers to embrace, for example, ideas of Vico, Hegel, Nietzsche, and movements such as Neo-Platonism and Thomism.

Philosophy can claim to have progressed with regard to its methodology. The imperatives of maximum explicitness, of sustained clarification, and of argumentative rigour have all been widely adopted, and they now characterize work across the full range of issues and approaches. In trying to account for why, this fact notwithstanding, philosophy has not solved its traditional problems—and *pace* Parfit, Churchland and Nagel, offers no obvious prospect of doing so—one may have recourse to a number of explanations, several of which are adverted to by Rescher and Smart in the articles I have cited. These include such ideas as that when a philosophical problem gets solved it ceases to be regarded as being (or even as having been) a philosophical issue. Again, it is suggested (usually under Kantian influence) that philosophical problems arise from antinomies in our conceptual schemes and hence cannot be solved from within them but only avoided by adopting other ways of thinking. To these may be added the thought that if philosophy seems to proceed in a circular movement that is not of itself incompatible with progress; for it may yet be spiralling upwards and returning periodically not to exactly the same positions but to ones in alignment with them at successively higher levels. I leave it to readers to test the plausibility of this last suggestion by reference to issues that especially interest them. For my own part, however, I can easily think of examples from the philosophies of mind and lan-

[22] Smart, op. cit., p. 82.

guage, the metaphysics of substance, identity and causation, and the theory of value, where this seems precisely to be the situation.

IV. Philosophy's uncertain identity

Relevant as these points may be, they do not get to the depths of the question of the intractability of philosophical differences and of the possibility of progress. In conclusion, therefore, I wish to offer a more radical answer—giving determinate shape to the suggestion made earlier that there is no such thing as *the* nature of philosophical enquiry. This was suggested to me by thinking about the account given by Anthony Kenny of the world of Western philosophy around the year 1960. He writes:

> You could represent the overall position by taking a square and dividing it into four quadrants [as follows]:[23]

EXISTENTIALISM	ANALYTIC PHILOSOPHY
MARXISM	SCHOLASTICISM

He then goes on to point out that the locations within the square represent features in respect of which the philosophies resemble or differ from one another: those in the top half share a concern for individual intellectual and moral autonomy, those in the bottom half are associated with doctrinal ideologies; those on the right-hand side are interested in abstract theory and logic; those on the left are characterized by practical commitments to the basic features of

[23] Anthony Kenny, *The Oxford Illustrated History of Western Philosophy* (Oxford: Oxford University Press, 1995) 363–4.

human experience. Kenny's observations in regard to these philosophies and his general purpose in identifying them are purely
descriptive, and he goes on to say how around the 1960s they 'began
to crumble, fissure, and shift' thereby leading to a more diverse and
less ideological state of affairs.

What I am struck by, however, is the thought that these four historical movements are but particular, cultural expressions of permanent and ineliminable possibilities for philosophy, and that
current differences about the proper role and possibilities for the
subject reflect attachments to these deeper forms or paradigms.
Consider then the following alternative diagram:

PHILOSOPHY AS ART	PHILOSOPHY AS SCIENCE
PHILOSOPHY AS POLITICS	PHILOSOPHY AS RELIGION

The styles of presentation adopted by these broad approaches and
the particular doctrines advanced by proponents of them are likely
to admit of a fair degree of contingency. By contrast, their objects
or dominant ends and their governing values are much closer to
defining them. These 'objects' are, in clockwise rotation: *beauty*,
nature, *god* and *justice*. Here I shall not even begin to explore these,
but only note that each concept is highly abstract, and admits of
many conceptions and near equivalents.

In commending this broad analysis for further reflection, however,
I suggest that it enables us to understand certain recurrent features of
philosophical activity, the diversity of its forms and interests, and the
fact of disagreement about its goals. Consider, for example, that
whereas under the scientific conception it makes sense to suppose that

so far as knowledge is concerned the latest thought may well be the best, this assumption is dubious in relation to artistic or political conceptions. The reason lies in the differences between activities that are directed towards describing causal, compositional or logical structures, and those that are concerned with understanding or expressing aesthetic and practical values. Whereas the first deal with orders of being that are invariant with regard to human purposes and interests, the second engage attempts to make sense of human existence and to transform it. These latter are inevitably highly contextual: responding to disasters and triumphs and seeking to reject, endorse or develop prior forms of thought and action.

Consider also that the analogy with science serves to explain the cluster of concerns with rigour, sytematicity, theoretical grounding and explanatory power that are dominant within certain circles. Advocates of this conception of philosophy tend not to be especially concerned with embodying the subject in broad social practices and institutions, whereas this is characteristic of those practising philosophy as something akin to politics. Similarly, while practitioners of the scientific conception rarely express interest in the pursuit of personal wisdom, the meaning of life or the possibilities of transcendence, concerns with these ends are to be found in the work of other philosophers who are practising reflection in a broadly religious mode.

It is to be expected that in various times and places one or more of these conceptions may dominate to the near exclusion of others but no final victory can be expected since each answers to something too deep to be uprooted or eradicated. Since the human condition itself, in its most fundamental respects, is a kind of perpetual mystery in which we oscillate between permanent possibilities of understanding it, the idea of pursuing philosophical enquiry according to a single transcendentally preferred form is a false ambition. Likewise, while every enquiry and practice must see itself as directed towards its goal, and thereby envisage the possibility of advancing towards it, the notion of making 'undeniable progress' in terms of a transcendentally preferred form is an intellectual illusion. Equally, it is a mistake to suppose that religious ethics is something that philosophy has left behind in its mythic past and which cannot now be expected to make a significant contribution. Indeed, one of the most powerful calls of recent times to the practice of philosophy has come precisely from a religious source. The author writes as follows:

> One of the most significant aspects of our current situation, it should be noted, is the "crisis of meaning". Perspectives on life

John Haldane

and the world, often of a scientific temper, have so proliferated that we face an interesting fragmentation of knowledge. ...

... [P]hilosophy needs first of all to recover its sapiential dimension as a search for the ultimate and overarching meaning of life.[24]

The writer is, as it happens, a philosopher of phenomenological and neo-Aristotelian orientations, *viz.* Karol Wojtyla, and the text is *Fides et Ratio*.

---

[24] John Paul II, *Faith and Reason* (London: Catholic Truth Society, 1998) Ch. VII, section 81, p. 119. For some discussion of the encyclical relating it to secular philosophical concerns see John Haldane 'The Diversity of Philosophy and the Unity of its Vocation' in R. McInerny (ed.) *Faith and Reason* (Southbend, IN: St Augustine's Press, 2001).

Prospects for Beauty

ANTHONY O'HEAR

Ruskin said 'Great nations write their autobiographies in three manuscripts, the book of their deeds, the book of their words and the book of their art. Nor one of these books can be understood unless we read the two others, but of the three the only trustworthy one is the last.'

Kenneth Clark, who quoted these words at the beginning of his television series *Civilisation*, adds that 'writers and politicians may come out with all sorts of edifying sentiments, but they are what is known as declarations of intent. If I had to say which was talking the truth about society, a speech by a Minister of Housing or the actual buildings put up in his time, I should believe the buildings.'[1]

Well, his time, the time when he wrote those words was 1968–9. And we all know what the judgment of the year 2000 is of the buildings of the 1960's. What, though, of us, now? What do we read in the book of our art?

We read the blank opacity of the Millennium Dome, the sheer perversity of the V & A extension; and the squalor of Tracey Emin's life and bed; we read Chris Ofili's '*Madonna*' surrounded with elephant dung; we read the scatology of Gilbert and George, the filth of Irving Welsh and Will Self, and the adolescent outpourings of Salman Rushdie; in music, we read the pretentious cacophony of Sir Harrison Birtwhistle, in dance the confrontational spirit of much modern choreography and in the theatre, all manner of cruelty and perversion not elevated or redeemed, but gloried in. And these are only the 'highbrow', publicly lauded and often publicly funded examples. Go lower, go into popular taste, and you will find the unrelieved indignity and coarseness of EastEnders and Grange Hill (the very programmes highlighted by the BBC's new Director-General in launching his new crusade for education); we find pop videos and pop music characterized by crudity, pornographic suggestivity and lack of musicality; and far from any rediscovery of a vernacular architecture in either homes or shops, we find mass produced designs and items assembled without thought or sensitivity to place or history.

The above collection is a very mixed bag. But they do have one thing in common, I think. None could be described as aiming at, or

[1] Kenneth Clark, *Civilisation* (1969) in the Penguin Edition (1982), pp. 17–18.

at reaching the beautiful. Indeed, to raise the question of beauty in connection with them would be to miss their point, to criticize them from the wrong point of view. They are aiming at other things, and at things which, by and large, are incompatible with beauty.

To other ages than ours this would have seemed a strange, if not remarkable state of affairs. Art might be about lots of things, but one thing it is certainly about is beauty, at least if not all art, most art, most of the time. This, at any rate is an intuitive pre-reflective thought and a thought which might seem to have some connection or resonance with the experience of the Parthenon or the *Odes* of Horace or St Mark's in Venice or Chartres Cathedral or Botticelli's *Primavera* or Vermeer's *View of Delft* or Shakespeare's *Hamlet* or Mozart's *G minor symphony* (K550) or Constable's *Hadleigh Castle* Schumann's *Dichterliebe* or Renoir's *Boating Party*.

Of course, none of these works is the same or directly aiming at the same sort of thing. But in relation to each them the following words might be appropriately uttered

> What a piece of work is man! How noble in reason! How infinite in faculty! In form, in moving, how express and admirable! In action how like an angel! In apprehension how like a god! The beauty of the world! The paragon of animals!

Hamlet goes on

> And yet, to me, what is this quintessence of dust? Man delights me not; no nor woman neither, though by your smiling you seem to say so.

As a culture, are we stuck in Hamlet's slough of disgust? Do we even remember that there were once moments in our history when we might have believed in the nobility of man and in the potential of his works to uplift, and in which this sense of beauty might have transformed our attitude to the natural world and to fate itself?

I am aware of the very unphilosophical nature of these remarks, prejudices some might think them. So let us turn to philosophy to see if we might find help there. However three fairly representative philosophical quotations suggest that this might be something of a blind alley:

> Despite its ancient aura as one of the supreme values in human life and in the cosmos some philosophers give beauty short shrift.[2]

[2] Christopher Janaway, in 'Beauty' in *The Oxford Companion to Philosophy* (Oxford University Press, 1995), p. 80.

Beauty is a topic of great philosophical interest and one that is relatively unexplored. Few would deny its importance and yet the mere suggestion that it be defined drives intelligent people to witless babble.[3]

Until the eighteenth century, beauty was the single most important idea in the history of aesthetics ... (but as a consequence of the modern notion of fine art) beauty lost its traditional centrality in aesthetic theory and has never since regained it.[4]

There is a good justifiable reason for this sidelining of beauty in philosophical discourse. It is the Austinian point that describing a work of art or part of nature as beautiful is, in one sense, rather unhelpful. It doesn't point to any precise aspect of a work, and can often be little more than empty gushing (as critics of beauty would have it, not entirely unfairly).

Moreover, as Stolnitz points out, for some, beauty has become a rather narrow concept, denoting 'pleasure unmixed with pain and the absence of bizarre or discordant elements'. Excluding the sublime and much else, beauty then becomes irrelevant for the evaluation of many admired works of art, maybe even the tragic, and certainly the challenging, as happened when Plato, in his *Philebus* analysed beauty in terms of measure and proportion (64a) and excluded the tragic as a 'mixed' pleasure (50b).

On the other hand if, as Janaway suggests, beauty is to serve as a catch-all for absolutely any positive value a work of art can have, 'then beauty really becomes a vacuous ideas for philosophical purposes'.

Against the narrow 'unchallenging' interpretation of beauty, I would simply set Rilke's lines

For Beauty's nothing
But beginning of Terror we're just still able to bear,
And why we adore it so is because it serenely
Disdains to destroy us. (*First Duino Elegy, lines 4–7*)

Beauty, at least in the sense I want to discuss it, is not a kind of superior prettiness. It can co-exist with discordant and disproportionate elements and even with intimations of terror. It can, as in Homer and in Aeschylean tragedy, co-exist with the absence of pity

---

[3] Mary Motershill, in 'Beauty' in *A Companion to Aesthetics* (Blackwell: Oxford, 1992), p. 44.

[4] Jerome Stolnitz, in 'Beauty' in *The Encyclopedia of Philosophy* (Macmillan Publishers: New York, 1967), Vol. I, p. 262.

Anthony O'Hear

and the presence of an implacable fate before which we are crushed, and in the face of which the hero sinks to sleep, but not in shame.

Does this, though, mean that in my scheme of things anything can be beautiful? Or that beauty is simply the name given to any aesthetic quality? These two interpretations of the beautiful are not, of course, the same. It may be that anything can be made to look beautiful. Certainly we are familiar with the way in which a Chardin or a Morandi can invest the most commonplace, and even untidy of things with a timeless beauty, a half eaten fish on a dinner plate or an old jar, for example. Could somebody find beauty in a scene of rape or murder? Here again we have to distinguish: between finding a bit of the scene beautiful (for example, a drop of red blood on a carpet of green grass), and finding the scene itself beautiful. The latter, which cannot be ruled out *a priori*, cannot be ruled out *a posteriori* either—at least not for a culture for whom tragedy is a high point of its art, and for whom the crucifixion is its central religious image. From the crucifixion, down to a beggar's lameness, all the tortures and maladies of man were to be made, at least in part, the subjects of art. The point seems to be that while any subject may become beautiful, it all depends on the way it is treated. I suppose that Titian's *Tarquin and Lucretia* does not glorify the murder and for all its energy has some of the poise and pathos and rightness of judgment of tragedy. But there is also the morally questionable possibility of making the intolerable tolerable through beautifying it, or perhaps more common, of simply reducing its significance through making it into a work of art. I am not just thinking of crass entertainment, like the Titanic film here: although it has been tried—by Kenneth MacMillan among others—I would express profound reservations about making a ballet about a rape or a concentration camp. The very combination of beautiful bodies and horrific scenes is bound to be deeply problematic.

While the extent of beautiful subject matter may be unlimited, it is not the case that any evaluation on aesthetic grounds signifies the presence of beauty. After all, ugliness is an aesthetic quality, the opposite of the beautiful. And so are types of dreariness, ungainliness, clumsiness, barbarity, discordance, terror, aggression, sentimentality, exaggeration, irony and grotesquerie. The presence of any of these features in a work of art will militate against its being beautiful, and unless balanced by more positive qualities, may even make it impossible.

It is not my view that any work of art is beautiful. I have already given plenty of examples of works which are not beautiful, and it is not part of my thesis that every work of art ought to be beautiful or

178

to be aiming at beauty. After all, if *Eine Kleine Nachtmusik* (K525) is a work of art, so is its purported companion piece, *Ein Musikalischer Spaß* (K522) and for its purpose, a jolly good one too, described by Alfred Einstein as the negative key to Mozart's whole aesthetic. And indeed over the last couple of centuries many artists have attempted to produce works which are anything but beautiful, precisely in response to various horrors and disasters, and also in an attempt to portray the inhumanity and ignobility of man. One thinks of some of the works of Goya and of Picasso, of Otto Dix, of Georg Grosz, of Leon Golub, of Philip Guston and of Francis Bacon, to take only examples from the visual arts.

I am not claiming that Goya's *Execution of Third of May* or Picasso's *Guernica* are not considerable works of art. My claim is rather that the repudiation in these works of the beautiful, the refusal in them to gothicize or to prettify is part of what constitutes their power (though prettyfying the ugly is not a temptation to which Goya was always immune). If you look at a deliberately unbeautiful work of art, you will begin to see that beauty is associated with such qualities as nobility, grace, balance, harmony, dignity, humanity, sympathy. ... Not with all of them always and at all times, but overall with what might be called positive and uplifting qualities, rather than with their opposites. It is this positivity of beauty which explains its most obvious, but often un-or under-remarked feature: namely that something or someone beautiful is, for that reason and at least to that extent, attractive. Beauty attracts, but not in any way, because things which are not beautiful can also attract. Beauty attracts in such a way as to inspire love (in Mary Mothersill's helpful phrase) as opposed to the ghoulish fascination or delightful horror evoked by works which glorify violence or are complicit with perversity.

In saying that beauty attracts and that it is a life-enhancing quality, I do not mean to deny the classical Kantian analysis. Three points from it stand out. The favourable aesthetic judgment—of which the judgment that something is beautiful is the central example—will be disinterested, universal and noncognitive.

To take disinterestedness first. What this amounts to is that in admiring something for its beauty, one is admiring it for what it is, in itself, and not for some other purpose the object might serve. It thus enables us to discriminate between two possible responses to a work of art on the part of its owner, say. The work might be admired aesthetically, but it might also be admired because of what it is worth, or because of the kudos its possession brings. This is obvious enough, but the disinterestedness of the aesthetic also means that in admiring a work's beauty, one is abstracting from the way it might be used for purposes other than simply being admired for what it is.

The purity of Kant's position might seem to be compromised by the distinction he draws between free and dependent beauty. Free beauty is when a beautiful object is admired simply for its form. (Kant's example is a flower, as judged beautiful by a non-botanist: non-botanists have no idea what its function is, or what the functions of its parts are, so if we admire it, we admire it simply for its form, its sheer appearance). But in addition to purely formal beauty of this sort, we can also find things beautiful because they appear as precisely adapted to their purpose: that is dependent beauty.

So, in admiring a horse or a church because it looks just like a horse or a church ought to look are we admitting a compromising kind of interest in our assessment of its beauty? The answer to this question is surely that we can still admire the church or the horse for what it is, and for its beautiful appropriateness to what it is, quite irrespective of any other way the object might be useful or relevant to other interests or purposes one might have in regard to that thing. For example, even if my horse had just been defeated by Desert Orchid, say, I could still expatiate on Dessie's beauty (as in sport people often do even in defeat).

The admission by Kant of a class of dependent beauty rescues his aesthetics from which might otherwise be a rather sterile formalism, verging on a doctrine of art for art's sake. For, in recognizing dependent beauty as a genuine type of beauty, it means that in making aesthetic judgments we are not barred from taking into account more than the pure form of the object. We can appeal to considerations drawn from the moral, the teleological and the human more generally. Thus, I might admire the technical and formal qualities of a Kokoschka portrait or a Bacon coupling but be disturbed by the lack of any humanly elevating quality in it; or, to take Kant's own example we might find the adornment of the human body with tattoos of spirals and straight lines unpleasing because it was on the figure of a man.

Nevertheless, although the disinterestedness of beauty does not imply a purely formal attitude to the beautiful, it does mean that in being attracted to something for its beauty we are admiring it for what it is in itself and not because it might be expensive or a good piece of propaganda or a brilliant expression of my current state of my mind or a release from some overwhelming sense of guilt or, as much current pop music, a stimulus to sexual license and drug-taking.

The beautiful is also universal. By this Kant means that in judging something to be beautiful we are presupposing that anyone who looks at the object with sufficient care, knowledge and attention will come to the same conclusion. The aesthetic judgment is thus, in Kant's eyes, to be distinguished from a mere preference of taste. Beauty matters, and in our pre-philosophic frame of mind, before we are introduced to the fashionable relativism of the age, we all know this. That is to say, we understand the difference between a preference for dark over milk chocolate—mere taste—and the judgment that almost anything by Beethoven is a superior piece of music to almost anything written by Lord Lloyd Webber or sung by Sir Elton John. This judgment also raises the possibility that it or we or someone else might be mistaken in making it. But these are judgments which can be defended, argued about and justified or criticized in terms of salient features of the works in question: their complexity, musical skill, timeless appeal, intellectual interest, emotional depth, human resonance, and so on.

After disinterestedness and universality, we come to non-cognitiveness. Two connected features of the Kantian analysis here are that these judgments cannot be explicated in terms of general principles, and also that the making of them requires personal acquaintance with the work or works in question. That is to say, there is no rule which could determine whether something is beautiful in advance of the appreciation of the precise character of the work, and we will be in a position to make or defend a judgment of aesthetic quality only when we have actually seen or heard the work. I imagine that most artists and art-lovers would agree with both these points, which taken together constitute the Kantian claim that aesthetic judgments are non-cognitive (or at least the acceptable aspect of that claim); that is, they cannot be justified by appeal to any general rule of principle applied independently of the experience of this particular work of art.

For example, one might judge, as Ruskin did, that in a Veronese painting what would in other hands be a mass of 'trivial or even ludicrous detail' in no way detracts from the nobleness of the whole. (Ruskin was writing of *The Presentation of the Queen of Sheba* in Turin, but the same point could be made of *The Family of Darius Before Alexander* in London, and of many other of Veronese's great set pieces).

But what would be the amount of detail that would have been trivial and ludicrous, even in Veronese's hands? What is it about the composition of a Veronese set piece which preserves balance in the midst of the sort of detail which, in the hands of a Frith, say, might have rendered the painting wholly ununified, in the unpainterly sense a mere narrative, hardly more than a piece of photographic reportage?

There is no general answer to these questions, and the only recourse to the critic is an appeal to precise aspects of the composition of *Derby Day* and how they cumulate in a particular experience, as opposed to *The Presentation of the Queen of Sheba*.

I will leave aside the other aspect of Kant's non-cognitivism, the thought that aesthetic judgment 'can be no other than subjective'; I suspect that the implication here that aesthetic judgments are not true or false but merely a part of a subjective reaction arises from Kant's recognition of the non-generalizable nature of aesthetic judgments together with the way that they have to be based in experience. Taken with the belief that only scientific (i.e. measurable and generalizable) judgments can properly be seen as true (or false), aesthetic judgments would then indeed turn out to be neither true nor false. But we need not accede to this implication of the Kantian analysis, which its basic tenets do not, in any case, require. We can simply take from Kant the thought that aesthetic judgments are universal in intent, are disinterested and need to be based on personal direct experience. Taking these claims together will help us to understand why so much contemporary art is not beautiful, and could not be, at least as long as it follows the professed intent of those who create and appreciate it.

As a way into my theme here, I cannot do better than refer to some things Arthur Danto says in a recent essay on the Jewish Museum in New York, entitled '*Post-modern Art and Concrete Selves*'.[5] In this essay Danto is discussing whether there could or should be a museum specifically of Jewish art. In an earlier incarnation that museum had adopted what Danto calls a purist attitude to its art: the art exhibited was by Jewish artists (such as Ad Reinhardt and Philip Guston); there was, as Danto says, nothing particularly Jewish about the art: a pride, no doubt that Jews were up there with the Pollocks and the de Koonings, but the art exhibited could have been exhibited anywhere at that time.

This all changed in the late 1960's. At that time the museum's trustees began to insist on the art exhibited being specifically Jewish in some sense. Now, while art which reflected a particularly Jewish experience could be universal (just as, perhaps, Spinoza's philosophy) by the time Danto came to write his essay in 1993, this was no longer what was wanted. What was wanted were works which, in a

[5] in Arthur C Danto's *Philosophizing Art* (University of California Press: Berkeley and Los Angeles, 1999), pp. 123–43.

way, remained enclosed in their Jewishness, and which would not reach out to or interest non-Jews, except as examples of ethnography.

Connecting what had happened to moral and political philosophy post-Rawls and post-Kant (when pretensions to a universal value system had also been given up and also to education, with the growth of women's studies, black studies, working-class studies, Chicago studies, where the work reinforces identities, bringing them more and more into consciousness), Danto says this of the art exhibited in the Jewish museum in the 1990's:

> Their conception of art is very much one of interestedness, and is not at all universal. The art, like the museum, speaks in a special way to the group whose art and museum it is. To experience the art is from the start to have an interest … (an) interest that has as its object the furtherance of the group to which one belongs. The art is there for the sake of that interest.

And, most revealing from my point of view,

> It follows that, from this perspective, the primary concern of art (not the art, notice) is not that it be beautiful—or in any case—its being so is secondary. It follows further that artistic experience is not aesthetic either: it is instead political and instrumental … Needless to say, the art made present to the visitors related to it through interest need not be great art by universal criteria at all.[6]

Danto goes on to comment about the similarly separatist Museum of Women's Art in Washington D.C.: 'critics sometimes noted that the work was not always of the highest quality'.[7] But, as he says, to make a judgment of this sort or at least to regard it as in any way damning or negative is to miss the point: it is to impose an irrelevant conception of art on the art it contains. For this art—be it Jewish, Women's, American/Indian, homosexual or whatever—is precisely not trying to be universal and it is certainly not trying to be disinterested. On the contrary, its whole point is the furtherance of the group to which one belongs.

So, in so far as universality and disinterestedness are part of the conditions of being beautiful, it is hardly surprising if it is mostly not beautiful, or if it is beautiful, it is beautiful only *per accidens*, as it were, through looking at and judging the work against criteria its creators might well reject.

[6] ibid., p. 134.
[7] ibid., p. 135.

Anthony O'Hear

Indeed, far from merely being interested, as opposed to disinterested, for Danto whole swathes of contemporary art are what in another article ('Bad Aesthetic Times in the USA?'[8]) he calls 'disturbational'. That is to say, it is art which is not just interested and particular, but which intentionally transgresses the aesthetic distance which makes disinterested contemplation possible:

> My concept of disturbation is derived from its natural English rhyme, where images have physical consequences ... and in the main the use of disturbing things is a means to an end. So often, feminist art, when performative, is funky, aggressive, contestive, flagrant, shocking, daring, extreme and meant to be responded to as dangerous: it uses frontal nudity, blood, menstrual fluid, and the like almost magically ... the traditional aesthetic categories do not apply to it. It is not intended to be beautiful, symmetrical, composed, tasteful, let alone pretty or perfect or elegant. It is everything that a painting by Matisse, for example, is not. So it is in its favour that it should be ugly, distorted, offensive, not to mention tacky, flawed and raucous.[9]

And he goes on to say that:

> The transformation of consciousness and social reality at which feminism, at which post-modernism aims, *requires* that the work be perceived as aesthetically bad ... the injunction is to sneer at the genius, to make fun of the masterpiece, to giggle at aesthetic values altogether. The injunction is to begin a non-exploitative history in which art is something put to immediate human ends, rather than something destined for the brilliant collection ... the sanctuary of the museum, the graphic tomb of the expensive art book.[10]

Of course, in other contexts many of those Danto is praising would say that in art, political servitude means bad aesthetics; they would probably be thinking of the art of the 1930's produced in accordance with the wishes of the dictatorships of Russia, Germany and Italy. But Danto shows that aesthetics can be subverted by politics of a non-dictatorial, impeccably liberal, impeccably liberational kind. More to the point, precisely by using the Kantian analysis of the judgment of taste Danto shows convincingly enough why politically motivated art and art of ethnic identity is unlikely to be beau-

[8] In *Modern Painters*, Vol. 2, No. 2, Summer 1989, pp. 55–9.
[9] Ibid., pp. 55–6.
[10] Ibid., p. 57.

tiful. It is unlikely to be beautiful because it is not trying to be beautiful. It has no interest in the universality or disinterestedness characteristic of beautiful things. And nor, of course, does art (in this case primarily music) whose whole aim is to stimulate and impel people into drug use or sexual license. In that case, as in different ways in the others, the art seeks to deny the possibility of being contemplated disinterestedly. It aims to overwhelm the hearer, to take him or her over, to cancel the psychic distance which aesthetic experience requires. It is, in a very direct sense, disturbational. It is in the disturbing sense consciousness-altering, in the same way that political agit-prop aims to be, in the jargon, 'consciousness raising'.

It might, though, be said that similar points could be made about religious art, some at least of which most people would have little hesitation in recognizing as beautiful. Can religious art aspire to the disinterest and universality demanded by Kant? Universality may not be a problem; non-believers clearly have no difficulty in admiring Chartres Cathedral or the *St Matthew Passion*. But are these things disinterested in the relevant sense?

It must be admitted that some religious art is very preacherly, directly and obviously missionary, just like feminist or socialist agit-prop. That would certainly detract from its potential for beauty. But religious art does not have to be didactic or indoctrinatory. It can be, and often is, contemplative, in the sense of being simply for the glory of God, as would be said. And here there would be both truth and the disinterestedness characteristic of the beautiful. Things would be portrayed for themselves as they are in themselves. Religious commission and subject-matter do not of themselves impede an artist in pursuing the virtues of his art: in using his strength, and muscular precision and skill and insight and ruthlessness to paint as he sees fit, cutting himself entirely away, as Ruskin says 'from all love of his fellow creatures'. Indeed a certain interpretation of the religious impulse—the one which accepted the world and humanity in all its light and all its shadow, without anxiety or lust or spite or remorse—would actually encourage that type of disinterested and universalizing artistic impulse.

I have dwelt at some length with the ways in which much contemporary art and music repudiates any drive towards Kantian disinterestedness and universality, and in so doing makes it hard for it to be perceived as beautiful, except unintentionally, or by default as it were.

But there is also another way in which beauty can be avoided by the artist flouting the satisfaction of another of the Kantian conditions for a truly aesthetic experience. In discussing what I called the non-cognitiveness of the aesthetic experience, I intended to focus on precisely that: the experience. For aesthetic judgments are judgments which require experience of the object, and the significance of the experience is not in any straightforward sense the transmission of information. It is because I have heard it that I know that Mozart's *Jupiter* Symphony is beautiful because of its sublime balance of melody, rhythm, harmony and counterpoint, its unponderous gravity and its exquisite fusion of learned and galant styles. If I had not heard it, I could not know any of these things, although I might know a great deal about its history, its place in Mozart's œuvre, its scoring, and much else besides.

A crucial aspect of the non-cognitive, non-informational nature of the aesthetic experience is that one can hear a work like the *Jupiter* countless times without its attraction palling, whereas there would be no point in reading and re-reading a newspaper or a text book, say, once its informational content had been assimilated.

There are at least two strong tendencies in 20th century art which militate against the experiential requirement. There is first the assumption, dominant in serialism in music, but not without its influence and counterparts in architecture and the visual arts, that what counts in a work is not its perceived or perceivable surface, but its underlying and imperceptible structure (as in later Schoenberg) or more generally its adherence to some abstract blueprint, such as in architecture the doctrine of functionality.

The difficulty with these approaches from the aesthetic point of view, and hence from the perspective of beauty, is that what comes to dominate in the composing of a piece of music or in the designing of a building is not primarily what can be perceived. In the case of the Second Viennese School the innate musicality of a Berg could triumph over theory and dogma. His Violin Concerto is, as anyone who has heard it will know, a work of elegaic beauty, as beautiful as anything written in the last century, but this is surely because of how it sounds, not because it adheres to the Schoenbergian dogma. In fact, it does not sound like a piece of serialism, which prompts the conclusion that its conformity to the principles of dodecaphony is irrelevant to the way we hear it, a triumph indeed of Berg's musicality over theoretical constraint.

With much twentieth century architecture, function took (or was supposed to take) precedence over appearance. It wasn't, as in Kant's dependent beauty, that a building had to look like what it was. It was rather that in it appearance was to be determined by analysis of a set of goals for the building which in themselves dictate no particular appearance, but which are derived from technology and a quasi-scientific account of human need. This doctrine is memorably if rather bathetically expressed in the Pevsnerian injunction that if you want to build a nursery school, you 'must find out all about nursery school work'. This 'research into function' as Pevsner calls it, is all nonsense and should be distinguished from Kant's notion of dependent beauty.

Dependent beauty arises when an object looks as it ought to look when it looks like what it is supposed to be and it is constructed with regard to how it looks. But what Pevsner means by research into function is the view associated with Le Corbusier in his *Unité d'Habitation* phase: that you scientifically determine the optimal amounts of light, air, space, heating and so on for an apartment or a school room. Having discovered these desiderata, you then design your building to fulfil them in the simplest way possible. Aesthetic properties are supposed to play no part in this: ornament is crime, after all; what must be attended to are simply the building's 'practical requirements' not any of the images of enjoyment or entertainment or education or domesticity or worship, which for most people and, one suspects for Kant, would be required by a building looking like what it is for. That is, it would be via its aesthetic properties and its style that it would achieve dependent beauty, not by the elimination of them. Of course, there was actually an aesthetic underlying this 20th century functionalism. It was the aesthetic in which anything pertaining to the beautiful or taste of old-fashioned human beings was mere clutter, untidiness to be ruthlessly eliminated by the new rationalism, a rationalism in both its genesis and its effects not surprisingly not unlike that of Schoenberg's musical rationalism.

The upshot was that schools built in the 1960's on reductively functionalist principle are conducive to anything but the education of children, in part one suspects because they lack not just aesthetic qualities in general, but in particular those which might go along with a humane education (such as an architectural style embodying a sense of tradition, some evocation of dignity and authority and a sensitivity to the complexities of light and shade and surface). But then of course, on the doctrine of research into function consideration of aesthetic qualities or effects plays no role at all.

In aiming at theory and function, rather than appearance, art will make the achievement of beauty that much more unlikely. But so will it if the aim is to convey an idea or (as Sir Nicholas Serota likes to put it) to challenge its audience's preconceptions. This 'theory art' reaches its *reductio ad absurdum* in the joke slogans of Jenny Holzer, which once seen do not need to be seen again—or, more accurately, which once heard, do not need to be seen at all. But quasi-philosophical challenge is routinely trotted out as the aim and justification of a host of contemporary works of art, from Damien Hirst's medicine cabinets, to Rachel Whiteread's casts of the underside of chairs, to Gilbert and George's homosexual scatology, to Jeff Koons' vacuum cleaners and pornographic photographs.

In these cases, too, there is really no need to see the objects in question, or even if there is an initial visual impact it rapidly diminshes in interest, much as the typical arresting advertisement and for much the same reason. People come into a gallery full of modern installation art and, once they have got the idea, are at a loss to know what to look at: quite the reverse of what happens when people examine a Monet or a Renoir, for example, where fascination with and interest in the surface and what is seen in it appears virtually endless.

I have tried to show that there are aspects of fashion in contemporary art which militate against the achievement of beauty. These are a repudiation of disinterestedness in favour of work which serves some political or therapeutic purpose, an emphasis on art as the embodiment of particular identities, and a focus on non-perceptual properties, such as the underlying imperceptible structure of a work of art, or its satisfaction of functional demands in a utilitarian sense. In all these ways much contemporary art flouts the requirements for the beautiful correctly identified by Kant.

But these, of course, are purely formal requirements. They say nothing about a work's content. A work would in the appropriate sense be disinterested, universal and aiming at what could actually be perceived, and yet still not be beautiful. It could fail to be beautiful because its maker may have wanted it to be ugly and discordant or raucous or unsettling. And he or she may have wanted it to be these or analogous things because of some view the composer or artist had about his and our time or situation. After Auschwitz should we be even aiming at beauty? More profoundly; perhaps, a cultivation of beauty seems to imply that ultimately all is or could be well with the world. Again, this is suggested by Kant's analysis of beauty: that in judging something to be beautiful, we find a harmony between our judgment and it. But how, it would be said, can there be any such harmony except as a temporary and lying diversion, given the lack of any harmony obtaining between the world and us, between us and the rest of our kind, between our deepest yearnings and our inevitable fate, and post-Darwin, within the world itself?

So, in short, even if there are temporary experiences of beauty, these are inevitably tinged with an almost sickly nostalgia and world-weariness—as in the final trio in *Der Rosenkavalier*—and are ultimately no better than a childish avoidance of what we really know (like the elderly Ruskin's advocacy of Kate Greenaway). In other words, we won't have beauty because beauty belongs to our and mankind's infancy.

I cannot say that any of this is wrong. In our post-religious age such an attitude can come to seem all but forced upon us. That so many artists and musicians seem to take this attitude may help to explain why it is that when most of us seek aesthetic delight—or beauty—we do not turn to works of our own time. So, on this view, the prospects for beauty are bleak, and it may go some way towards explaining why it is that art tends these days to be disturbational rather than Kantian.

But there is another possible view, and it is the view associated with Plato. That is, the experience of beauty itself is part of a background which elevates us, which as Nietzsche puts it, justifies our world.

What Plato (or rather Diotima) suggests in *The Symposium* is that the lover of beauty is first captivated by the beauties of individual bodies (a more realistic account of the genesis of a taste for beauty than the rather austere Kantian account). But then, 'by scanning beauty's wide horizon' the aesthete detaches him or herself from the 'slavish and illiberal devotion to the individual loveliness of a single boy', and turns the eye disinterestedly to the 'open sea of beauty'. True aesthetic appreciation has then been reached until it in turn comes to be love for something which is not physical at all.

Now, as far as aesthetics is concerned this non-physical attraction is surely a step too far. However, what is suggestive in the Platonic account is the way a sense for beauty is represented as moving from intense sensual attraction to a sense which diffuses itself over aspects of the whole of creation. But, to come back to our earlier question, does this sense of harmony with things point to anything fundamentally right about the world? To see things in the world, things made by us, and above all to see attempts to confront our fate head on as beautiful, as ultimately redeemable is to show the world as not ultimately alien, and ourselves as not necessarily alienated.

The aesthetic sense points to and presupposes the type of ultimate harmony and meaning in the universe which, in other more direct ways, religions symbolize. Of course, to say *that* is not to say that the religious sense is justified, or that our consolation in aesthetic experience is not, at root, an illusion: in the aesthetic case, wish fulfilment powered by the type of release certain shapes and colours and sounds produce in the chemistry of the brain.

Anthony O'Hear

So we come back to our age and its lack of care for the beautiful. We lack the type of shared symbolic order which in previous ages sustained artistic styles and forged aesthetic communities. More profoundly, publicly at least we lack the type of vision, religious or otherwise which might have filled out the aesthetic sense into something intimating transcendence and meaning, in Ruskin's terms, transforming *aesthesis*—'the mere animal consciousness of the pleasantness'—into *theoria*—the sense that beauty has a moral or at least a spiritual core, bearing 'witness to the glory of God'. So, as Ruskin predicted as early as 1846 (long before art for art's sake or Whistler), our arts have sunk into 'mere amusement, ministers to morbid sensibilities, ticklers and fanners of the soul's sleep'.[11]

But this may not be the end of the story. The great works of art of the past, those conceived within a transcendent framework, still for many of us have a charge and a vivacity quite missing from the sensations of to-day. Even as the public culture denies any such thing, many of us have private experiences of *theoria*.

And perhaps, as the Kantian system intimates, the aesthetic, or more precisely the experience of the beautiful, does provide a resolution to at least some of our dilemmas; it suggests an approach to life which is neither that of science, with its downgrading of appearance and unattainable thing in itself, nor that of morality with its stern and unfulfillable duties and the endless, apparently pointless suffering to which humanity is subject and demands. For in the experience of beauty we get a sense that, despite the problems of alienation thrown up in different ways by science and morality, we are nevertheless at home in the world.

By 'at home', I mean that the world is not just the blind, random, humanly indifferent entity described by modern science, that it is in some sense responsive to our concerns, that consciousness (our consciousness) does take us to the essence of the world, that meaning and intelligibility are not simply imposed by us on a world which is ultimately meaningless and indifferent. (Even the world of Homer, heartless though it is, does respond to our noblest aspirations: the blood of the heroes, as Ruskin said, though poured out on the ground, rose into hyacinthine flowers; all nature became divine, and 'the gods whom they had never ceased to love, came down to love them...')

I suppose that something of the sort *can* be suggested by aesthetic experience, aesthetic experience intimating a type and a depth of feeling and meaning beyond the everyday. Of course, there may be

[11] On this aspect of Ruskin's thought, see Peter Fuller's *Theoria* (Chatto & Windsor: London, 1988), esp Ch. 4.

nothing which corresponds to these feelings, in which case aesthetic experience has no more significance than a warm bath or Prozac or some other way of affecting the chemistry of the brain. All I can say about that is that this is not how the experience of say, *King Lear*, or Beethoven's *Op 132* actually *feels*; perhaps in the case of Lear the experience is of an ultimate if heartless justice in which despite the appearance to the world, Lear and Cordelia do not die like dogs, but die with meaning and a certain dignity; or in the case of Beethoven, *Heilige Dankgesang*, praise for the spirit which harmonizes and elevates the universe; and in both cases we are close to Rilke's beginning of Terror, serenely disdaining to destroy us, close though it may come to it.

Dogmatic religion is not implied by these or analogous feelings, nor is traditional theism. Perhaps all that is suggested is something akin to and as vague as William James's 'piecemeal supernaturalism' —that is the belief that there is a power in the universe which works towards the good and helps achieve it, and that in our conscious experience we can somehow link in to that power. My point is that positive aesthetic experience—the experience above all of beauty— will for many people be a pointer to the existence of such a reality, and because of the embodied basis of aesthetic feeling one which unlike much religious thought, does not seek to play down the reality or significance of the material world.

Of course, for those whose horizons are bounded by a narrow physicalism, none of this will begin to be credible. It may not even make any sense. The point of the last few pages has been to suggest that from such a perspective, both art and beauty may be transformed; more precisely art as a quest for universal and disinterested experiences of beauty will become problematic only if the world can sustain no sense of the beautiful beyond mere *aesthesis*, which will look increasingly like a highly temporary and indulgent retreat from the reality of our condition. So we get instead the shark in formaldehyde or the soiled bed or close ups of the artist's orifices, which at least have the virtue of not suggesting that there is anything more to life than what they show, and are certainly not presented as an escape from an ultimately meaningless existence.

What, then, are the prospects for beauty? Are we destined to find its most lively expressions *only* in the art of the ever-receding past? Or will the new millennium bring about a renaissance of beauty?

The Future of Ideals

JOHN SKORUPSKI

I

The early part of the twentieth century was as revolutionary in the domain of ethical ideas as in other realms. An ethical culture inherited from the preceding century was to all appearance destroyed. This culture, the high-bourgeois culture of the nineteenth century, had emerged gradually from years of revolution and counter-revolution, and seemed then to be developing steadily and expanding its reach towards the end of the century and up to the first world war. Yet what followed it, and in fact overlapped with it, being already presaged well before the war, was quite other: the mainly 20th century phase we call 'Modernism', acutely fragmented not only in aesthetic but also in ethical terms, marked in politics by nationalist, collectivist and populist clashes. However, Modernism too, and in particular, many of the ideas in ethics which were characteristic of it, now belongs to history. That much has for some time been clear; the change is complicated, confused, hard to outline; discernibly though, we're in a new period and have been for perhaps a third of a century—quite how long depends on which aspect of change one considers, and on how one interprets its character.

The ethical culture of this new period is still a conundrum, not least, it seems to me, because the outcomes of many issues crucial to it remain unclear. Cultures change holistically and it is mostly impossible to say what effects, proximate or remote, changes in one aspect will have on others. In this talk I want to raise just one question about it. The question is about the future of *ideals*. It is only one question, but an important one, in that high-bourgeois culture and modernism were most evidently at odds in the field of ideals, while the emerging ethical culture of the present time is hardest to make out in exactly that field, the field of ideals.

II

By ideals I mean conceptions of how it is admirable, excellent, to live, ideas of what constitutes a life that one could be proud of, that one could find dignity, self-respect, self-realization, or at least sig-

193

nificance—*importance*—in. Ideals, one may say, constitute one of three fundamental ethical categories, of which the other two are morality and ends. It is usual to contrast morality, or the right, with the good. I am further distinguishing, within the good, between ends of life and ideals of life. In practice ends and ideals are often seamlessly interwoven; yet one can have ends without having ideals and one can have ideals without making them one's ends. Indeed the ideals of most people only fitfully and sporadically shape their ends. Nevertheless ideals constantly and quietly shape any culture, and they can also break into the public arena and become revolutionary historical forces.

The primitive element of this contrast lies in the difference between desire and admiration. That is, the philosophical theory of ends is the theory of what is truly, genuinely desirable; the philosophical theory of ideals is the theory of what is truly, genuinely admirable. For example many of us can agree that pleasure is a desirable thing as such, in as much as living a pleasant life is a reasonable end for anyone have—but we don't hold that there is anything either admirable or disadmirable in itself about living a pleasant life (though of course what gives a person pleasure may be more or less admirable). Thus a pleasant life is for us an end but not an ideal. Ideals can *become* ends, in that something that is admirable can become through one or another psychological process something that I reasonably desire to attain—something desirable for me. But they don't *have* to be ends. I can find a way of life admirable without desiring to lead a life like that. I may admire the effortlessness, ease and grace of an athlete or violinist to the point of hero-worship without desiring to have those qualities in anything I myself do. Nor, shifting to the normative level, does the fact that those qualities are genuinely admirable entail that it *is* desirable for me to attain them, whether or not I actually do desire to attain them. The connection between the admirable and the desirable is very puzzling and ethically interesting. It would be strange if there was no connection at all—but it is certainly not one of simple entailment. An equally interesting connection is between the admirable and the mandatory. How is it that an ideal I acknowledge, in the sense of recognizing that it stands for a genuinely worthwhile attainment, comes to be something that I *must* try to attain in my own life? The mere fact that it is worthwhile and that I could attain it does not seem to be enough.

Whereas ideals and ends are grounded in admiration and desire, morality is concerned with obligations whose infraction properly attracts guilt and blame. Failure to achieve an ideal, in particular an ideal experienced as mandatory, may attract disdain and shame, the opposite of admiration; failure to achieve a desirable end may involve merely regret, the opposite of satisfaction. Neither of these failures mobilises the specific emotional resources involved in blame. And the relative importance of these three categories is itself an ethical question. Nietzsche's critique of morality is a critique from the standpoint of the ideal. Morality, in this view, stands in the way of self-making and it is self-making, not morality, that is really mandatory. There can also be a very different, utilitarian, critique of morality from the standpoint of well-being, in which guilt and blame are seen as 'unhelpful' and 'unproductive'. And it is an everyday fact of our culture that middlebrow versions of these two critiques very easily combine. But equally, or rather, more rarely, there is an idealism of morality, in which moral virtue, duty, rectitude or in a certain sense piety, or a Platonic vision of the good, become themselves the content of an ideal of life. That is, virtue itself comes to be seen as what gives one's life importance and meaning, and in a moralistic extreme, the only thing that gives life meaning. But then there is also a common attitude which treats the category of the ideal, as against the category of morality, with scepticism, or perhaps suspects it of divisiveness. This is an ethics of morality and well-being alone, which either recognizes no distinction between ideals and well-being or at most recognizes the ideal of service to others. And there are many other ways in which these three categories can relate in a whole ethical vision.

I hope that helps to make clear what it is that I want to consider the future of. Now, to become concrete, I want to consider some historical ideals. It will help us to think about the question of what ideals if any have a future if we address it against the background of the two previous periods which I mentioned at the beginning—that which I referred to as the high-bourgeois culture of the nineteenth century (this is to label it in infamously external and approximate terms—but I have no better word) and that of twentieth century Modernism. So I shall recapitulate some salient ethical ideas of those periods before moving on to consider some aspects of our present situation.

III

The civil society of the first period I'm considering came together in the nineteenth century and lasted to the outbreak of the first world war, though in its high-cultural aspects—ethical and philosophical, but above all aesthetic—there had been signs of crisis or revolution quite a while before that catastrophic turning point. Some of its main political aspects—the division of Europe into sovereign nation states competing to extend their territorial sovereignty and spheres of influence, and the further division of those nation-states into dominant and excluded classes—were obviously dangerous. I am, by the way, focusing here on the European story, for throughout this period American culture developed steadily on its own rather distinct path. Though the results of that development may well now be almost as formative for European culture as is Europe's own internal history, they have to be studied in their own right.

The framework of European high-bourgeois culture was the structure Hegel describes as Abstract Right: the rule of law not of persons—in particular the rule of laws of property and contract. It framed a seemingly stable social hierarchy, resulting from unequally distributed but great and growing wealth. Its political expression was representative government, with a franchise restricted by property and/or educational qualifications, but gradually extending. On its branches nested the safety of the bourgeois family: the paradigm of ethical good order and the expression of an ideal of domestic or private love. Love, intimacy, shared interiority against an outside world of impersonal imperatives was the content of this ideal of the family. In fact, the family as an ideal in this sense is a special case of what I shall call *the ideal of private intimacy*. It is really a class of ideals, allowing considerable internal development. Of course, as the case of the family shows, an ideal, while constituting in itself an important reality, can nevertheless fail to reflect various realities. In this ethical order the ideal of private intimacy, actualized in the family, involved further ideals of masculinity and femininity which have been fiercely criticized. These in turn connected private intimacy to a function, that of bringing up children, which both sustained it and weighed on it. And that helped to produce regions of human exclusion. Not just directly, of those within the bourgeois ethical order for whom private intimacy could not be embodied in an ideal of heterosexual family life, but also indirectly, in helping to lock out the dangerous or undomesticated classes below this ethical order who sustained it yet were not incorporated into it.[1]

Beyond the family the practical life of business and politics called for a morality of individual responsibility. It turned on duty to family, business and state. But it also cumulated in, or gave substance to, an ideal which I will call *the ideal of the autonomous person and citizen*. The autonomous person and citizen has two key features.

[1] Which is not to say that *any* ideal of private intimacy must have these particular limitations.

First he (and it was then almost exclusively he) has a capacity of immediate insight into the moral law. That is, when there is in his concrete situation some specific thing that he has a moral obligation to do, he is capable of knowing that there is, just by thinking it through. He doesn't have to be told by experts. He has personal moral insight, acknowledging for himself the moral law and its authority, and responding effectively to it. Second, he is at one with his social order (which he affirms as rational) and he has an ethical disposition to do within it that which he can see for himself to be fitting and right. The ideal of the autonomous person and citizen does not just say that this is an admirable, worthy, fulfilling way to be. It sees identification with the social order as a liberation, a 'being at home in the other', in which the self is preserved as well as superseded. Thus it is an ideal of at-homeness in one's city, of being able to recognize in its law one's own law, an ideal of self-realizing membership. By 'city' I mean something to which one belongs and perceives as existing as its own end, not as some sort of collective cause, movement or mission with an end beyond itself.

These twin ideals of the bourgeois order, the ideal of private intimacy and the ideal of person and citizen, can be contrasted as private and public ideals. And the distinction between private and public is important for what I want to discuss. But it is not easy to tease out—in this talk I will rely largely on exemplifying rather than analysing it. Note first that if something is admirable then anyone has reason to admire it—the admirable does not relativize in the way the desirable does; an end can be desirable for me but not desirable for you, an ideal can't be admirable for me but not admirable for you. One of us may accept that it is admirable and the other may not, but in that case one of us is wrong. If something is a genuine ideal success in realizing it is something there's reason for everyone to admire. This therefore is not the point on which the distinction between public and private ideals turns. Nor is the difference between a private and a public ideal a difference in respect of mandatoriness. Whereas domestic intimacy, or ascetic contemplation in the desert, would characteristically—or even, given their content, necessarily—be private ideals, excellence in athletics or poetry have in many cultures been public ideals. Even then it is not mandatory that everyone should strive for them—public ideals don't have to become totalistic. So what makes them public when they are? They become public when excellence in them comes to be seen as contributing to a common culture and not just a shared culture. They are seen not just as ideals of the private individual but as ideals of the society. They appropriately fit into public acts, they

197

contribute to the common cultural wealth of the nation. As such they can be publicly funded.

Public ideals are ideals of the individual-in-society. Now certainly it is true that neither the family, nor indeed any intimate, companionate relationship is outside civil society. It would be a mistake to think any such relationship can be governed solely by love; it may also in certain eventualities have to have justice imposed on it by law. Allowing for that however, the ideal of private intimacy is still the ideal of forms of relationship in which on the one hand, others have, justice apart, no business to meddle, and on the other hand— more relevantly for present purposes—there is no onus to contribute something to the *common* culture, the *common* good, the *res publica*. By contrast, an ideal is conceived as public if it is conceived as an admirable contribution to a common culture, a common stock—if only as a model or even as just one of a number of diverse models of living. Thus a small community living on an outer Scottish island might be funded not for profit but because it represents one of the ideals of worthwhile living to which the larger community is committed. This does not of course mean that everyone should feel some onus to live that way. Or a free-love community might be putting itself forward, more or less explicitly, as a model for others, whereas a relationship conceived solely under the ideal of private intimacy is not. In this sense actual bourgeois families, with their children, relatives and servants, were obviously only partly informed by the ideal of private intimacy. The family was and remains also an institution of civil society. Still, this ideal of private intimacy had a significantly greater place in the bourgeois ethical order than it had had in earlier ethical orders and it was centred on the family.

These twin ideals of the bourgeois order, that of intimacy and that of person and citizen, are widely intelligible and capable, for many people, of giving enough significance to life. But one could progress to a higher key. The bourgeois order also contained a level of high ideals and the contrast between private and public can also be made at this level of high ideals. The public ideals of high bourgeois culture included a certain Periclean or Schillerian humanism—an ideal of *Bildung*, or to borrow Mill's word, of individuality. I will call it *the ideal of realised spontaneity* and I shall be coming back to it; it was at the heart of that period's classical liberalism. Not that it was by any means the only high public ideal of the time—notably, for example, there was also a kind of Catholic-mediaeval, or Gothic-communitarian, response to this liberal humanism. These were both public ideals which could be expressed in architecture and public monuments, and which related an ideal of individual excellence to an ideal of service in society. Thus the debate between classical and gothic architecture had an ethical dimension—the decision to rebuild the Houses of Parliament in gothic style on a classical carcase was a good old British compromise.[2]

These high ideals belonged to the public domain. But then there was also a high ideal in the private domain. One might call it the ideal of the inner life of the spirit, or *the ideal of innerness* for short. It occupied a region beyond the public world of person and citizen, and it was also distinct from the ideal of intimacy, whether that be the intimacy of family or friendship. Like the ideal of intimacy the ideal of innerness can develop in a variety of forms, but central to it is the notion of a personal quest for at-oneness with life, with existence, or with being as such, with the world beyond the merely social world. One might question whether an ideal of innerness has to be thought of as a private ideal. Was not institutional religion a basic structure in the bourgeois order? And is not religion the affirmation of spirituality in the public domain—the conferment of inner or other-worldly meaning on the common wealth?

It is, and the Catholic-mediaeval or Gothic-communitarian response to liberal humanism just mentioned was an attempt to reinstate it. But the high-bourgeois ideal of innerness also registered a weakening of just that public-religious ideal of spirituality. In general a highly significant ethical development of the last phase of the bourgeois order, especially in its high culture, was the increasing power of private ideals, of intimacy on the one hand and innerness on the other. Consider for example the overwhelming role of intimacy and innerness[3] in Proust. Note the external stance Proust's narrator takes, from his high-bourgeois niche, on social worlds governed by public ideals—the aristocratic salon, diplomacy, military life—worlds which he finds attractive but sooner or later also finds hollow. Whereas the ideal of family intimacy, love and sincerity remains a pillar of his life. Even friendship comes to be seen as 'destructive of the spiritual life', that is, destructive of innerness. Its

> whole effort ... is directed towards making us sacrifice the only part of ourselves that is real and incommunicable (otherwise than

[2] 'All Grecian, sir; Tudor details on a classic body', Pugin apparently said. N. Pevsner, *The Buildings of England*, London, vol. 1, 3rd edn. (Penguin 1973), p. 523.
[3] Not of religion: which, unlike churches, is wholly absent as a theme.

John Skorupski

by means of art) to a superficial self which, unlike the other, finds
no joy in its own being, but rather a vague, sentimental glow at
feeling itself supported by external props, hospitalised in an
extraneous individuality, where, happy in the protection that is
afforded it there, it expresses its well-being in warm approval and
marvels at qualities which it would denounce as failings and seek
to correct in itself. (*Rememberance of Things Past*, Vol. III 455–56)

Friendship is hostile to purity of spirit just because it competes with
and compromises it in the inner sphere. This interestingly jaun-
diced passage gives us pause, because the idealism of friendship,
unlike the intimacy of family, is so much a part of our current ethical thought. In fact there's a lot to reflect on in it. To a considerable extent we still inherit the recoil against the public ideal of person and citizen which developed in late bourgeois society and which
became, as I shall shortly be discussing, a major constitutent of
modernist ethics. But since the ideal of the family has also come
badly apart, and the ideal of innerness has at least become deeply
problematic, and since in general the neutralist liberalism which has
recently been so influential has some trouble in acknowledging the
very idea of a *public* ideal, it's not suprising that the ideal of friendship should have acquired the sentimental dominance it now has.

Nevertheless, one striking fact about the new period that we're in
is the extent to which the twin bourgeois ideals of the autonomous
person and citizen, and of family intimacy, or in an interestingly
broadened way, of intimacy in settled and equal domestic relationships, are being *revived*. But before I turn to the period of modernism, in which they were at their low, I want to note how well the
major texts of moral philosophy from the nineteenth century
express the spirit of that earlier ethical period and criticize it from
within. And they *are* major texts, because this is a formative ethical
period in the modern world. How brilliantly Hegel's *Philosophy of
Right* sets out its basic ethical categories and ideals right at its
beginning—contrary to his own well-known comments about philosophy being wise only after the event. As readers of Hegel will
have recognized, I have relied on him heavily in my description of
this ethical order. Then we have Mill's quartet of *Utilitarianism,
Liberty, Representative Government* and the *Subjection of Women*,
which comes at the apogee of this ethical culture, and Green's
Prolegomena to Ethics, together with his political writings, which
come towards its end. All three philosophers apply a philosophically comprehensive ethical vision to understanding and criticizing
this ethical order; they all accept the moral philosopher's responsi-

bility to take account of *all* the ethical categories of his ethical world, and to interpret and criticize them in a unifying philosophical perspective. Further, all three of them criticize it 'immanently', from within its own categories. Mill and Green criticize it for its exclusiveness: both of them want to make the ideal of person and citizen available to everyone.[4] Similarly, Mill's criticism of marriage is made from the standpoint of private intimacy. Though it emphasizes companionate equality it does not reject the ideal of intimate family love. What do Green and Hegel, as against Green and Mill share? For Hegel a major problem of the high culture, or idealism, of the bourgeois ethical order is a tendency towards mere subjectivity. The growing role of the ideals of private intimacy and spiritual innerness, which I referred to when I quoted from Proust, might well have struck him as cases of that. Green wrote at a time when this strain between innerness and citizenship was evident, and he tried to reconcile these ideals. But the only scope he offered for innerness was whatever could be found in the ideal of service to others. This was a diminution from Hegel's vision of the world of ideals, for Hegel gives a role beyond citizenship to what he calls 'Absolute Spirit', that is, to the inner realization of identity with the whole which can be grasped in art, religion, or finally in speculative philosophy.

IV

The dominant ideals of bourgeois ethical culture as I have sketched them, then, were the public ideal of person and citizen and the private ideal of family intimacy. At a higher level of bourgeois culture could be found, among other ideals of the public substance of shared living, the liberal ideal of realised spontaneity. Also at this higher level, but private rather than public in their orientation, were various forms of the ideal of innerness.

When we turn to modernism and its moral philosophers we get a variety of different, even mutually opposed, ideals. The one thing that these various ethical visions in modernism share is an attitude to the ideal of person and citizen which ranges from bored indifference to outright hostility. I am talking here about the *ideal*—about personhood in civil society and citizenship in a city envisaged as

---

[4] 'Positive freedom', the freedom actualized in the person and citizen, was by no means a concept alien to high-bourgeois ethical culture, though it may have been alien to purely economic liberals.

forms of life with the potential to inspire and ennoble, as against instrumentally necessary duties. And I am distinguishing the ideal of person and citizen from a different ideal, an ideal of life-enhancing, self-abandoning, adherence to some revolutionary or transformative cause. The latter ideal, the ideal of revolutionary struggle or 'praxis' was of course by no means absent from modernism. One might say that it was precisely what replaced, for many people, the ideal of person and citizen. For the ideal of person and citizen is an ideal of reconciliation with, at-homeness-in, one's society and oneself, and they could not be reconciled to their society or themselves. The rejection not just of this ideal but of the whole philosophical conception which underpinned it—of a unitary, determinately developmental, self-controlling individual placed *in* the world—is a kind of tidal wave in modernist art, philosophy, speculative psychology and indeed politics.

There were many other changes. The ideal of intimacy was displaced from its domestic and family focus to the intimacy of friendship or, closer to the public domain—not really private intimacy any more, but something inherently more wooden—to the already-noted companionship in a cause. And the ideal of innerness gained hugely in strength and variety, while at the same time tending towards greater alienation from society.

In early-modernist moral philosophy Moore's *Principia Ethica* illustrates the way in which the ideal of intimacy comes to be embodied in an ideal of private personal relations distinct from that of family love. Further and importantly, Moore's treatment of duty effectively casts doubt on the possibility of immediate insight into the moral law which is essential to the ideal of person and citizen. Notoriously on his account, our duty is something we can hardly ever know. Only by noting the destructive effect of this doctrine on the ideal of the autonomous person and citizen, it seems to me, can one understand the relish with which he lays this out. Finally his Platonistic realism about the good is a modernist form of the ideal of spiritual innerness. Psychologically if not logically it tends to introduce a kind of cleansing other-worldliness which was quite foreign to the nineteenth century thinkers we have just considered.[5] Similar points could be made about the ethical remarks in Wittgenstein's *Tractatus*. The rejection of the psychological subject is also a rejection of the autonomous person and citizen; ethics as

[5] Thus I agree with Alasdair MacIntyre (*After Virtue*, London: Duckworth, 1981) about the exemplary importance of *Principia Ethica* (though not with his diagnosis of what it was that was exemplary and important).

transcendental is an inner ideal of personal purity. Moore and Wittgenstein powerfully express the ideals of pure private intimacy and spiritual innerness which dominated early modernism.

However the main shift I want to discuss is one that developed later. Whereas these early-modernist ideals could be seen as developments of high-bourgeois ideals of intimacy and innerness, the later shift came to have a more collectivize and populist tinge. One can see it as a shift from the Schillerian ideal of realized spontaneity to the modernist ideal of authenticity. And by one of those endlessly subtle modulations of ethical thought, which always seem so deceptively intelligible in retrospect, this later shift, with its demotic aspirations, nevertheless had Nietzsche as one of its important sources.

As with all modernist ethics, the ideal of *authenticity* rejects the idea of *autonomy* and of equal respect based on that autonomy— that is, it rejects the idea which is foundational to the liberal idealism of personhood and citizenship. Whatever else it is, Nietzsche's critique of morality and objectivity is an assault on that—in that respect he is simply a particularly vehement voice in a universal modernist recoil. On the other hand Nietzsche does not repudiate this public ideal from the standpoint of privacy, whether of personal intimacy or spiritual innerness (as with Moore or Wittgenstein). His ideal of authenticity is crucially a mandatory public ideal, though at the same time (as with all aristocratic ideals) an ideal only few can live by. The point is worth stressing given the tendency of some of his current readers to make the Nietzschean ethic of nobility into a personal and private ideal, locatable within a liberal social order. Such readers show more about themselves and their time than about Nietzsche; Nietzsche's ideal is a way of being in the world and society which carries with it a *social* order of rank and power.

Within the ethics of authenticity more generally there is something of a division between authenticity as being true to oneself and authenticity as being at one with the real (the authentic, the true). Obviously these can be thought to go together, and Nietzsche did think that, in that he thought that recognizing oneself as one's own self-maker, and having the strength to be true to that recognition, is also achieving reconciliation with the world in all its aspects of suffering and exhilaration, without fantasizing a 'Beyond'. Also however there is possible divergence here—for example between the heroically individualist ideal of self-making in Sartre and the mystical ideal of reconciliation with Being, that which discloses itself, in Heidegger. But both these philosophers, like Nietzsche, present a public ideal, an ideal of living together.

John Skorupski

These public ideals of authenticity war with the public ideal of person and citizen. They do so in a way which differs from the retreat into the intense private world of intimacy or innerness which characterizes early modernism, because they challenge the ideal of person and citizen on its own public ground. In this respect, one important element in the ideal of authenticity, at least in its Nietzschean and Sartrean versions, is its voluntarism. Voluntarism removes the idea of duty or obligation as something impersonal, which I can acknowledge, recognize, *submit* to as something other and yet something in which I can find that which is my own. To remove that idea is also to remove the high-bourgeois conception of reconciliation with an impersonally law-governed social order, in which the self is both preserved and transcended. instead, authenticity as a public ideal tends to slide either towards arbitrary oppositionism or towards a fascist version of reconciliation—identification with the People rather than the Law, losing oneself in the collective. The latter direction is supported by the idea that the life of the people contains the authentic in the second sense, that of being at one with being, with truth. Whereas the high-bourgeois conception assumes the rationality of an impersonally law-governed disciplinary social order, a *Rechtstaat*, with which one can identify just because of its impersonal rationality, authenticity conflates impersonality as such with estrangement: its politics is a revolutionary one, involving fantasies of completely trans-legal community, or of authenticity in the praxis of revolution as such.

Authenticity is the dominant ethical ideal of middle and later twentieth century culture. But what is noteworthy is that in the later phase it has come to dominate in a privatized or domesticated form which stems from a kind of combination of existentialism and populism and fits in very well with liberal capitalism: consumerism, the ethics of 'choice'. This late twentieth century or 'post-modernist' compromise combines authenticity in the private domain with impersonal regulation (often thought of contractually) in the public. The general character of its ideal is that each of us deserves respect as a pure self-maker, an extensionless point which somehow expands itself by itself into a definite personal space. The state has a neutral pragmatic role in providing a rule of law within which this pursuit of personal self-definition takes place and in maintaining and refining the socio-economic and technological engines of prosperity which enable it to continue. This ideal is not an empty ideal in the sense that it has no ethical consequence. Importantly, it legitimates an assault on all forms of prejudicial discrimination and domination.[6] If I believe that meaning can be created only by self-definition then I'll object to people who attempt to force definitions of human being on others. Moreover, by a familiar existentialist fallacy, I may easily get a sense of self-definition out of that very activity of opposition, and the collective praxis it makes possible. But it *is* an empty ideal in the sense that it cannot provide self-realization—because it refuses to give any positive account of what is to be realized.

V

Objections of this kind to what I have called the ideal of authenticity are by now familiar. Of recent moral philosophers Iris Murdoch and Charles Taylor[7] have been among its most lucid and perceptive critics, but there have been many other critical voices, and not only or even mainly in philosophy. Moreover many current trends in moral philosophy are working against this modernist ideal, even if it is still dominates our contemporary common culture. One might mention in particular the very strong reassertion of cognitivism about the normative in meta-ethics, and the revival of interest in character as a vital ethical category: in Aristotle's virtuous person, Kant's autonomous individual, Hegel's person/subject/citizen.

These changes in moral philosophy correspond it seems to me to changes in the larger ethical and political culture. We are experiencing a renewed emphasis on character, individual responsibility and inclusion in a moral community, an emphasis on duty as well as rights, a willingness to envisage reductions of negative liberty for the sake of positive freedom (drugs are the prime example), all of which would be very understandable to a turn-of-the-century social liberal in the Kant/Hegel tradition—someone like T. H. Green. Indeed this programme or ethical climate, at least at its best, is nothing other than the attempt to bring up to date and universalize for everyone, without exclusion, the ideal of the person and citizen. That was the ambition of social liberals at the end of the nineteenth

[6] As far as *this* goes, any liberal must be on its side. But even here the ideal of authenticity is liable, by its negative nature, to be undiscriminating about what prejudice is. The very word 'discrimination' is an index of this. It has come to *mean* 'prejudicial discrimination', acquiring thereby rightly ugly overtones but losing some of its usefully positive ones.
[7] Iris Murdoch, *Existentialists and Mystics* (Chatto & Windus, 1997); Charles Taylor, *Sources of the Self* (Cambridge University Press, 1989), *The Ethics of Authenticity* (Harvard University Press, 1992).

century and after the modernist assault on the ideal of person and citizen, or at any rate on its possibility in society as we know it, we are witnessing a striking return to that ambition.[8]

But this leaves questions open about the future of other ideals. On my earlier taxonomy one can ask what sorts of forms the private ideals of intimacy and spiritual innerness are likely to take. However one can also ask what future there is for public ideals at all, other than the ideal of person and citizen as such; and in particular what future there is for the liberal ideal of realized spontaneity. The older bourgeois order, as we saw, while it did give considerable respect to this particular public ideal among others, had a strong tendency overall to shift its emotional investment from public to private ideals. Will this also be true of the new bourgeois order?

It's very hard to tell because we're still, I believe, in a period of rapidly changing ethical ideas. Consider for example feminist and gay critiques of the family, or of ethical attitudes to the body. They may clearly work some lasting change, greater or lesser, on our private ideals, both of intimacy and of inner spirituality. The same goes for environmentalists' ethical ideas about nature, since achievement of some sort of spiritual at-one-ness with nature has always been one major form of the contemplative ideal of innerness. But clearly these discussions may also have important implications in turn for the Schillerian public ideal of the classical liberal. Do they show up something facile, something narrow and limiting about its humanism and its individualism?

Before we could begin to answer that question we would have to investigate the ideal and its potential—a task involving history as well as moral philosophy. I remarked earlier that Iris Murdoch and Charles Taylor are among the most interesting critics of authenticity. However I would want to argue, if I had the time, that both of them link the ethics of authenticity far too closely to classical liberalism's ideals of spontaneity, often treating the one as a form of the other, though they also both from time to time point out differences.[9] It's easy to do this, since both ideals are concerned with self-development. As we noted earlier, however, the Schillerian ideal of realized spontaneity is not voluntaristic. Its accent is on self-discov-

[8] Even Rawls' political liberalism, though neutral about most 'conceptions of the good', works a version of this ideal into its 'political' conception of the person.

[9] In *Ethics of Authenticity* Taylor seems to use the term 'authenticity' to cover both what I have called realized spontaneity and and what I have called authenticity, but in practice he distinguishes them, favouring the former while deploring the latter as a bad or corrupt form.

ery and self-realization, not on self-invention. And just because one aspect of the spontaneity that one develops in oneself is autonomy of the will, this ideal can accommodate and complement the ideal of person and citizen, even if the two are always liable to pull in rather different directions. In contrast the ideal of authenticity is fatefully opposed to the ideal of person and citizen; if it has anything to say about civil and public order at all it tends to treat it instrumentally.

The Schillerian ideal did survive in some modernist movements—in those parts of Marxist tradition which maintained a romantic-hellenic, world-affirming humanism, or rather differently, in those public ideals of architectural modernism which affirmed a liberating vision of health, light, space and grace. Since those more ethical forms of Marxism shared the Schillerian ideal with classical liberalism, it was easy for a Marxist like Lukacs to see the gulf between the idea of freedom put forward in that ideal on the one side and in the Sartrean existential notion of freedom on the other; easy also for him to see why the former can support a political programme whereas the latter cannot. This is well noted by Iris Murdoch[10].

But why did such Schillerian ideals come for many people over the last four or five decades to seem hollow, sentimental or even sinister? Was it for reasons of accident or essence?

I think one reason is precisely that this Schillerian liberal ideal is public. Its pursuit is inherently collective as well as individual, both in the nature of the end that is pursued and in the collective decisions that have to be made in its pursuit. It inevitably shapes public space with a definite, non-neutral vision. In contrast we observed that authenticity has been domesticated into an article of private consumption—'doing it your way'—even though in such visionaries as Nietzsche, Heidegger or Sartre it originally appeared as a public ideal. By virtue of this privacy it is unmenacing and potentially comforting; also, because it is never realized in any public act or outcome, and does not put itself forward for public criticism, it can escape the disillusionment that inevitably attends the attempt to actualize, give public shape to, an ideal. The Schillerian ideal is public yet difficult, both to achieve and to understand—and because difficult, disenchanting and divisive.

VI

One of the most important tasks of moral philosophy is to understand, criticize and regenerate or even generate ideals. In *Sources of the Self*, Charles Taylor remarked:

[10] 'The Existentialist Political Myth' reprinted in Iris Murdoch, *Existentialists and Mystics*, (London 1997)—see e.g. pp. 137–139.

Close and patient articulation of the goods which underpin different spiritual families in our time tends ... to make their claims more palpable. The trouble with most of the views that I consider inadequate, and that I want to define mine in contrast to .... is that their sympathies are too narrow. They find their way through the dilemmas of modernity by invalidating some of the crucial goods in the contest.[11]

I agree with Taylor on the need for that broad-mindedness, and also with his view that we suffer from a philosophical 'inarticulacy', in his words, about our own and other people's ideals. So one thing that I hope moral philosophy will try to do in the new millennium is to find ways of talking about important ideals, making them more palpable. They are after all among the major movers of human action. Yet one could easily read a lot of current moral philosophy without even realizing that they exist. Not that that necessarily matters if there is also a lot of moral philosophy which makes them its main subject, whether in a first-order normative way or as an object of historical and philosophical study. There is such moral philosophy, and it has widespread influence—witness among others the philosophers referred to in this talk, MacIntyre, Murdoch and Taylor[12]. Widely influential moral philosophy of this kind exists, then—yet I'm still not sure that the need to do it, and the importance of doing it really well, is sufficiently recognized within philosophy. Is 'know thyself' central to philosophy? If so—if self-understanding is one of philosophy's important tasks—then understanding one's ideals and articulating the philosophical and ethical visions which give them life and power is important to philosophy.

[11] *Sources of the Self*, pp. 502–3.
[12] Also Bernard Williams' more recent work, notably *Shame and Necessity* (Cambridge University Press).

The Philosophy of Cognitive Science

MARGARET A. BODEN

i: *What's in a Name?*

If the Trade Descriptions Act were applied to academic labels, cognitive scientists would be in trouble. For what they do is much wider than the name suggests—and wider, too, than most philosophers assume. They give you more for your money than you may have expected.

In a bureaucrat's Utopia where all products fitted their labels, 'cognitive science' would be the science of cognition. It would study knowledge—as opposed to motivation, emotion, and social interaction. Most people unfamiliar with the field believe this is so. But they're mistaken. In fact, cognitive science is the interdisciplinary study of mind, informed by concepts drawn from computer science and AI. The core claim is that all aspects of mind can be understood in these terms.

That emotion is essential for intelligence, for example, was argued on computational grounds in the earliest days of GOFAI (Good Old-Fashioned AI[1]). It was recognized that emotion can be crucial in accepting something as a 'problem', and in assessing candidate 'solutions'.[2] Recent neuroscientific work on 'emotional intelligence'[3] is widely seen both as a new insight and as a nail in AI's coffin. It would be fairer to see it as a critique of the type of AI that ignores how problems arise within the whole mind. Since not all AI is like that, emotional intelligence can't be used to beat it into the ground—nor to exclude emotion *in principle* from cognitive science.

Anxiety, neurotic defences, motivational conflict, personality, cooperation, and social roles were all modelled by the very earliest AI.[4] Since these are even more complex than 'single-minded' prob-

---

[1] J. Haugeland, *Artificial Intelligence: The Very Idea* (Cambridge, Mass.: MIT Press, 1985).

[2] For example, H. A. Simon, 'Motivational and Emotional Controls of Cognition', *Psychological Review*, 74 (1967), 29–39; W. R. Reitman, *Cognition and Thought: An Information-Processing Approach* (New York: Wiley, 1965).

[3] For example, A. Damasio, *Descartes' Error: Emotion, Reason, and the Human Brain* (New York: Putnam, 1994).

[4] S. S. Tomkins and S. Messick (eds), *Computer Simulation of Personality: Frontier of Psychological Research* (New York: Wiley, 1963); M. A. Boden, *Artificial Intelligence and Natural Man*, 2nd edn., enlarged (London: MIT Press, 1987), chaps. 2–4.

Margaret A. Boden

lem-solving, they soon dropped out of the picture. Only a few stalwarts retained an interest. But the *fin de siècle* has seen a renewal of AI-work on such matters.[5] Grief and mourning, for instance, have recently been analysed as natural consequences of the mind's computational architecture.[6] The mind (on this view) is a hierarchy, or 'society', of virtual machines, and the key questions concern their computational roles, and how they influence each other. Some research-groups have implemented promising (though primitive) models of emotional intelligence.[7] But it's the architectural ideas that are crucial: they precede, and inform, the implementation of the models.

Talk of implementation suggests another reason for not interpreting the label 'cognitive science' too strictly. Since cognition is a psychological category, the Trade Inspector might expect that neuroscience and biology won't be found inside the can. Again, many people would agree with him—and not just because of the label. For they assume that 'the' philosophy of cognitive science is functionalism, which stresses multiple realizability. 'Since the hardware details don't matter', they say, 'how could neuroscience or biology possibly be relevant?'

It's true that most cognitive scientists have adopted functionalism

[5] For example, A. Sloman, 'Motives, Mechanisms, and Emotions', *Cognition and Emotion*, 1 (1987), 217–233. Reprinted in M. A. Boden (ed.), *The Philosophy of Artificial Intelligence* (Oxford: Oxford University Press, 1990), pp. 231–247; A. Sloman, 'Architectural Requirements for Human-like Agents Both Natural and Artificial. (What sorts of machines can love?)'. In K. Dautenhahn (ed.), *Human Cognition and Social Agent Technology: Advances in Consciousness Research* (Amsterdam: John Benjamins, 1999), pp. 163–195; H. A. Simon, 'Bottleneck of Attention: Connecting Thought with Motivation'. In W. D. Spaulding (ed.), *Integrative Views of Motivation, Cognition, and Emotion* (Lincoln, NE: University of Nebraska Press, 1994), pp. 1–21.

[6] I. P. Wright, A. Sloman and L. P. Beaudoin, 'Towards a Design-Based Analysis of Emotional Episodes', *Philosophy, Psychiatry, and Psychology*, 3 (1996), 101–137.

[7] I. P. Wright, *Emotional Agents*. PhD thesis, School of Computer Science, University of Birmingham (1997). (Available at http://www.cs.bham.ac.uk/research/cogaff/); I. P. Wright and A. Sloman, *MINDER1: An Implementation of a Protoemotional Agent Architecture.* Technical Report CSRP-97-1, School of Computer Science, University of Birmingham (1997). (Available from ftp://ftp.cs.bham.ac.uk/pub/tech-reports/1997/CSRP-97-01.ps.gz)

in some form. McCulloch and Pitts[8] saw the whole of psychology as the specification of logical networks. Putnam's[9] functionalism glossed all mental concepts (not just cognition) in computational terms. And Newell and Simon's theory of Physical Symbol Systems (PSSs) downplayed the physical mechanisms.[10] However, cognitive scientists sometimes consider neurophysiology. Even Newell and Simon designed their later models to reflect properties of the brain,[11] and Marr[12] (among many others) asked what types of computation a certain neural mechanism could—or could not—perform. In short, the functionalist dogma of multiple realizability needs to be taken with a large pinch of salt. Neuroscience can provide crucial information about the functional organization of the cognitive system, not just about how it happens to be implemented.[13] (This intellectual traffic goes both ways: the discovery of single-cell feature-detectors, for example, was inspired by computational ideas.)[14] As for biology,

[8] W. S. McCulloch and W. H. Pitts, 'A Logical Calculus of the Ideas Immanent in Nervous Activity', *Bulletin of Mathematical Biophysics*, **5** (1943), 115–133. Reprinted in Boden, *Philosophy of Artificial Intelligence*, pp. 22–39.

[9] H. Putnam, 'Minds and Machines'. In S. Hook (ed.), *Dimensions of Mind: A Symposium* (New York: New York University Press, 1960), pp. 148–179. Reprinted in H. Putnam, *Mind, Language, and Reality: Philosophical Papers*, Volume 2 (Cambridge: Cambridge University Press, 1975), pp. 362–385; H. Putnam, 'The Nature of Mental States'. First published as 'Psychological Predicates' in W. H. Capitan and D. Merrill (eds), *Art, Mind, and Religion* (Pittsburgh: University of Pittsburgh Press, 1967), pp. 37–48. Reprinted in Putnam, *Mind, Language, and Reality*, pp. 429–440.

[10] A. Newell and H. A. Simon, 'Computer Science as Empirical Enquiry: Symbols and Search', *Communications of the Association for Computing Machinery*, **19** (1976), 113–126. Reprinted in Boden, *Philosophy of Artificial Intelligence*, pp. 105–132; A. Newell, 'Physical Symbol Systems', *Cognitive Science*, **4** (1980), 135–183.

[11] A. Newell and H. A. Simon, *Human Problem Solving* (Englewood Cliffs, NJ: Prentice-Hall, 1972).

[12] D. Marr, *Vision: A Computational Investigation into the Human Representation and Processing of Visual Information* (San Francisco: Freeman, 1982).

[13] W. Bechtel and J. Mundale, 'Multiple Realizability Revisited: Linking Cognitive and Neural States', *Philosophy of Science*, **66** (1999), 175–207.

[14] J. Y. Lettvin, H. R. Maturana, W. S. McCulloch and W. H. Pitts. 'What the Frog's Eye Tells the Frog's Brain', *Proceedings of the Institute of Radio Engineers*, **47**, 1940–1959 (1959). Reprinted in W. S. McCulloch, *Embodiments of Mind* (Cambridge, Mass.: MIT Press, 1965), pp. 230–255; compare O. G. Selfridge, 'Pandemonium: A Paradigm for Learning'. In D.

research in artificial life (A-Life) focuses on self-organization and adaptive evolution, each of which has psychological relevance. Arguably, so does the concept of life itself, since many would claim that only living things can be intelligent.

Moreover, A-Life's emphasis on embodiment has helped put the phenomenologist cat among the functionalist pigeons. So have certain types of work in 'programmed' AI. Similar critiques are even arising within the theory of computation as such. These interactionist, participatory, ideas are being used not negatively, to dismiss cognitive science, but constructively, to develop new ways of doing it (see Sections iii & iv).

Given these explicit philosophical disagreements, one might question the *science* as well as the *cognitive*. 'Surely', the Trade Inspector might say, 'a *science* must posit some fundamental philosophy and methodology on which all its practitioners can agree.' Even if they did agree, they might conceivably be mistaken in calling their activity a science. (Modularity theorists have argued that while there can be a science of vision or language, there can't be a science of belief, or higher mental processes.[15]) But since they don't, there's some ground for seeing 'science' as an undeserved honorific, expressing hope rather than achievement and obscuring the fundamental diversity involved. Indeed, this objection is tacitly recognized by those who prefer to speak, in the plural, of the cognitive *sciences*.

Clearly, then, there's more in the can than is suggested on the label. 'Cognitive science' doesn't pick out only one topic of empirical research, only one methodology, or only one philosophical position. Richly stimulating and controversial, it is. Neat and tidy, it is not. So this paper, too, could fall foul of the Trade Descriptions Act: it should rather be called '*Philosophies* of Cognitive Science'.

The controversial 'philosophies' I'll mention concern the relevance of representations (Section ii); the 'new phenomenology' (Section iii); the nature of computation (Section iv); and the relation between life and mind (Section v).

ii: *The Relevance of Representations*

At this point, you may object that I'm playing fast and loose with the notion of cognitive science. After all, cognitive science was

[15] J. A. Fodor, *The Modularity of Mind: An Essay in Faculty Psychology* (Cambridge, Mass.: MIT Press, 1983).

V. Blake and A. M. Uttley (eds), *Proceedings of the Symposium on Mechanisation of Thought Processes* (London: H. M. Stationery Office, 1959), pp. 511–529.

defined long ago—by key AI-workers, as well as by philosophers—as the study of formal computations over representations.[16] Cognition is therefore the core topic, and motivation and emotion are excluded. Moreover, because of multiple realizability, neuroscience and biology are irrelevant. Even computer implementations are mere 'existence proofs' that formal logics can have a foothold in the physical world.

Those who defined cognitive science—or 'computational psychology'—in this way took representations to be symbolic structures, with a compositional semantics. In other words, representations are *literally* describable by the terminology used to specify symbol-manipulation in GOFAI. They are implemented, in brains and computers, as distinct physical entities, with distinct causal powers. However, they are individuated not by their physical properties but by abstract structural criteria.

Notoriously, however, this concept of representation was eventually challenged, for being overly restrictive. It implies, for example, that attempts to distinguish different types of representation must be a waste of time. So experimental studies of imagery as analogue representation are apparently doomed from the start.[17] Likewise, neuroscientific evidence for functionally distinct kinds of representation is an embarrassment.[18] It ruled out of court a host of computer models widely regarded as significant contributions to cognitive science: PDP-connectionism, for instance, employs representations very different from GOFAI symbols.[19] It meant that if cognitive scientists were to discover that

[16] Newell and Simon, *Human Problem Solving*; Newell and Simon, 'Computer Science as Empirical Enquiry'; J. A. Fodor, *Psychological Explanation: An Introduction to the Philosophy of Psychology* (New York: Random House, 1968); J. A. Fodor, *The Language of Thought* (Hassocks, Sussex: Harvester Press, 1976); Z. W. Pylyshyn, 'Computation and Cognition: Issues in the Foundations of Cognitive Science', *Behavioral and Brain Sciences*, 3 (1980), 111–132; Z. W. Pylyshyn, *Computation and Cognition: Toward a Foundation for Cognitive Science* (Cambridge, Mass.: MIT Press, 1984).

[17] M. A. Boden, *Computer Models of Mind: Computational Approaches in Theoretical Psychology* (Cambridge: Cambridge University Press, 1988), pp. 27–44.

[18] A. Clark, *Being There: Putting Brain, Body, and World Together Again* (Cambridge, Mass.: MIT Press, 1997).

[19] G. E. Hinton, J. L. McClelland and D. E. Rumelhart, 'Distributed Representations'. In D. E. Rumelhart & J. E. McClelland (eds), *Parallel Distributed Processing: Explorations in the Microstructure of Cognition*, Vol. 1, *Foundations* (Cambridge, Mass.: MIT Press, 1986), pp. 77–109. Reprinted in Boden, *Philosophy of Artificial Intelligence*, pp. 248–280.

Margaret A. Boden

a certain type of behaviour does not involve representations, it should cease to interest them. So situated robotics and dynamical systems theory, which deny the importance of internal representations, would not count as 'cognitive science'. And, for good measure, it took for granted a concept of computation that may not be appropriate (see Section iv).

There's still no agreed account of what a representation is. Some take it to be an identifiable internal state that causes behaviour to be adaptively coordinated with some environmental feature, even on occasions when that feature is absent. This would exclude internal states that enable coordination with the environment only when the relevant feature is present, and perceptible. There's neuroscientific evidence that such internal states do indeed exist[20] but they would not be classed as 'representations'. It would also exclude cases (highlighted by the dynamical approach) where there is a complex interaction of body, brain, and environment.[21]

Even if there is some inner state standing in for the environmental feature, it may not be identifiable as a Turing-computable symbolic structure. It may, for instance, be a pattern of activation statistically defined over many computational units, none of which can be assigned a constant meaning or regarded as a symbol for some nameable concept.[22] And it may not be the same physical state on different occasions. A GOFAI-expression can be stored in a specific memory-register, but 'one and the same' representation in a PDP-model can be implemented as equilibrium-patterns involving different sub-units and/or weights. Finally, temporal structure may be important: for instance, an inner state may undergo spontaneous changes that correlate with (unperceived) changes taking place in the external world.[23]

[20] A. Clark and R. Grush, 'Towards a Cognitive Robotics', *Adaptive Behavior*, 7 (1999), 15–16.

[21] A. Clark and M. Wheeler, 'Genic Representation: Reconciling Content and Causal Complexity', *British Journal for the Philosophy of Science*, 50 (1999), 103–135.

[22] Hinton *et al.*, 'Distributed Representations'; A. J. Clark, *Microcognition: Philosophy, Cognitive Science, and Parallel Distributed Processing* (Cambridge, Mass.: MIT Press, 1989); A. Cussins, 'The Connectionist Construction of Concepts'. In Boden, *Philosophy of Artificial Intelligence*, pp. 368–440.

[23] J. J. Freyd, 'Dynamic Mental Representations', *Psychological Review*, 94 (1987), 427–438; G. F. Miller and J. J. Freyd, *Dynamic Mental Representations of Animate Motion: The Interplay Among Evolutionary, Cognitive, and Behavioral Dynamics*. Cognitive Science Research Paper CSRP-290.(Brighton: University of Sussex, 1993).

But what does temporality (as opposed to succession) have to do with formal symbols?

As these examples show, novel candidates for 'representation' have already resulted from the ingenuity of computer scientists, neuroscientists, and experimental psychologists. The future may see still more. Philosophers of cognitive science should not restrict 'representation' to the formal definition, or 'content' to symbolic structures, without first considering all the candidates available. If that is done, the most likely, most reasonable, outcome is that they will distinguish various senses of the crucial term, exemplified by a range of natural and artificial mechanisms. This will be a dialectical, cooperative enterprise (as it's been in the past). That is, the philosophers' imagination will be continually prompted and refreshed by new empirical findings.

iii: *Embodiment and Cartesianism*

A few years ago, some colleagues and I were listening to a reading (in the Sussex dialect) of *Alice's Adventures in Wonderland*. Alice had just glimpsed the beautiful garden, but couldn't get her head through the doorway—'and even if my head *would* go through', she thought, 'it would be of very little use, without my shoulders.' One quick-witted listener tartly remarked that cognitive scientists wouldn't agree.

As you may have guessed, he is a phenomenologist at heart. Phenomenologists hold that the whole body is involved in our mental life, which emerges from our bodily presence and action in the world, and which constructs that world as 'objective'. For many years, cognitive scientists took a more Cartesian view, in which the mind was conceptualized without reference to the body, and *Subject* and *Object* were taken as given.

Multiple realizability was only part of it. More to the point, there was no suggestion that the essential nature of mental states and processes depends on the fact that we have bodies (as opposed to brains), and live in a physical environment. It was admitted, of course, that sensory transducers and motor effectors enter the empirical story. But the prime theoretical focus lay inside the head. Mental life was seen as a repeated cycle of *perception, thought, action*—and *thought* was where the interest lay.

So most early AI had no sensory-motor dimension, confining itself to text-based examples. When sensory-motor aspects were included, much of the information in the real-world stimulus was discarded. Computer vision relied instead on pre-stored representations of objects and projective geometry. In effect, seeing was reasoning.[24]

[24] Boden, *Artificial Intelligence and Natural Man*, chaps. 8 & 9.

Margaret A. Boden

Even robotics concentrated on reasoning and planning, using abstract representations of the robots' highly simplified environment. The messy details of the real world, and of the changes caused by bodily movement in it, were excluded whenever possible. Those which remained were explicitly anticipated in the planning process.

That, at least, was the intention. But GOFAI-robotics encountered the frame problem.[25] Real-world details didn't always occur as anticipated, and many weren't anticipated at all. Perhaps it was impossible to represent every situation the robot might encounter? Moreover, many creatures—beetles, for instance—seem to move around successfully without planning. Apparently, their continuous interaction with the world suffices.

Accordingly, some roboticists took a leaf out of the beetles' book. Avoiding centralized control and internal representation, the new 'situated' robots relied on direct motor responses to environmental cues.[26] Support for this approach came from an insightful AI-critique of the planning paradigm.[27] This remarked (for instance) upon the high speed at which people can play computer-games like *Pengo* or *Tetris*. There seems to be no time for reasoning or planning: the relevant buttons are pressed 'automatically', triggered by visual cues. Certainly, there's no consciousness of planning or decision-making—introspective evidence which this critique took seriously. Interactionist versions of AI, of which situated robotics is one example, were recommended instead.

Phenomenological philosophers were triumphant. The return of the body (even a beetle-body), and the rejection of reason and representation, was what they would have expected. Indeed, Dreyfus [28]

[25] P. J. Hayes, 'The Naive Physics Manifesto'. In D. Michie (ed.), *Expert Systems in the Micro-Electronic Age* (Edinburgh: Edinburgh University Press, 1979), pp. 242–270. Reprinted in Boden, *Philosophy of Artificial Intelligence*, pp. 171-205; Z. W. Pylyshyn (ed.) *The Robot's Dilemma: The Frame Problem in Artificial Intelligence* (Norwood, NJ: Ablex, 1987).

[26] R. A. Brooks, 'Intelligence Without Representation' *Artificial Intelligence*, **47** (1991), 139–159.

[27] P. E. Agre, *The Dynamic Structure of Everyday Life*. PhD dissertation, Dept. of Electrical Engineering & Computer Science. (Cambridge, Mass.: MIT, 1988); P. E. Agre, *Computation and Human Experience* (Cambridge: Cambridge University Press, 1997); compare L. A. Suchman, *Plans and Situated Actions: The Problem of Human-Machine Communication* (Cambridge: Cambridge University Press, 1987).

[28] H. L. Dreyfus, 'Why Computers Must Have Bodies in Order to be Intelligent', *Review of Metaphysics*, **21** (1967), 13–32; H. L. Dreyfus, *What Computers Can't Do: A Critique of Artificial Reason* (New York: Harper & Row, 1972).

had expected it, up to a point. However, although he had complained that AI neglects the body, he didn't illuminate how the body is involved. He took the Heideggerian line that we don't plan our behaviour, we 'just do it'.

For a cognitive scientist, of whatever philosophical persuasion, there's no 'just' about it. Even beetles don't move around by magic. How is skilled behaviour possible? Dreyfus denied that computations over representations are involved, but offered no alternative explanation. *A fortiori*, he didn't ask when, and why, a 'just do it' approach might fail to account for behaviour. By contrast, the neo-phenomenological movement in recent cognitive science has tried to address these questions constructively.

That's not to say that there's agreement here, for there isn't. (Trade Descriptions, again!) The Cartesian approach is not dead and buried. The anti-representational arguments of the 'new' robotics have been explicitly rebutted by some GOFAI-researchers and philosophers.[29] Indeed, situated roboticists now admit that internal representations may be needed for some human behaviour.

Moreover, there are distinct positions *within* the neo-phenomenological movement. Situated robotics includes both subsumption architectures[30] and the dynamical systems approach.[31] The former allows some reflex-responses to inhibit the triggering of others, while the latter exploits dynamic coupling between robot and world. Some sympathetic philosophers also stress epigenesis: a series of interactions between organism and environment that 'boot-straps' development.[32] And those who (like Dreyfus) cite Heidegger's attack on the 'Subject-Object' distinction sometimes reject his claim that animals, lacking language, can't construct their own

[29] A. H. Vera and H. A. Simon, 'Situated Action: A Symbolic Interpretation', *Cognitive Science*, **17** (1993), 7–48; D. Kirsh, 'Today the Earwig, Tomorrow Man?', *Artificial Intelligence*, **47** (1991), 161–184. Reprinted in M. A. Boden, *The Philosophy of Artificial Life* (Oxford: Oxford University Press, 1996), pp. 237–261.
[30] Brooks, 'Intelligence Without Representation', *Artificial Intelligence*, **47**, 139–159.
[31] R. D. Beer, *Intelligence as Adaptive Behavior: An Experiment in Computational Neuroethology* (Boston: Academic Press, 1990); R. D. Beer, 'Computational and Dynamical Languages for Autonomous Agents'. In R. F. Port & T. J. van Gelder (eds), *Mind as Motion: Explorations in the Dynamics of Cognition* (Cambridge, Mass.: MIT Press, 1995), pp. 121–148.
[32] H. Hendriks-Jansen, *Catching Ourselves in the Act: Situated Activity, Interactive Emergence, Evolution, and Human Thought* (Cambridge, Mass.: MIT Press, 1996).

Margaret A. Boden

'worlds' by their world-inhabiting activities.[33] (Fodor[34] once remarked 'I don't know what *Dasein* is, but I'm sure there's lots of it around.' For these neo-Heideggerians, that's certainly so.)

Another aspect of 'Cartesian' cognitive science is its assumption that the mind/self stops at the skull—or anyway, at the skin. Admittedly, Newell and Simon[35] claimed long ago that objects in the outside world (from pencil and paper to typewriter-keys) comprise an 'external memory', crucial to problem-solving and bodily skills. But they didn't press the implication: that mind, thought, and self are largely *constituted* by one's engagement with the physical and cultural environment.

That idea was already familiar to social psychologists and philosophers,[36] but wasn't prominent in the analytic tradition. Some twenty-five years ago, however, philosophers of language offered an externalist account of meaning, according to which '"meanings" just ain't in the head'.[37] An even stronger type of externalism has now arisen within cognitive science.

Dynamical approaches in general argue that identifying the organism-environment boundary is problematic, even arbitrary. Two closely coupled dynamical systems can always be regarded as one all-embracing system. The decision where to locate a boundary, then, boils down to asking how close is 'close'. And the answer will depend on one's purposes. For an autopoietic biology, the crucial boundary is the cell-membrane (see Section v), but the limits of 'organ' and 'organism' may be less evident. For a dynamical psychology or philosophy of mind, the system-boundary is still less clear-cut.

Some cognitive scientists have recently argued that the mind, or

[33] M. Wheeler, 'From Robots to Rothko: The Bringing Forth of Worlds'. In Boden, *Philosophy of Artificial Life*, pp. 209–236; M. Wheeler, *Reconstructing the Cognitive World: the Next Step* (Cambridge, Mass.: MIT Press, in press).

[34] J. A. Fodor, 'Methodological Solipsism Considered as a Research Strategy in Cognitive Psychology', *Behavioral and Brain Sciences*, 3 (1980), 63–72. Reprinted in J. A. Fodor, *Representations: Philosophical Essays on the Foundations of Cognitive Science* (Brighton: Harvester Press, 1981), pp. 225–253.

[35] Newell and Simon, *Human Problem Solving*.

[36] M. Hollis, *Models of Man: Philosophical Thoughts on Social Action* (Cambridge: Cambridge University Press, 1977).

[37] H. Putnam, 'The Meaning of "Meaning"'. In K. Gunderson (ed.), *Language, Mind, and Knowledge*, Minnesota Studies in the Philosophy of Science, VII (Minneapolis: University of Minnesota Press, 1975). Reprinted in Putnam, *Mind, Language, and Reality*, pp. 215–271; see p. 219.

self, is not a Cartesian ego but 'a coupling of biological organism and external resources'.[38] As such, it is 'spread into' the world in which we're embedded—which includes natural objects, cultural artefacts, and virtual objects defined (for instance) by language, science, and myth. Empirical research has studied how all these aspects of our environment play an active role in driving cognitive processes. Competent seafaring, for example, involves a complex coupling of individual personalities, social roles and conventions, maps and instruments, mariners' knowledge, problem-solving (often spread across several crew-members), and a variety of bodily capacities and skills.[39]

iv: *What is Computation?*

Cognitive science is grounded in computational concepts—but what is computation? Broadly speaking, cognitive scientists have offered three answers. The first is clear, and to many seems 'obvious'. The second is important, but kind-of-boring. The third is sometimes far from clear—and far from boring.

The first answer is Turing's.[40] He defined computation in formal terms, as an exercise in pure mathematics. When digital computers appeared, computation as such was still mathematically understood. A program was a series of well-formed formulae of some logical calculus, or programming language—that is, a set of uninterpreted mathematical expressions. Putnam[41] took this answer for granted in defining functionalism, Fodor[42] in proclaiming methodological solipsism, and Searle[43] in saying AI-programs are 'all syntax and no semantics'.

For historical reasons, the first answer is strongly associated with

[38] Clark, *Being There*; A. Clark and D. J. Chalmers, 'The Extended Mind', *Analysis*, **58** (1998), 7–19.

[39] E. Hutchins, *Cognition in the Wild* (Cambridge, Mass.: MIT Press, 1995).

[40] A. M. Turing, 'On Computable Numbers with an Application to the Entscheidungsproblem', *Proceedings of the London Mathematical Society*, **42** (1936), 230–265. Reprinted in M. Davis (ed.), *The Undecidable: Basic Papers on Undecidable Propositions, Unsolvable Problems, and Computable Functions* (Hewlett, NY: Raven Press, 1965), pp. 116–153.

[41] Putnam, 'Minds and Machines'.

[42] Fodor, 'Methodological Solipsism Considered as a Research Strategy'.

[43] J. R. Searle, 'Minds, Brains, and Programs', *Behavioral and Brain Sciences*, **3** (1980), 417–424. Reprinted in Boden, *Philosophy of Artificial Intelligence*, pp. 67–88.

traditional AI. People who favour it generally see computation as typified by GOFAI.

The second answer is less restrictive, for it amounts to 'Whatever methods are used in computer-modelling'. GOFAI is included, of course. But so are the several kinds of connectionism; the various styles of evolutionary programming; and the many types of cellular automata. Sometimes, situated robotics and dynamical models inspired by physics are included also.

This undiscriminating answer may seem boring, for it doesn't imply any particular philosophical position. It may even seem perverse, given that proponents of some of these methodologies distance themselves not only from classical AI but also from the notion of computation itself.[44] But all these models are describable as Turing machines, and are usually implemented in von Neumann computers. More importantly, they involve significantly different virtual machines. A PDP-system, for example, has strengths and weaknesses largely complementary to those of a GOFAI-program, and cellular automata behave differently according to the types of rule they embody. Interesting questions arise, then, about the types of virtual machine involved in human minds.

To restrict 'computation' to the approaches now available—or worse, only one of them: GOFAI—is as unreasonable as restricting 'mathematics' to its early varieties. When Galileo said that mathematics is the language of nature, he didn't mean that *his* mathematics would suffice for physics but that physicists needed to explore mathematical pathways. Analogously, cognitive science employs concepts and models that are computational in a general sense.

What of the third answer? This treats our question as a deep philosophical puzzle: 'What *is* computation, *really?*' The puzzlement concerns the paradigm case (GOFAI), no less than exotic varieties. 'Cognition is computation' is here interpreted not (opaquely) in terms of how we currently think about computation, but (transparently) in terms of whatever theory turns out to be the best account of the phenomenon of computation (intuitively understood as *what computers do*)—which may differ from what we expect.[45] In general, this answer conflates *what computers do* with

[44] T. J. van Gelder, 'What Might Cognition Be If Not Computation? *Journal of Philosophy*, **92** (1995), 345–81.

[45] R. L. Chrisley, 'Transparent Computationalism', In M. Scheutz (ed.), *Proceedings of the Workshop 'New Trends in Cognitive Science 1999: Computationalism—The Next Generation'*. To appear in Conceptus Studien Sonderheft (in press).

what minds do, via some account of intentionality that supposedly applies to both.

One version of the third answer was given by Newell and Simon, the high-priests of strong AI. Their AI-programs specified formal computational systems of the type defined by Turing. As psychologists, however, they were interested in computations capable of directing behaviour. Accordingly, they outlined a semantic theory according to which intentionality is achieved by implementing certain types of computation.[46]

In arguing that both minds and computers are PSSs, Newell and Simon defined *symbols* as physical patterns with causal effects. The meaning of a symbol, they said, is the set of changes it enables the information-processing system to effect, either *to* or *in response to* some object or process (outside or inside the system itself). Analogously, *representation, interpretation*, and *designation*—equivalent, they declared, to *reference* and *aboutness*—were defined in fundamentally causal terms.

The meaning of an atomic symbol depends on its causal history and effects, while that of a complex symbolic expression depends on the meaning of its components *and the abstract relations between them*. It was the complex expressions which interested them, as the inner core of intelligence or mentality.

In practice, then, Newell and Simon focused on the formal properties of their programs (psychological theories). That's why they are often seen (by Searle, for instance) as proponents of the first answer, not the third. On that view, PSS-theory holds that causation grounds the interpretation of computations, once implemented, not that it's involved in defining computation *as such*.

The most ambitious version of the third answer has been developed over the past twenty years by the computer scientist Brian Smith. Deeply influenced by his practical knowledge of what Silicon Valley's various artefacts actually do, Smith's position is an example of neo-phenomenological, interactionist AI.

In his early work on the semantics of programming languages, he distinguished Turing-computability from computation as such.[47] Computation, he said, *makes things happen* in computers, and computer scientists should define basic terms (such as 'variable') accordingly. Even then, he had philosophical aims: he was trying to

[46] Newell and Simon, 'Computer Science as Empirical Enquiry'; Newell 'Physical Symbol Systems'.
[47] B. C. Smith, *Reflection and Semantics in a Procedural Language*. PhD dissertation and Technical Report LCS/TR-272 (Cambridge, Mass.: MIT, 1982).

put intentional flesh onto dry logicist bones, and to show how self-reflective knowledge is possible. He eventually came to believe that one must understand metaphysics to understand computation—and vice versa. He has developed a novel approach to the nature of objects, individuation, particularity, subjectivity, and meaning.[48] These matters, he argues, are all inescapable if one wants to say what computers actually do.

On his view, neither physical objects nor intentional subjects are metaphysically given. They all arise from the 'participatory engagement' of distinguishable areas of the metaphysically basic dynamic flux. This flux is the subject-matter of theoretical physics, and as such has neither individuality nor particularity. Objects emerge, or are constructed, as a result of dynamic participatory relations—some of which involve minds. Smith claims to have retained the major insights of both Continental and empirical-analytic traditions, without their problematic ontological assumptions.

Justified or not, Smith's metaphysical concept of *computation* is challenging. The widespread notion that philosophers of cognitive science can begin with a quick definition of 'computation', and then get on to the *really* interesting philosophical issues, takes far too much for granted.

v: *Life and Mind*

All the minds we know about are found in living organisms. This may be no accident. Many philosophers argue, or at least imply, that life is an essential precondition of mind.[49] If this is correct, then A-Life is essential to cognitive science, and in principle should ground AI.

Consider evolution and intentionality, for example. Some philosophers ground knowledge and intentionality in evolutionary history, describing language and thought as 'biological' categories.[50] These ideas can be related to A-Life research in evolutionary robotics. The robot's neural-network 'brain', and sometimes its sense-organs too, evolves over many generations of variation and selection so as to perform its task efficiently. Such robots challenge Searle's view

[48] B. C. Smith, *On the Origin of Objects* (Cambridge, Mass.: MIT Press, 1996).
[49] P. Godfrey-Smith, 'Spencer and Dewey on Life and Mind'. In R. A. Brooks & P. Maes (eds), *Artificial Life IV* (Cambridge, Mass.: MIT Press, 1994), pp. 80–89. Reprinted in Boden, *Philosophy of Artificial Life*, pp. 314–331.
[50] R. G. Millikan, *Language, Thought, and Other Biological Categories* (Cambridge, Mass.: MIT Press, 1984).

that the 'meaning' of a computer model must always be derivative, and arbitrary to boot.[51]

For Searle, meaning is ascribed *by us* to AI-programs because their structures match phenomena we're interested in. A given program might map equally well onto the tax-laws, a dance-routine, or a tourist's itinerary. With respect to the program itself, which of these we choose to say it 'represents' is arbitrary. As a statement about traditional AI-programs, this is correct. But it's not obvious that it applies to classical robots—and still less, to evolved ones.

Consider, for instance, an evolving population of robots selected for their ability to navigate an environment containing a white cardboard triangle.[52] Each robot's 'eye' was very simple, distinguishing light from dark in only two pixels. Before evolution started, every eye was randomly linked to its bearer's (randomly interconnected) neural network. To the roboticists' surprise, on one occasion the population evolved a feature-detector analogous to those found in mammalian visual cortex. This mini-network was sensitive to a light-dark gradient at a particular orientation. It evolved as part of an integrated visuomotor mechanism, enabling the robots to use the triangle as a navigation-aid.

One could debate whether the feature-detector means 'light-dark gradient sloping up and to the right' as opposed to 'left side of the white triangle'. But similar difficulties attend the ascription of intentional content to animals. The point is that the meanings one might want to ascribe to the robot aren't arbitrary. Nor are they derivative, based only in the human purposes involved in their design. They aren't based purely on causal regularities, either. They spring to mind as candidate meanings because the mini-networks concerned have evolved, within that task-environment, to discriminate certain visual features and guide the robot's movements accordingly. That is, they are environmentally and enactively grounded.

To say these meanings aren't arbitrary isn't to say they're genuine. They're certainly primitive, and arguably metaphorical, for today's A-Life robots have only very limited 'cognitive' powers. But suppose this technology were to result in much more animal-like creatures: what

---

[51] Searle, 'Minds, Brains, and Programs'.

[52] I. P. Harvey, P. Husbands and D. Cliff, 'Seeing the Light: Artificial Evolution, Real Vision'. In D. Cliff, P. Husbands, J.-A. Meyer & S. W. Wilson (eds), *From Animals to Animats 3: Proceedings of the Third International Conference on Simulation of Adaptive Behavior* (Cambridge, Mass.: MIT Press, 1994) pp. 392–401; P. Husbands, I. Harvey and D. Cliff, 'Circle in the Round: State Space Attractors for Evolved Sighted Robots', *Robotics and Autonomous Systems*, **15** (1995), 83–106.

then? If intentionality is grounded in evolution, perhaps full-blooded meanings could be ascribed to such evolved robots.—Why not?

Many will reply (first) that bearers of meaning must be alive, and (second) that this excludes robots. But neither of these claims is universally agreed within cognitive science.

The justification for the first claim is unclear. Life is an example of self-organization (the autonomous emergence of higher levels of order). But just what sort of self-organization is it? And why (if at all) is it necessary for meaning and mind? Both those questions arise in A-Life, but there's no consensus on how to answer them. For A-Life work on the nature of life is guided by two radically opposed philosophies: functionalism and autopoietic theory. (There's also a third way, as we'll see: functionalism tempered by a respect for metabolism.)

Functionalists see life as a type of self-organization definable in logical terms. A robot that implemented these abstract criteria (whatever they are: definitions differ) would be alive. Some even claim that genuine life could be ascribed to virtual 'creatures' inside computer-memory—a position termed strong A-Life, by analogy to strong AI.[53]

For proponents of autopoiesis, however, strong A-Life is an absurdity. And robotic life is impossible too, if the robots are assembled (or self-assembled) from manufactured parts. Autopoiesis is defined as the continuous self-production of an autonomous entity.[54] Life thus requires the self-creation of a unitary physical system, by the spontaneous formation of a boundary (at base, the cell-membrane) and the continuous generation and maintenance of the body's own components.

Because of its stress on the generation of the system's self-constituting boundary, autopoietic theory has some counter-intuitive implications. For instance, it denies that reproduction is essential for life. The argument is that reproduction is not (as functionalists claim) informational self-copying, but the formation of new autopoietic unities from previous ones. Life is therefore prior to

[53] C. G. Langton, 'Artificial Life', In C. G. Langton (ed.), *Artificial Life: Proceedings of an Interdisciplinary Workshop on the Synthesis and Simulation of Living Systems* (Redwood City, Calif.: Addison-Wesley, 1989). Reprinted (revised) in Boden, *Philosophy of Artificial Life*, pp. 39–94; T. S. Ray, 'An Approach to the Synthesis of Life'. In C. G. Langton, C. Taylor, J. D. Farmer & S. Rasmussen (eds), *Artificial Life II* (Redwood City, Calif.: Addison-Wesley, 1992) pp. 371–408. Reprinted in Boden, *Philosophy of Artificial Life*, pp. 111–145.

[54] H. R. Maturana and F. J. Varela, *Autopoiesis and Cognition: The Realization of the Living* (Boston: Reidel, 1980). (First published in Spanish, 1972.)

reproduction. This is not merely a conceptual point, but an empirical claim: that the earliest living organisms need not have been able to reproduce.[55] Evolution is excluded too, because it requires reproduction. This is less controversial, since there are independent arguments against defining life in terms of evolution. Nevertheless, some philosophers of A-Life take evolution to be the sort of self-organization that characterizes life.[56]

The 'third way' takes metabolism to be essential for life. Metabolism is the self-production of the physical body by energy budgeting, involving self-equilibrating energy exchanges of some (necessary) complexity. (This concept resembles autopoiesis, but without emphasizing *boundaries*.) It can't be glossed in functionalist terms, since it's irredeemably physical. Strong A-Life is possible only if virtual systems can metabolize, or if metabolism is inessential for life. The third way holds that neither of these alternatives is tenable.[57] It also excludes 'tin-can' robots: only robots powered by complex biochemical cycles of synthesis and breakdown would be truly alive (and truly embodied).

What of the relation between life and mind? Again, there's disagreement here. If evolution is seen as a criterion of life, and if an evolutionary semantics is accepted also, then mind can arise from life. But that it can arise *only* from life would require that evolution be confined to living things. For autopoietic theorists, and for 'pure' A-Life functionalists, this is so. But third-way functionalists could allow that evolved robots aren't alive (because they don't metabolize), yet ascribe genuine meanings to them.

The situation changes, of course, if evolutionary semantics is rejected. Cognitive scientists who adopt a causal or model-theoretic semantics may well share the commonsense intuition that mind is restricted to living things. But their theory of meaning can't be used to support it.

vi: *Not the Conclusion*

Cognitive science is much more than its label implies. However, some people see it as much *less*, insisting—because of the philo-

---

[55] M. A. Boden, 'Autopoiesis and Life', *Cognitive Science Quarterly*, 1 (2000), 115–143.

[56] M. A. Bedau, 'The Nature of Life'. In Boden, *Philosophy of Artificial Life*, pp. 332–357.

[57] M. A. Boden, 'Is Metabolism Necessary?', *British Journal for the Philosophy of Science*, **50:2** (1999), 231–248.

sophical disagreements within the field—that it's not a science at all (see Section i). But cognitive science is addressing the most complex system we know: the human mind/brain. It's hardly surprising if no single theoretical paradigm has yet emerged.[58]

Will the new millennium see one, at last?—'Who knows!' The ground is littered with the dead leaves of mistaken predictions. But if we must risk adding more leaves to the compost heap, I'd say four things.

First, that we'll see many new modelling methodologies, many new types of virtual machine. Second, that we'll achieve a better understanding of the interactions between cognition, motivation, and emotion. Third, that the rapprochement between analytic and Continental philosophy will advance. And fourth, that we may even come to understand how conscious experience as such (discussed in another lecture in this series) is possible. *Pace* Dennett[59] and Sloman,[60] however, I believe this would require a fundamental conceptual revolution in philosophy and neuroscience, probably involving the rapprochement just mentioned.[61]

It should be clear why I said this paper could have been called *'Philosophies* of Cognitive Science'. At the turn of the next century—or of the next millennium?—that alternative may be less apt. We may, by then, be able to identify a single philosophical position that unifies all the research in this area. But, for sure, not yet.

[58] See M. A. Boden, *Cognitive Science in Context: A Historical Perspective*. In preparation; to be published by Oxford University Press.

[59] D. C. Dennett, *Consciousness Explained* (London: Allen Lane, 1991). See also Dennett's chapter in this volume.

[60] A. Sloman, 'Architectural Requirements'. In Dautenhahn, *Human Cognition and Social Agent Technology*, pp. 163–195.

[61] M. A. Boden, 'Consciousness and Human Identity: An Interdisciplinary Perspective'. In J. Cornwell (ed.), *Consciousness and Human Identity* (Oxford: Oxford University Press, 1998) pp. 1–20.

Language, Thought and Compositionality

JERRY FODOR

Introduction

Consider the task under which I labour: These are supposed to be talks in the millennial spirit. My charge is to find, somewhere in the philosophical landscape, a problem of whose current status I can give some coherent account, and to point the direction in which it seems to me that further research might usefully proceed, And I'm to try to sound reasonably cheerful and optimistic in the course of doing so. No sooner did I begin to ponder these terms of engagement, than it occurred to me that cheer and optimism aren't really my thing; also that I hadn't heard of a topic in the philosophy of mind (which is the only part of philosophy that even I think that I know anything about) which seems to me to be other than a god-awful mess. It struck me that my best course would be for me to change my name and go into hiding. Thus my first choice of a title for this lecture, which was 'To Be Announced'.

But by dint of unflagging efforts, I have actually found an issue of respectable philosophical provenance, on which it seems to me that there has been some progress; one which, I think, it is becoming possible to contemplate resolving in the foreseeable future, if not by demonstration then still with arguments that an impartial bystander might reasonably find persuasive, at least if he is impartial in my direction. So that's what I'll talk about this evening.

My topic is: Which comes first, the chicken or the egg?

Or, by way of narrowing the field a bit, it's the chicken and egg problem as it arises in the philosophy of mind; namely: 'Which comes, first, thought or language?' Or, by way of narrowing the field still further, 'Which comes first *in order of explanation*, the content of thought or the content of language?' (I'll borrow a way of speaking from John Searle and sometimes put this question as: 'Is it thoughts or sentences that have "content in the first instance" or that have "underived" content?')

Two caveats: I'm taking for granted that either sentences mean what they do because they express the thoughts that they do, or vice versa (whatever, exactly, vice versa comes to here). There are, of course, other positions in logical space; it could be that the content of thought and language both derive from some *third thing*; or that neither thought nor language has any content; or that nothing has any content; or that thought has content in the first instance for thinkers who speak English but language has content in the first instance for thinkers who speak Urdu. And so forth. But none of these options strikes me as attractive and I won't discuss them in what follows.

Also I think we can reasonably expect, having once answered the question about the relative priority of thought and language in the explanation of content, that connected issues about which comes first in the order of ontogenetic or phylogenetic explanation should then fall into place. But I won't argue for that here either.

So now, here's the prospectus: In Part 1, I will tell you why I think we are in a better position to sort out the thought/language issue now than we have been till recently. Roughly, my point will be that we are a little clearer than we used to be about one of the conditions of adequacy that an acceptable theory of content must satisfy. Then, in Part 2, I'll tell you why, now that we are a little clearer about that, the question whether it's thoughts or sentences that have content in the first instance begins to look capable of being solved: There are persuasive empirical reasons suggesting that, although a theory of the content of thought might be able to satisfy the adequacy condition in question, it's unlikely that a theory of the content of language could do so. Which is to say that, as between the two, only thought *has* content strictly speaking. Which is, *a fortiori*, to say that, as between the two, only thought has content 'in the first instance'.

But I do want to stress, here at the outset, the empiricalness of the reasons I'll have on offer. It has often been supposed that there might be an *a priori* resolution of the thought/language issue, For example, that there might be a persuasive transcendental argument of more or less the form:

—*Only what can meet the conditions for radical translation (or for radical interpretation, or for being learned by induction from behavioural data; or whatever) can have meaning in the first instance;*
—*Only (public) languages can meet such conditions;*
—*Therefore, linguistic content must be prior to thought content.*

I claim that since their conclusion is empirically false, such arguments must be unsound; but, in the present paper, I'll have nothing else against them. So if it's your view that philosophy needs a firmer grip on truth than matters of fact can provide, I'm afraid you'll find what follows unconvincing. I apologize in advance; but one of the (many) things that I'm not optimistic about is the philosophical reliability of transcendental arguments.

Part 1: Content

Kierkegaard says somewhere that purity of the heart is to will one thing only. By this (no doubt too stringent) standard, there's long been a lot of *mauvais foi* in the metaphysics of meaning. No doubt, philosophers want a theory of content for its very own sake and quite apart from any other of their problems that it might help them to solve. It would be sort of interesting to know what content is, and where it fits in the natural order; and if it doesn't fit in the natural order, it would be sort of interesting to know that, too. But also, at least since Hume, many philosophers have wanted to know what content is because they've thought knowing that is a prerequisite for constructing a theory of *justification*. Justification is what such philosophers *really* care about; more, even, than they care about purity of the heart.

The putative connection between content and justification has, perhaps, never been formulated very precisely. But the intuition is familiar, so I'll just gesture in its direction. Justification consists in giving reasons. But not *any* reason justifies; only *justified* reasons do. If my claim that P is to justify my claim that Q, then my claim that P must itself be justified (or, at a minimum, justifiable); and its justification *had better not be my claim that Q*. But though this principle seems plausible, and is untendentious in some circles, one sniffs, straight off, the threat of a regress: If every reason needs a reason, how does giving reasons end? Arguably, if we're to block the regress, we need to suppose that at least some claims, at least sometimes, at least *prima facie*, justify themselves. As Christopher Peacocke rightly says: 'This is actually a form of a classical rationalist principle ... to the effect that all *a posteriori* reason-giving relations rest ultimately on *a priori* reason-giving relations.[1]

But what would a reason that justifies itself be like? This is where the metaphysics of content is supposed to come floating in, like Lohengrin on his swan, to save the epistemologist's bacon. Actually, there are supposed to be two kinds of self-justifying claims, either of which may serve to avoid the regress. One kind is claims that are true 'solely in virtue of what they mean'; and the other kind is

[1] Peacocke, C. (2000): 'Fodor on concepts, philosophical aspects', *Mind and Language*, 15, 327–40.

claims that can be 'just seen' to be true. Well, here's the point I've been aiming for: Both the fact, that a claim is true solely in virtue of what it means, and the fact that a claim can be 'just seen' to be true, are supposed to depend on the identity (specifically, on the content) of the concepts that are the claim's constituents. It's (let's say) self-justifying that if John is a bachelor, then John is unmarried. Then anybody who knows what the words 'bachelor' and 'unmarried' mean (or 'anybody who knows what the content of the corresponding concepts is'; or 'anybody who "has" the corresponding concepts;' philosophers have a variety of ways of saying this) *thereby* knows that the claim that if John is a bachelor then he is unmarried is self-warranting. Likewise, if it's true that RED is a concept that can be 'just seen' to apply, then (in appropriate circumstances, blah, blah) its appearing to apply is (*ceteris paribus*, blah, blah), warrant for applying it.

The aspect of this I'd like you please to attend to, is that being the kind of concept that can serve as a constituent of a self-justifying claim is supposed to be *concept-constitutive*. Thus it's constitutive of the concept BACHELOR that *if it's a bachelor, then it's unmarried* is a conceptual truth; and, by a natural extension, it's constitutive of having that concept that one is disposed to draw, and to acquiesce in, tokens of that inference. Likewise, if it's part and parcel of the concept RED that it's 'observational', then having RED is (*inter alia*) being able (at least some of the time) to apply it just by looking. So the moral is that you can maybe get the theory of content to underwrite the theory of justification; and that this is a consummation devoutly to be wished (*ceteris paribus*). The way to do so is: you allow epistemic clauses in the definitions of such notions as 'concept individuation' and 'concept possession'.

That is, of course, a kind of foundationalism. Like Descartes' kind, it proposes to block epistemological regresses by endorsing appeals to self-justifying claims, and thereby undertakes an obligation to explain how on earth there could be such things. The difference is that, whereas Descartes thought theology might discharge this burden (via there being innate ideas and God's not being a deceiver), the prevailing view since Hume is that it's the theory of meaning that ought to do so. It is to follow *from the theory of meaning* that 'red' is an observation term, and that 'bachelor' implies *unmarried*. If you assume that what follows from the theory of meaning is *ipso facto a priori*, that explains why such claims are able to warrant themselves.

The idea that semantics might underwrite justification, thereby doing for us what God wasn't able to do for Descartes, is most of what is called philosophy's 'linguistic turn'. It's visible, in one form or other, from Hume to Carnap to Quine (inclusive) and from Wittgenstein to Ryle to Davidson to Dummett (likewise inclusive). It is, even now I think, properly stigmatized as the received view. This is not quite to say that everybody, everywhere believes it. Old hands will recall a flurry of interest, in the '60s, largely under Hilary Putnam's tutelage, in 'theoretical' inferences, also known as 'arguments to the best explanation'. The suggestion was that, because it is holistic, this kind of '*a posteriori* reason giving', does *not* need to be grounded in '*a priori* reason giving'. 'Holism' is what you call circularity if you are commending it (likewise, 'circularity' is what you call holism if you are condemning it). Circles don't stop anywhere, so maybe epistemology can do without foundations if it tolerates a few. And maybe it can tolerate a few if they're big enough. Here too the general picture is familiar, so I'll spare you further exposition.

Suffice it, in any case, that you can't expect semantics to do all that work for you for free. The cost, if you insist that it underwrite your theory of justification, is learning to live with a touch of verificationism about meaning and with a touch of analytic/synthetic distinction as well; the former because the possession conditions for 'observational' concepts include being able to apply them correctly, the latter because 'true in virtue of meaning' is supposed to be what 'analytic' means. Over the years, philosophers have invested quite a lot of sophistication in trying to convince themselves that buying a semantic foundation for epistemology at this price is a good bargain. Many have learned to say 'criterion' and the like in public, and not to blush when they do so. My own view is that it's a doomed strategy: The account of content it requires isn't true; and, anyhow, the kind of justification it can buy you isn't worth having. If my tooth hurts, I want it to be that my behaviour justifies (indeed, patently, irresistibly justifies) the dentist's believing that I'm in pain. It is, however, no use his belief being justified because 'toothache behaviour' is *what we call* the way I've been behaving. I want it to be justified *because I'm behaving this way because my tooth hurts*. Likewise in more dignified cases; $p < 0.05$ is what they *call* statistical justification by the data. But what you want is not an experimental hypotheses that is justified by the data by definition; what you want is a hypothesis that is justified by the data *because it's true*. Stipulating a 'level of significance' will never buy you that, of course. Truth requires that the world cooperate.

This does all seem to me to be self-evident, and unavoidable, and why it's so hard to take 'analytic epistemology' seriously. But never mind; I'm prepared to agree that others could think otherwise. I hereby concede that it's possible to believe that a foundational account of justification is worth what theories of meaning would have to pay for it. Or, rather, I hereby concede that it *used to be possible* to believe that. But, to come to the main line of my argument, we now know more than we used to about the adequacy conditions that theories of content must satisfy. And, as it turns out, some of these are *incompatible* with recognizing epistemic constraints on either concept individuation or concept possession. That it does turn out this way is, of course, of considerable interest quite aside from how its doing so bears on the thought and language problem. Quite a lot of modern philosophy has been devoted to the quest for a 'critical' method; one that would dismiss, *a priori*, metaphysical theses that might otherwise have seemed worth considering. 'When we run over libraries persuaded of these principles, what havoc must we make?' Just like the prospects for a foundationalist philosophy of justification, and for the same reasons, the prospects for a 'critical' philosophy turned first on God's not being a deceiver; and then, when that didn't work, on ideas being copies of impressions, and then, when that didn't work, on content being epistemically constituted. If, as I'm suggesting, that doesn't work either, then probably there *can't be* a critical philosophy. So a venerable philosophical tradition comes to an end.

But, though I take these considerations very seriously indeed, it's the thought-and-language issue that I care about for present purposes. I'm going to argue that the same considerations that guarantee that no epistemic conditions are constitutive of the content of words or concepts, strongly suggest that thoughts must be what have content in the first instance. So the prospectus for what's left of the lecture is this: first I'll tell you why content can't be epistemically constituted; and then I'll tell you why the reason that it can't be decides the priority between thought and language.

Part 2: Compositionality

I've suggested that it's possible for rational people to disagree about whether semantic notions like content can underwrite epistemic notions like inference and justification. But here is one thing that we know about content for *sure*: It is compositional in whatever has it intrinsically. If it's linguistic expressions that have content in the first instance, then the content of a sentence must be exhaustively determined by the content of its constituent expressions together with its syntax; and if it's thoughts that have content in the first instance, then the content of a thought must be determined by the content of its constituent concepts together with its 'logical' syntax. And if, as between language and thought, only one of the two has compositional content, then that must be the one whose content is underived. Unlike the thesis that semantics should underwrite justification, the thesis that underived content is compositional is not negotiable. So if, as I'm about to argue, these two theses come into conflict, then it's the first that has to be rejected.

So not-negotiable is compositionality that I'm not even going to tell you what it is. Suffice it that the things that the expression (*mutatis mutandis* the concept) 'brown cow' applies to are exactly the things to which the expressions 'brown' and 'cow' apply. Likewise, the things that 'brown cow in New Jersey' applies to are exactly the ones that 'brown' 'cow' and 'in New Jersey' apply to. Compositionality is the name of whatever exactly it is that requires this kind of thing to be the general case. It says (to repeat) that the semantic value of a thought (/sentence) is determined by the semantic values of its constituents, together with their arrangement. Whatever, exactly, semantic values are; and whatever, exactly 'determined by' means (both these being matters of some obscurity).

Nobody knows exactly what compositionality demands, but everybody knows why its demands have to be satisfied. Here too the arguments are familiar; and, in my view, they're decisive. Both human thought and human language are, invariably, productive and systematic; and the only way that they could be is by being compositional. (Productivity is the property that a system of representations has iff it includes infinitely many syntactically and semantically distinct symbols. Systematicity is the property that a system of representations has (whether or not it is productive) iff each of the symbols it contains occur with the same semantic value as a constituent of many different hosts.)

For present purposes, we can collapse systematicity and productivity together,[2] and make the point like this: There are, for better or worse, indefinitely many things that English allows you to say about pigeons and the weather in Manhattan. For example: 'The weather in Manhattan is nice for the pigeons early in the summer' and 'The weather is nice in the early summer in Manhattan if you are a pigeon' … and so forth. English being compositional is what

[2] The difference between them matters primarily in polemical contexts where an argument is required for the compositionality of a representational system that is *not* granted to be productive. See (Fodor, J. and Pylyshyn, Z., 1988): 'Connectionism and cognitive architecture', Cognition, 28, 3–71.

Jerry Fodor

explains why so many of the sentences that you can use to say things about pigeons and the weather in Manhattan, share some or all of their vocabulary. So, in particular, the word 'weather' occurs in many, many of these sentences; and in more or less every case where it does, it contributes the very same semantical property to its sentential host; viz a reference to the weather. Barring idioms and such, this is the general case. A word's occurring in one sentence license its occurrences in many others, and its semantic contribution is the same in all of them. Were this not so, we couldn't explain the familiar pattern according to which natural languages exhibit open ended clusters of semantically and syntactically related forms. Ditto, *mutatis mutandis*, for thoughts.[3] So that, in brief, is why compositionality is not negotiable.

We can now begin to put some of the pieces together. Here's what we have so far:

—As between the two, at least one of thought and language must be compositional. If *only* one of them is, then that's the one that has content in the first instance.

—In a compositional representational system, whatever belongs to the content of a complex symbol is inherited from the contents of its constituents symbols.

These being so, we can establish the first of the major claims of which I would like to convince you: *None of their epistemic properties are constitutive of the contents either of words or of concepts.* The argument for this is utterly straightforward: the *epistemic properties of symbols do not, in general, compose.* In particular, the epistemic properties of sentences are not, in general, predictable from those of the words that they contain; and the epistemic properties of thoughts are not, in general, predictable from the concepts they contain. I'll tell you a moment why this is so; suffice it, for now, just to argue from examples. I'll take *being observational* (i.e. being the kind of term/concept that can be 'just seen' to apply) as the epistemic property in question; but the argument generalizes straightforwardly to cases where the epistemic property that's supposed to be content constitutive involves inferential dispositions.

Here's a first approximation to the argument: Suppose (for *reductio*) that everyone who has the concept Ø is *ipso facto* able to recognize Ø things in favourable circumstances. Then, *a fortiori*, whoever has the concept RED SQUARE is *ipso facto* able to recognize red squares in favourable circumstances. Well, but compositionality

[3] More precisely, ditto for thoughts assuming that the representational theory of mind is true.

says that the content-constitutive properties of concepts are exhaustively inherited from their constituents. So, whoever has these concepts must *ipso facto* be able to recognize red things and square things in favourable circumstances.

But now it seems that something's wrong. For, as a matter of fact, having the concepts RED and SQUARE is *not* sufficient for being able to recognize red squares in favourable circumstances; not even on the assumption that having the concept RED is sufficient for being able to recognize red things in favourable circumstances and having the concept SQUARE is sufficient for being able to recognize square things in favourable circumstances. Indeed, it's perfectly possible that the favourable conditions for applying RED 'screen off' the favourable conditions for applying SQUARE or *vice versa*; eg. that the circumstances that are favourable for recognizing red things are *ipso facto* *un*favorable for recognizing square things. If that were so then, *a fortiori*, the favourable conditions for recognizing RED SQUARE could not be inherited from the favourable conditions for recognizing RED and the favourable conditions for recognizing SQUARE. But, that would be contrary to compositionality, for compositionality requires that complex concepts have *only* such semantic properties as they inherit from their constituents. And compositionality isn't negotiable. I conclude that the possession conditions for *at least some* concepts (in effect, the complex ones; the ones that have compositional structure) are *not* constituted by recognitional capacities. Arguments similar in spirit apply, *mutatis mutandis*, to preclude other putative epistemic conditions on the possession of complex concepts.[4]

What I haven't shown, however, is what I promised you that I'd argue for: namely, that *no* concepts are constituted by epistemic possession conditions. For, the following possibility remains open: Having RED requires being good at recognizing red things; and having SQUARE requires being good at recognizing square things. But having RED SQUARE doesn't require being good at recognizing red squares. In effect, according to this account there are possession conditions on primitive concepts that they don't transmit to their hosts. So an epistemic semantics might work for the former even if compositionality rules it out for the latter.

But this won't do. In fact, (and this is no small matter) the connection that compositionality imposes on the relations between the possession conditions of constituent concepts and the possession

[4] For extensive discussion of these issues, see Fodor *Concepts: Where Cognitive Science Went Wrong* (Oxford University Press, 1998), chapters 4 and 5.

conditions of their hosts goes *in both directions*. That is, it requires not just that having the constituent concepts is sufficient for having a host concept, but also (and even more obviously) that having the host concept is sufficient for having its constituents.

Or, to put it slightly differently, compositionality requires that host concepts receive their semantic properties solely from their constituents, *and also that constituent concepts transmit all their semantic properties to their hosts*. The argument is straightforward: If constituent concepts didn't transmit all their possession conditions to their hosts, there would be nothing to stop you from having a host concept without having its constituents.

You can't have the concept RED SQUARE unless you have the concept RED. But it certainly looks as though you could have RED SQUARE without having a recognitional capacity for red things at large (in favourable circumstances or otherwise). For example, you might have a concept RED that occurs *only* in host contexts. In that case, you'd be able to think *red square* and *red triangle* but not *red tout court*. (That kind of mind wouldn't even be very surprising since thoughts about red tout court are more abstract than thoughts about red squares.) Well, if this *is* possible, and if observational capacities are content constitutive, then you could have RED SQUARE without meeting the (putative) epistemic conditions on RED. But biconditional compositionality requires that satisfying the possession conditions for RED SQUARE *entails* satisfying the possession conditions for RED. The moral would seem to be that there aren't any epistemic possession conditions on RED. Since this form of argument is perfectly general, I conclude that there aren't any epistemic possession conditions on any primitive concepts.

I remarked that trying to exhibit epistemic constraints on possession conditions for concepts has been the central project in critical philosophy since Hume. That being so, its worth emphasizing not only that it doesn't work, as it were, *de facto*, but that there are principled reasons why nobody should ever have expected it to work. The basic point is this: Epistemic capacities are internally connected to the notion of *a good instance*. Except for God, having a concept clearly does not require being able to recognize its instances *come what may*. What's moot is whether it requires being able to recognize *good* instances *in favourable circumstances*.

But whereas 'good instancehood' is presumably what's central to epistemology, what matters to semantics is plausibly *instancehood per se*. It's surely at least a necessary condition for an expression having the same content as 'bird' that it apply to all and only birds. An expression which applied to all and only *good instances* of birds would, *ipso facto*, not *mean* 'bird'; at best, it might mean *good instance of a bird*. The reason that there's a clash between compositionality and epistemic semantics is resident exactly here. For, whereas *instancehood* is compositional, goodinstancehood is not. Whatever is an instance of RED SQUARE is *ipso facto* an instance of RED and of SQUARE. But it is *not* the case that whatever is a *good* instance of RED SQUARE is *ipso facto* a good instance either of RED or of SQUARE. Good instances of PET FISH are neither good instances of PET nor good instances of FISH.

All that being so, it was one of the worst ideas about the metaphysics of meaning that anybody has ever had that the concept of an instance of a concept should somehow be understood in terms of the concept of a good instance of that concept. I guess Plato was the first philosopher to have this bad idea; but you got it in Wittgenstein, and you still do in the unholy alliance between prototype theories of concepts and connectionist theories of mental architecture. It is, indeed, currently the standard view of conceptual content. But it can't be true since, to repeat, goodinstancehood doesn't compose, and compositionality isn't negotiable.

Compositionality rules out an epistemically based semantics. I've been going on about this not only because it's directly germane to the main topic of whether it's thought or language that comes first, but because so many philosophers have supposed that semantics *has to be* epistemically based, on pain of loosing the connection between meaning and justification, and on pain of abandoning the project of constructing a critical philosophy. Well, so be it; I think the idea that there is an interesting connection between meaning and justification is probably mistaken root and branch; what justifies what depends on how things are connected in the world. As for critical philosophy, I wouldn't buy it at a discount, Probably, if you want to refute a metaphysics, you are going to have to read it first.

I do think, however, that there's a consolation for having to give up on epistemological semantics: We now know, with reasonable certainty, whether it's thought or language that comes first.

Part 3: Thought and Language

Here's the argument: If, as between thought and language, only one of them can plausibly be supposed to be compositional, then that is, *ipso facto* the one that comes first in order of the explanation of content; the other has only such secondary content as it 'derives' from the first. But, as a matter of empirical fact, language is pretty clearly *not* compositional, so it can't have content in the first instance.

Jerry Fodor

Q.E.D. It's been a great pleasure being here, and I thank you for your kind attention.

What's that? You wish to hear my empirical premise defended? But I am a philosopher, and hence not in the empirical-premise-defending line of work. Still, I'll give it a try if you insist.

David Pears has a recent book called *Hume's System*. His main point, if I read him right, is that scholars have grossly underestimated the influence of the later Wittgenstein on Hume; and that Hume would have done still better if Wittgenstein's influence had been still greater. According to Pears, 'Hume's method ... is to use a kind of introspection which is direct and independent of language. ... [But] ... is it really likely that anything so intricate [as thought] can be investigated in one mind independently of the language in which it would be passed from that mind to another one?' The question is rhetorical. Pears' 'criticism is that [Hume] exaggerates the perspicuity of the mind and then, when he finds himself forced to pay heed to language, he does little more than glance at it in an oblique and perfunctory way.' Now, comes the bit that I'd like you to think about; Pears offers an argument for claiming that looking closely at language structure is a good way of discovering the structure of thought; namely that 'the linguistic expression of a thought has to transmit it in its entirety and so cannot afford to omit or blur anything that is essential to its structure [i.e. to the structure of the thought that the expression transmits] (all quotes from p. 74).'

I have two points to put to you, the first is this: I'm prepared to believe that the function of sentences is primarily to express thoughts; and I am likewise prepared to believe that the content of a sentence is, plus or minus a bit, the thought that it is used to express. Indeed, I am prepared to shout all that that from the rooftops. I'm therefore also perfectly willing to believe in the heuristic value of drawing inferences from the structure of language to the structure of thought as a research strategy in philosophy. (It couldn't, in any case, be more of a waste of time than the currently fashionable project of trying to infer the structure of thought from pictures of the brain; and it's sure to be a great deal cheaper.) For all that, what Pears claims about how language succeeds in expressing thought is flagrantly and ubiquitously untrue. It is, in fact, *not* the case that 'the linguistic expression of a thought has to transmit it' in some way that requires the sentence 'not ... [to] omit or blur anything that is essential to [the thoughts] structure.' To the contrary, language is strikingly eliptical and inexplicit about the thoughts it expresses; though, to be sure, it manages to express them all the same.

The second point is that it couldn't be true that language is strikingly elliptical and inexplicit about the thoughts that it expresses if language were compositional in anything like strict detail. For, if it were (and assuming that the content of a sentence is, or is the same as, the content of the corresponding thought) the structure of a sentence would indeed have to be explicit about the structure of the thought it expresses; in particular, the constituents of the sentence would have to correspond in a straightforward way to the thought's constituents. For, if there are constituents of your thought that don't correspond to constituents of the sentence you utter, it must be that there was something in the content of the thought that the sentence left out. So you've said less than you intended to. And, likewise, if there's some constituent of the sentence that doesn't correspond to a constituent of the thought, it must be that there's something in the content of the sentence than isn't in the thought. So you've said more than you intended to.

The moral is that if language is compositional (and if what a sentence means is the thought that it expresses) then how a sentence is put together must be very explicit about how the corresponding thought is put together. But, as a simple matter of fact, in the general case, sentences are remarkably *in*explicit with respect to how the thoughts they express are put together. So either the content of the thought is different from the content of the sentence that expresses it, or the sentence isn't compositional. I take it that the first disjunct is preposterous so I take it that the second disjunct must be true.

Actually, I think this is all pretty untendentious. Everyone knows that a speaker doesn't generally say everything he's thinking. That's true even if what he's thinking is precisely what he intends to communicate. So, for example, you ask me what's the time, and I say 'it's three o'clock'. This reply is inexplicit in two rather different ways. For one thing, the sentence is *syntactically* inexplicit; presumably what I've uttered is an abbreviated form of something like 'it's three o'clock here and now.' Second, although the thought I intended to convey is that it's three o'clock *in the afternoon,* Grice requires me to leave some of that out. That's because, even though you don't know exactly what the time is, you presumably do know what time it is plus or minus twelve hours; and I know that you know that; and you know that I know you know that; and so on. Given all that, communicative efficiency constrains the form of words I use to tell you what you asked. What's obvious in the shared intentional context is generally not something that one bothers to say, even if it is part of what one intends to communicate.

Jerry Fodor

My point, however, is rather different. My point is that a perfectly uneliptical, unmetaphorical, undeictic sentence that is being used to express exactly the thought that it is conventionally used to express, often doesn't express the thought that it would if the sentence were compositional, Either (the typical case; see just above) it vastly underdetermines the right thought; or the thought it determines when compositionally construed isn't in fact, the one that it conventionally expresses. Since it's an open secret among formal semanticists that this sort of thing happens all over the place, I'll give just one example by way of pointing to the sort of phenomena I have in mind.

Russell taught us how to read definite descriptions compositionally; an expression of the form 'the x (Fx)' is satisfied by, and only by, the unique individual that is F. There is, however, a light industry devoted to exhibiting the various ways in which this construal does not work. In particular, 'the book is on the table' does not, usually, convey the thought that there exists exactly one book and exactly one table, and the former is on the latter. What happens, instead, is that the speaker uses the expression when he wants to speak of a certain table and a certain book, each of which has somehow been picked out *other than by its being the unique x such that (Fx)*; and, correspondingly, it is those objects that the hearer understands that the speaker intends to communicate a thought about; namely, the thought that the one is on the other,

Now, definite descriptions aren't freaks; to the contrary, the point they illustrate is really ubiquitous. If you read a sentence as though it were compositional, then the thought that it *ought* to be conventionally used to express often turns out not to be the one that *is* conventionally used to express. If I could borrow one of Noam Chomsky's intelligent Martians, I bet what he'd say upon considering the way definite descriptions and lots of other expressions work, is that English just isn't compositional. And I think he'd be right to say that.

Four points about all this, and then I will stop pestering you.

i. The more or less patent uncompositionality of English isn't something that formal semanticists like to admit. Rather, as far as I can tell, it's the house rule in formal semantics that you hold onto the compositionality of natural language, whatever the cost in face implausibility may be. So, for example, there are semanticsts according to whom 'the x (Fx)' actually is compositional in its conventional meaning; it's just that 'the x' in what we loosely call a definite description is in fact some kind of a singular term; maybe it's a funny looking demonstrative. Why on earth any remotely sane language would use as a demonstrative an expression with the syntactic structure of a quantifier is, however, not explained.

I guess what motivates this sort of move is the reflection that if the semantics of English isn't compositional, and if compositionality is not negotiable, then English hasn't got a semantics. And if English hasn't got a semantics, what exactly is the study of the semantics of English the study of? I think there's a perfectly clear answer to this; namely, it's the study of the (compositional) semantics of thought.

In a way, that is bad news; whereas sentences have the determinants of their content more or less up front (they wear their constituent structure more or less on their sleeves), what determines the compositional structure of thoughts is obscure. (One might take the view that that's part of what makes studying the semantics of thought so interesting; but try selling that to a granting agency.) Also, whereas lots of sentences manifest themselves in behaviours (viz by getting uttered) the behavioural manifestations of thought are notoriously indirect. And practically everybody in cognitive science and the philosophy of mind is a behaviourist of one sort or another. (A 'sophisticated behaviourist' to use Dan Dennett's oxymoron.)

ii. No such objections as I've been urging against the compositionality of language can hold against the compositionality of thought. For, whereas the content of a sentence may be inexplicit with respect to the content of the thought it expresses, a thought can't be inexplicit with respect to its own content; there can't be more—or less—to a thought than there is to its content because a thought just *is* its content. If you put this in the language of a representational theory of mind, it comes out something like: A mental representation is *ipso facto* compositional with respect to the content that a correct semantics would assign to it. This is not a metaphysical mystery; it just spells out what is implicit in claiming that the content of thoughts, unlike that of sentences, is underived.

iii. Even if language isn't compositional, it doesn't follow that there's a principled problem about how linguistic communication works. Linguistic communication works by negotiation. Since, it's a convention of English that you use 'the x (Fx)' to refer to some F that you have in mind, I know that there has to be such an F if what you say when you utter the formula is true. It may be—indeed, it typically is—contextually obvious which F you're talking about; and if it's not contextually obvious, I can say so, and you can specify further. Eventually, we'll converge on the same F, and you will then be able to tell me (for example) that that F is G. Your thought that the

F is G may well contain constituents (ones that you use to think of the F) of which the sentence that you use to express the thought exhibits no counterparts, That's alright if the shared intentional context allows me to figure out what the unexpressed constituents are. (Indeed, it may be alright even if it doesn't. Communication needn't require that I recognize the whole of the thought that prompted your utterance. Referential consensus as to which F is the F in question suffices for most purposes. I needn't also know how you represent that F in the thought that you intend to communicate.)

iv. Finally, to reiterate the implications for the thought and language problem (which I'm beginning to be afraid that you're beginning to be afraid that I may have forgotten) here's the syllogism:

—As between thought and language, whichever is compositional is the one that has content in the first instance.
—The evidence suggests strongly that language is not compositional.
—So, unless the evidence is misleading, it's thought, rather than language, that has content in the first instance.

Which is just what we Cartesians have always supposed. There, that's a cheery, optimistic conclusion, isn't it?[5]

[5] A version of this paper appears in the journal *Mind and Language*, Vol. **16**, No. 1, February 2001.

Index

Index

www.ingramcontent.com/pod-product-compliance
Ingram Content Group UK Ltd.
Pitfield, Milton Keynes, MK11 3LW, UK
UKHW010040140625
459647UK00012BA/1510